THE VIRGINIA GUN OWNER'S Guide

**Who
can bear arms?**

❖

**Where
are guns forbidden?**

❖

**When
can you shoot?**

by *Alan Korwin*
and Steve Maniscalco

illustrations by Gregg Myers and Ralph Richardson

BLOOMFIELD PRESS
Scottsdale, Arizona

BLOOMFIELD PRESS
4848 E. Cactus #505-440
Scottsdale, AZ 85254
602-996-4020 Offices
602-494-0679 Fax
1-800-707-4020 Order Hotline
info@gunlaws.com
gunlaws.com

ISBN 10: 1-889632-22-8
ISBN 13: 978-1-889632-22-3
Library of Congress Catalog Card Number: 96-86264

Photograph of Mr. Korwin by Michael Ives

ATTENTION
Clubs, Organizations, Firearms Training Instructors,
Educators and all interested parties:
Contact the publisher for information on quantity discounts!

Every gun owner needs this book—
"It doesn't make sense to own a gun and not know the rules."

NOTE: Was a new law passed yesterday?
Send us a stamped, self-addressed envelope for update information when it becomes available—or sign up for free email updates at our website!

Printed and bound in the United States of America
at Bang Printing, Brainerd, Minnesota

Seventh Edition

by Alan Korwin
and Steve Maniscalco

2011 Update • Changes to Edition 7

Call, email, fax or write for our **free full-color catalog**.
Always check our website for the latest news and changes.
Copyright 2011 Alan Korwin

BLOOMFIELD PRESS • GunLaws.com

4848 E. Cactus #505-440 • Scottsdale, AZ 85254
602-996-4020 • 1-800-707-4020 • Fax 602-494-0679

Sincere thanks to **The Virginia Citizens Defense League** for compiling the info below.
If you're not a member, join—this is how you keep your gun laws righteous. vcdl.org

HB1856 • CH234 • Concealed handgun permits; lost or destroyed permits. Allows a CHP holder to obtain a replacement permit in the event the original permit is lost or destroyed. The permit holder would submit a notarized statement to the clerk of the court that the permit was lost or destroyed and pay a fee not to exceed $5, and the clerk would be required to issue a replacement within 10 business days. The replacement will have the same expiration date as the original permit. *VCDL Comments:* This bill clarifies that the Circuit Court Clerk must replace a lost or stolen permit within ten days of getting a notarized statement of the loss, for a fee of $5.00.

SB757 • CH832 • Pneumatic gun regulations. Prohibits a locality from adopting an ordinance to ban shooting pneumatic guns on private property, with permission of the property owner, if reasonable care is taken to prevent a projectile from crossing the property bounds. The bill invalidates any existing local ordinances that conflict with this act. *VCDL Comments:* This bill frees someone on private property to discharge an air gun as long as they have permission from the property owner and reasonable care is taken to ensure the projectile does not cross the bounds of the property. Any local ordinances to the contrary, such as Fairfax County has, would be invalid.

SB839 • CH835 • Homestead exemptions. Adds one firearm, not to exceed $3,000 in value, to the list of items every householder shall be entitled to hold exempt from creditor process. The bill also increases the maximum exemption for a motor vehicle from $2,000 to $6,000. This bill is identical to HB1422, CH761. *VCDL Comments:* This bill allows a person to keep one firearm for household use if they are subject to a creditor process (updates Virginia's Homestead laws).

HB1411 • CH684 • Reckless handling of firearms; revocation of hunting license. Provides that a person's hunting or trapping license, or privilege to hunt or trap while possessing a firearm, may be revoked for a period of one to five years for a violation of §18.2-56.1 (reckless handling of firearms) while hunting. Revocation for a person whose privilege to hunt has been revoked, who hunts with a firearm, will be for a period of one year to life. Currently, the penalties are revocation for a period of one year to life, and for hunting with a firearm while the privilege is revoked, an additional period of one to five years. *VCDL Comments:* This bill limits the penalty for reckless handling of a firearm while hunting or trapping to a maximum of five years of prohibition from carrying while hunting/trapping, down from the current one year to *life* prohibition. However, if the person then hunts during the prohibition period, they can be prohibited from carrying while hunting/trapping for one year to life, up from the current one to five additional years.

HB1552 • CH231 • Issuance of concealed handgun permits. Amends language relating to the issuance of *de facto* concealed-handgun permits. Current law states that if a court does not issue a permit or find that the applicant is disqualified, within 45 days of receipt of the application, the clerk is to certify the application and send it to the applicant. The certified application then serves as a *de facto* permit until the actual permit is issued or the applicant is found to be disqualified. The clerk must mail or e-mail the certified application to the applicant within five business days of the expiration of the 45-day period. *VCDL Comments:* This bill specifies that the Circuit Court Clerk is to mail a certified concealed-handgun-permit application to serve as a temporary concealed-handgun permit, within five days of the expiration of the application-processing period.

HB1699 • CH775 • Restoration of firearms rights; hearings. Smooths the process for requesting and conducting a hearing, sought by a person to restore the right to possess or carry a firearm after being acquitted due to insanity, adjudicated legally incompetent or mentally incapacitated, or involuntarily committed for mandatory treatment. *VCDL Comments:* This bill cleans up conflicting/inconsistent wording dealing with a person who has been acquitted by reason of insanity from certain charges, to petition to have gun rights restored after completing treatment.

HB1779 • CH402 • Preliminary protective orders. Applies the ban on purchasing and transporting a firearm to persons subject to preliminary protective orders, where a petition alleging abuse or neglect has been filed. Under current law, persons subject to a preliminary protective order are prohibited from purchasing or transporting a firearm regardless of any allegation. This bill is identical to SB 754, CH373. *VCDL Comments:* This bill is an improvement to current law dealing with abuse-based protective orders, which restrict purchase or transport of firearms. The bill makes such restrictions only after an *actual finding* of abuse (not just an accusation). However, the bill should be changed to require that the finding of abuse be made at an adjudicatory hearing (so that the order cannot be made *ex parte*, i.e. by one party only).

HB1857 • CH235 • Transfer of firearms; documentation of residence. Clarifies that a member of the military may show permanent orders of assignment to the Pentagon as documentation of residency, when purchasing a firearm from a licensed dealer. *VCDL Comments:* This bill clarifies that someone with permanent orders to a Pentagon duty post can use their ID as photo-identification to purchase a firearm in Virginia.

VCDL supports the bills above, and is neutral on the bills below:

HB1777 • CH401 • Fake birth certificate; penalty. Provides that any person who manufactures, sells, or transfers a fictitious birth certificate or the birth certificate of another for the purpose of establishing a false identity for himself or for another person is guilty of a Class 6 felony. Current law punishes obtaining, possessing, transferring and selling as a Class 1 misdemeanor. *VCDL Comments:* This bill cleans up some wording dealing with penalty for faking a birth certificate to obtain a gun illegally.

HB1889 • CH459 • Tracking dogs. Allows the use of tracking dogs on a lead to find wounded or dead bear or deer during archery, muzzleloader, or firearm bear-or-deer hunting seasons, so long as those who are conducting the retrieval effort have permission to hunt on or have access to the land, and don't have a weapon in their possession. *VCDL Comments:* This bill deals with retrieving certain wounded animals while hunting using tracking dogs and while armed with a gun.

SB903 • CH282 • Definition of violent felony; penalty. Removes an "and" in the list of violent felonies to make it clear that a person does not need to be convicted of both §18.2-308.1 (possession of weapon on school property) and §18.2-308.2 (possession of firearm by a felon) in order to have the offense qualify as a violent felony for the purpose of the sentencing guidelines. The bill also provides that using a firearm in a threatening manner in a school is the only felony in §18.2-308.1 that qualifies as a violent felony. *VCDL Comments:* Fixed to make only someone who intends or attempts to harm someone with a gun on K-12 school grounds a violent felon.

TABLE OF CONTENTS

ILLUSTRATIONS

ACKNOWLEDGMENTS

This book is very much a result of the help we received, great and small, from all of the good people who provided their thoughts, answered our endless questions, and generously shared resources with us.
Thank you.

Leon App, Conservation and Development Program Supervisor
Dept. of Conservation and Recreation

Ray Cahen, Legislative Director, Virginia Shooting Sports Association

Darrell Carden, Vice Commodore, Hopewell Yacht Club

Lucien J. Charette, Executive Director,
Virginia Shooting Sports Association

Barton Cooley, Mayor, Hillsville, Virginia

Harper Corder, Special Agent, United States Forest Service

Col. William Deneke, Founder, Virginia Shooting Sports Association

Thomas W. Evans

James J. Fotis, Executive Director,
Law Enforcement Alliance of America

Jeff Freeman, Virginia Legislative Liaison
National Rifle Association

Dennis Fusaro, Director, Gun Owners of America

Richard E. Gardiner, Attorney at Law

Fred Griisser

Charly Gullett, Author

Stephen P. Halbrook, Ph.D., Attorney at Law

Larry Hart, Virginia Dept. of Game and Inland Fisheries

Rich Jefferson, Coordinator of External Affairs and Marketing,
Virginia Dept. of Game and Inland Fisheries

Bruce Jones, Virginia Wildlife Federation

Cheryl and Tyler Brittany Korwin

Georgene Lockwood, Author

Larry Malinish

Leslie, Steven Blaise and Kevin Dale Maniscalco

Ted McCormack, Assistant Director, Commission on Local Gov't.

Tanya Metaksa, Executive Director, Institute for Legislative Action, National Rifle Association

Paul Moog, President, Northern Virginia Civilian Defense League

Major Justin B. Murphy, Staff Duty Officer, Fairfax County Police

Mark H. Overstreet, Researcher, National Rifle Association

Ernie Padgett, President, Virginia Shooting Sports Association

The Pensus Group, including Richard Shaw, Chris Shaw, David Maule-ffinch and Terrence Plas

Ron Pike

Erich M. Pratt, Director, Gun Owners of America

Larry Pratt, Executive Director, Gun Owners of America

Robert Saunders, Jr., Harbormaster of the City of Hopewell

Jim Snyder, Membership Director, Northern Virginia Civilian Defense League

Donna Tate, Office Manager, Virginia State Police

Easter Thompson, Vice President, Public Relations STG Marketing Communications, Inc.

Capt. R. Lewis Vass, Records Management Officer, Virginia State Police

Jeannie Whitehurst, Library Information Specialist, Virginia Beach Wahab Public Law Library

M.H. Wilkinson, Director, Commission on Local Gov't.

Gary R. Wright, Director of Administration, City of Norfolk Circuit Court

We found the Virginia State Police to be cooperative and professional during the research stages of this book, and very impressive with their diligence in implementing the various elements of Virginia gun law.

The Dept. of Game and Inland Fisheries is a wonderful resource for the state and their cooperation in the development of this book is much appreciated.

The National Rifle Association Institute allowed the use of material in their pamphlet, "Your State Firearms Laws," and the NRA itself has been invaluable in developing and exposing this book to the public.

A special note of thanks to Philip Van Cleave and the Virginia Citizens Defense League, a shining light of freedom in the struggle to preserve our precious right to keep and bear arms.

PREFACE

Virginia has strict gun laws. You have to obey the laws.
There are serious penalties for breaking the rules.

Many gun owners don't know all the rules.
Some have the wrong idea of what the rules are.
It doesn't make sense to own a gun and not know the rules.

Here at last is a comprehensive book, in plain English,
about the laws and regulations that control firearms in Virginia.

This book is published under the full protection of the
First Amendment with the expressed understanding that you, not
we, are completely responsible for your own actions.

The One-Glaring-Error theory says there's at least
one glaring error hidden in any complex piece of work.
This book is no different. Watch out for it.

"It will be of little avail to the people that the laws are made by men of their
own choice, if the laws be so voluminous that they cannot be read, or so
incoherent that they cannot be understood; if they be repealed or revised
before they are promulgated, or undergo such incessant changes that no
man who knows what the law is to-day can guess what it will be tomorrow." **–James Madison, Federalist Papers, #62**

"Do you really think that we want those laws to be observed? We want
them broken. We're after power and we mean it. There's no way to rule
innocent men. The only power any government has is the power to crack
down on criminals. Well, when there aren't enough criminals, one makes
them. One declares so many things to be a crime that it becomes impossible
for men to live without breaking laws. Who wants a nation of law-abiding
citizens? What's there in that for anyone? But just pass the kind of laws that
can neither be observed nor enforced nor objectively interpreted, and you
create a nation of law breakers—and then you cash in on guilt."
–Ayn Rand (*Atlas Shrugged*)

FOREWORD • WARNING! • DON'T MISS THIS!

This book is not "the law," and is not a substitute for the law. The law includes all the legal obligations imposed on you, a much greater volume of work than the mere firearms statutes contained in this book. You are fully accountable under the exact wording and current official interpretations of all applicable laws, regulations, court precedents, executive orders and more, when you deal with firearms under any circumstances.

Many people find laws hard to understand, and gathering all the relevant ones is a lot of work. This book helps you with these chores. Collected in one volume are copies, reporduced with great care, of the principal state laws controlling gun use in Virginia.

In addition, the laws and other regulations are expressed in regular conversational terms for your convenience, and cross referenced to the statutes. While great care has been taken to accomplish this with a high degree of accuracy, **no guarantee of accuracy is expressed or implied, and the explanatory sections of this book are not to be considered as legal advice or a restatement of law.** In explaining the general meanings of the laws, using plain English, differences inevitably arise, so **you must always check the actual laws.** Only edited pieces of the laws are included here. The author and publisher expressly disclaim any liability whatsoever arising out of reliance on information contained in this book. New laws and regulations may be enacted at any time by the authorities. **The author and publisher make no representation that this book includes all requirements and prohibitions that may exist.** Local ordinances, rules, regulations and policies are not covered.

This book concerns the gun laws as they apply to law-abiding private residents in Virginia only. It is not intended to and does not describe most situations relating to licensed gun dealers, museums or educational institutions, local or federal military personnel, American Indians, foreign nationals, the police or other peace officers, any person summoned by a peace officer to help in the performance of official duties, persons with special licenses (including collectors), non-residents, persons with special authorizations or permits, bequests or intestate succession, persons under indictment, felons, prisoners, escapees, dangerous or repetitive offenders, criminal street gang members, delinquent, incorrigible or unsupervised juveniles, government employees, or any other people restricted or prohibited from firearm possession.

While this book discusses possible criminal consequences of improper gun use, it avoids most issues related to deliberate gun crimes. This means that certain laws are excluded, or not explained in the text. Some examples are: criminally negligent homicide and capital murder; homicide; manslaughter; gun theft; gun running; concealment of stolen firearms; enhanced penalties for commission of crimes with firearms, including armed robbery, burglary, theft, kidnapping, drug offenses, assault and priors; smuggling firearms into public aircraft; threatening flight attendants with firearms; possession of contraband; possession of a firearm in a prison by a prisoner; false application for a firearm; shooting at a building as part of a criminal street gang; removal of a body after a shooting; drive by shootings; predicate crimes; and this is only a partial list.

The main relevant parts of Virginia statutes that relate to guns are reproduced in Appendix D. These are formally known as *Code of Virginia*. Other state laws which may apply in some cases, and official agency regulations, are discussed but may not be reproduced. Key federal laws are discussed, but the laws themselves are *not* reproduced. Case law decisions, which effect the interpretation of the statutes, are *not* included.

FIREARMS LAWS ARE SUBJECT TO CHANGE WITHOUT NOTICE. You are strongly urged to consult with a qualified attorney and local authorities to determine the current status and applicability of the law to specific situations which you may encounter. A list of the proper authorities appears in Appendix C.

Guns are deadly serious business and require the highest level of responsibility from you. Firearm ownership, possession and use are rights that carry awesome responsibility. Unfortunately, **what the law says and what the authorities and courts do aren't always an exact match.** You must remember that each legal case is different and may lack prior court precedents. A decision to prosecute a case and the charges brought may involve a degree of discretion from the authorities involved. Sometimes, there just isn't a plain, clear-cut answer you can rely upon. Abuses, ignorance, carelessness, human frailties and plain fate subject you to legal risks, which can be exacerbated when firearms are involved. Take nothing for granted, recognize that legal risk is attached to everything you do, and **ALWAYS ERR ON THE SIDE OF SAFETY.**

PUBLISHER'S NOTE TO THE SEVENTH EDITION

When future generations look back at this edition of *The Virginia Gun Owner's Guide*, it will represent "the way things used to be," as it seems quite likely that new laws and court cases will change the landscape in time to come. As we go to press, Congress is considering many new gun legislation schemes, with no end in sight. Books in general are guaranteed to age from the moment of their release.

That may make this edition a conversation piece and perhaps of collectible value, but it also brings out a dilemma you should not ignore. The accuracy of this book will diminish with time, and its value as a historical record is not a substitute for current information about gun laws.

We encourage you to notify us about anything you feel is inaccurate, incomplete or in need of attention in any way. Despite all our efforts at completeness and accuracy, we recognize that we aren't perfect and that corrections may be needed. You must recognize this too.

This book will be updated periodically, and news about updates is available from the publisher, Bloomfield Press. You are invited to send us an old-fashioned stamped self-addressed envelope which we will fill and return when news of updates is available. Updates are also posted to our website, gunlaws.com, and you can sign up there for free email alerts.

If you believe you have found an error or item needing adjustment, notify the publisher. A free copy of this book will be provided to any reader whose comments are used in the next edition.

Special Note on Pending Legislation

Bills have been proposed by law makers nationally who would:

- Outlaw specific or classes of firearms by price range, melting point, operating characteristics, accuracy, type of safety mechanism, type of sighting mechanism, point of origin, appearance and by name.
- Restrict the amount of ammunition a gun can hold, the devices for feeding ammunition and allowable types of ammunition
- Restrict the number of firearms and the amount of ammunition a person may buy or own
- Require proficiency testing and periodic licensing with expiration dates
- Register firearms and owners nationally
- Use taxation as a way to limit firearm and ammunition ownership
- Create new liabilities for firearm owners, manufacturers, dealers, parents and persons involved in firearms accidents
- Outlaw keeping firearms loaded or not locked away
- Censor classified ads for firearms and eliminate firearms publications and outlaw any dangerous speech or publication
- Melt down firearms that are confiscated by police
- Prohibit gun shows and abolish hunting
- Deny or criminalize civil rights for government-promised security
- Repeal or flatly ignore the Second Amendment to the U.S. Constitution

In contrast, less attention has been paid to laws that would:

- Mandate school-based safety training
- Provide general self-defense awareness and training
- Encourage personal responsibility in resisting crime
- Protect people who stand up and act against crime
- Guarantee people's right to travel legally armed for personal safety
- Fix the conditions that generate hard-core criminals
- Assure sentencing of serious criminals, increase the percentage of sentences actually served, provide more prison space and permanently remove habitual criminals from society
- Improve rehabilitation and reduce repeat offenses
- Reduce plea bargaining and parole abuses
- Close legal loopholes and reform criminal justice malpractice
- Reform the juvenile justice system
- Improve law enforcement quality and efficiency
- Establish and strengthen victims' rights and protection
- Hold the rights of all American citizens in unassailable esteem
- Provide for the common defense and buttress the Constitution

Some experts have noted that easy-to-enact but ineffectual "feel good" laws are sometimes pursued instead of the much tougher course of laws and social changes that would reduce crime and its root causes. Many laws aim at disarming honest people while ignoring the fact that gun possession by criminals is already strictly illegal and largely unenforced. Increasing attacks on the Constitution and civil liberties are threatening freedoms Americans have always had. You are advised to become aware of any new laws which may be enacted. Contact your legislators to express your views on proposed legislation.

To our children
and the potential they hold for the future

THE RIGHT TO KEEP AND BEAR ARMS 1

In the United States of America, people have always had the right to keep arms, and the right to bear arms. The Second Amendment to the U.S. Constitution is the historic foundation of this right to have and use guns. The Second Amendment is entitled *The Right To Keep And Bear Arms*. This is what it says:

"A well regulated Militia, being necessary to the security of a free State, the right of the people to keep and bear Arms, shall not be infringed."

The intentions of the revolutionaries who drafted the Constitution were clear at the time. It was this right to keep and bear arms that allowed those citizens 200 years ago to break away from British rule. An armed populace was a precondition for independence and freedom from oppressive government. The founders of the United States of America were unambiguous and unequivocal in their intent:

No free man shall be debarred the use of arms.
–Thomas Jefferson

The Constitution shall never be construed to authorize Congress to prevent the people of the United States, who are peaceable citizens, from keeping their own arms.
–Samuel Adams

Little more can reasonably be aimed at with respect to the people at large than to have them properly armed.
–Alexander Hamilton

Americans have the right and advantage of being armed.
–James Madison

The great object is that every man be armed.
Everyone who is able may have a gun.
–Patrick Henry

Today the issue is controversial and emotionally charged. There are powerful and vocal groups on all sides of the topic of guns. Some people have taken to saying that the Second Amendment doesn't mean what it always used to mean, and there have been calls to repeal it. The U.S. Supreme Court has heard more than 95 gun cases, and contrary to news reports, has recognized an individual right to arms consistently for two centuries. In the 2008 landmark *Heller* case, it was unequivocally recognized as a "specific enumerated right" of individuals, on a par with the right to counsel and free speech, and discarded the revisionist "collective rights" theory invented to attack this fundamental liberty. Importantly, all 50 states recognize a person's right to act in self defense, completely apart from firearms debates.

The Second Amendment of course means what it always used to mean, which explains the armed populace we observe today. This is also seen in the fact that most states have the right to keep and bear arms imbedded in their own Constitutions, often in terms more direct than the wording in the Bill of Rights itself. If our Second Amendment guarantee was ever torn asunder, the state constitutions would still be in place.

Excerpt from the Virginia State Constitution
Article 1, Section 13
MILITIA; STANDING ARMIES;
MILITARY SUBORDINATE TO CIVIL POWER.

That a well regulated militia, composed of the body of the people, trained to arms, is the proper, natural, and safe defense of a free state, therefore, the right of the people to keep and bear arms shall not be infringed; that standing armies, in time of peace, should be avoided as dangerous to liberty; and that in all cases the military should be under strict subordination to, and governed by, the civil power.

Nothing in Virginia law may conflict with our fundamental creed, the U.S. Constitution, and so the right to keep arms and the right to bear arms are passed down to Virginians, as they are to the people of all the states in the union. The states, however, have passed laws to regulate the arms that people keep and bear within their borders. That's what this book is about.

WELCOME TO THE STATE GUN LAWS

The majority of Virginia's "gun laws" (they are never actually called that) can be found in a book called *Title 18.2, Crimes and Offenses Generally*, part of the *Code of Virginia*. The complete *Code of Virginia* is contained in a four-foot wide, 31-volume set published by LexisNexis, 800-562-1197, often available in libraries. You can read or download the entire code online for free at gunlaws.com, under the National Directory button.

In addition to Title 18.2, Virginia has gun laws in at least 16 other titles of the state code, including:

> Alcoholic Beverage Control Code, Title 4.1
> Commonwealth Public Safety, Title 9.1
> Counties, Cities and Towns, Title 15.2
> Courts Not of Record, Title 16.1
> Courts of Record, Title 17.1
> Criminal Procedure, Title 19.2
> Education, Title 22.1
> Game, Inland Fisheries and Boating, Title 29.1
> Mental Health, Mental Retardation, and Substance Abuse
>   Services, Title 37.2
> Military and Emergency Laws, Title 44
> Motor Vehicles, Title 46
> Police (State), Title 52
> Prisons and Other Methods of Correction; Title 53.1
> Professions and Occupations, Title 54.1
> Property and Conveyances, Title 55
> Trade and Commerce, Title 59.1

You'll find the main relevant sections of all these laws printed in *The Virginia Gun Owner's Guide* in Appendix D. Many of the fine details concerning guns come from other sources, listed in Appendix C. In addition, "the law" includes many things that are not statutes passed by the legislature, and may not be covered in detail in this book, including court decisions, official regulations, common law, civil law, policies and more.

The state of Virginia has a *rule of preemption* about gun laws, in §15.2-915 of the state code. This prohibits local authorities from passing laws that aren't specifically allowed by state law. Power is delegated only to the state to regulate firearms, in the hope of providing uniform rules statewide, in theory at least.

The state does allow localities to regulate some things, such as where a firearm can be discharged. Localities generally cannot regulate the purchase, possession, transfer, ownership, transporting, storing, or carrying of firearms. Title 15.2 in Appendix D lists most of the ways that a locality can regulate firearms.

It is important to note that *The Virginia Gun Owner's Guide* deals primarily with laws at the state and federal levels, and not at the local level. To learn if there are laws in effect that relate to your community, you must contact the proper authorities and read any local ordinances that may exist. For a list of phone numbers and addresses of these authorities see Appendix C. Getting local authorities to provide copies of their local gun laws may be tougher than it sounds.

A Word About Federal Law

The Virginia Gun Owner's Guide covers federal laws directly related to your right to keep and bear arms. This is only a small portion of the more than 88,000 words of federal gun law. For an unabridged copy of federal firearm statutes, with plain English summaries of each law, get *Gun Laws of America,* listed in the back of this book.

Federal law generally does not control the day-to-day details of how you can carry a firearm in any given state, or the rules for self defense and crime resistance, or where you can go for target practice. The individual states control these things. Federal law focuses on the commercial aspects, interstate transportation, certain prohibited weapons, arming the proper authorities, crimes against the nation and other specifically defined areas.

Many people think that federal laws are "higher" than state laws, or that they somehow come first. Federal and state laws control different things. The states and the feds each have control over their respective areas. They may also disagree on where those lines are drawn.

The Dreaded "§" Section Symbol:
Code of Virginia §18.2-308

The character "§" means "section." You read it aloud (or to yourself) as "section" whenever it appears. Every individually named chunk of law in America is called a section and has a section number, so you see this symbol a lot. It's an integral part of the written name for every statute on the books. A section may be just a few words or may be extremely long, and it may be amended by new laws. Code of Virginia section eighteen point two dash three-oh-eight, the law shown above, is one of the main Virginia gun laws.

The section "§" symbol intimidates many people and as such, is valuable for keeping the law mysterious and seemingly unknowable to the general public. Don't let it scare you. Just think "section" whenever you see "§." To write a section symbol, make a capital "S" on top of another capital "S."

To make a "section" symbol
draw an "S" over another "S"

WHAT IS A FIREARM?

In general, §18.2-433.1 of Virginia law defines a *firearm* as:

"...any weapon that will or is designed to or may readily be converted to expel single or multiple projectiles by the action of an explosion of a combustible material, or the frame or receiver of any such weapon."

In addition, the "brandishing" law, §18.2-282, includes pneumatic weapons and any object that looks like a gun (in essence, anything that could fool a person into thinking it is a gun) whether it can be fired or not, as firearms. Sometimes, other sections of law that include a definition of a firearm exclude, "or the frame or receiver of any such weapon," or include their own qualifiers.

The concealed-carry law, §18.2-308 says *handgun* means:

"...any pistol or revolver or other firearm, except a machine gun, originally designed, made and intended to fire a projectile by means of an explosion of a combustible material from one or more barrels when held in one hand."

For students on school grounds, under §22.1-277.01, a starter pistol is included in the definition along with the frame or receiver of a firearm, a silencer, or any destructive device. Sawed-off long guns are defined in §18.2-299.

Antique firearms made before 1899 are not considered firearms for purposes of background checks and multiple handgun purchases, in §18.2-308.2:2, but do fit the Virginia definition of a firearm for other purposes. That statute has its own definitions of *firearm*, *handgun* and *assault weapon*, as well as technical descriptions for *antiques* and *curios or relics*.

Guns that have been thoroughly disabled and are only for show are not regarded as guns under federal law. Questions about how to make a specific gun unserviceable can be directed to the Firearms Technology Branch of the Bureau of Alcohol, Tobacco, Firearms and Explosives (BATFE).

In this book, the words *gun, firearm* and *arms* are used interchangeably to refer to all handguns and long guns. When you see the terms *handgun, rifle, shotgun, long gun, semiautomatic pistol* or *semiauto,* or *revolver,* the reference is to that specific type of firearm only.

Pneumatic Guns

BB and similar pneumatic-type guns may sometimes be treated almost as if they were regular firearms, especially if they are particularly realistic looking, by some authorities. Some types designed for hunting or competition are quite powerful and the safest course is always to treat them as if they are regular firearms. Don't panic the neighbors and attract a SWAT team.

Under §15.2-915.4 counties may prohibit shooting pneumatic guns anywhere they believe is too heavily populated to be safe. They may require adult supervision for the use of pneumatic guns by minors below the age of 16, and allow use by minors over 16 with written parental consent, in places designated for such use or on private property with the property owner's permission. The minor may be held accountable for all rules governing such use, with a maximum penalty of a class 3 misdemeanor. For county listings see Appendix C.

County ordinances may not ban the use of pneumatic guns at shooting ranges or on land where firearms may be discharged. The training of minors under 16 in the use of pneumatic guns may only be done under the direct supervision of a parent, guardian, JROTC instructor or certified instructor. Minors over 16 may be trained without direct supervision if approved by the responsible party as specified in the statute. Instructors my be certified by the NRA, state or federal agencies, and similar.

This 2004 law authorizes use of commercial and private paintball areas for recreation. Protective gear must be provided, along with posted warnings that paintball is in use and not to enter without protection.

Stun Weapons

The introduction of the TASER-brand electronic-control device has spurred new laws, basically to restrict stun-gun possession in certain areas where real guns are typically banned. Using compressed gas, a TASER fires a pair of darts on thin wire tethers, to deliver a high-voltage charge to a target up to 21 feet away. In 2007 the laws dropped the brand name in favor of "stun weapon" which is, "any device that emits a momentary or pulsed output, which is electrical, audible, optical or electromagnetic in nature and which is designed to temporarily incapacitate a person." Stun weapons are generally legal in Virginia and regulated under §§18.2-57.02, 18.2-283.1, 18.2-287.01, 18.2-308.1, 18.2-308.2, 19.2-386.28, and 19.2-386.29.

Toy Guns

Toy guns that can shoot blanks or balls by means of an explosive charge are regulated under §18.2-284. It is a class 4 misdemeanor to sell, trade or give this type of toy to anyone. The law specifically exempts cap pistols from the regulation.

Federal toy-gun laws since 1988 have required a blaze orange plug of at least 6mm in the muzzle of certain toys, except for theater, movie and TV use, or as modified by the Secretary of Commerce. Toy, look-alike and imitation guns, including water guns, as federally defined, specifically exclude traditional BB, paintball or pellet air guns. The sale of BB-type air guns or certain non-firing replicas have federal protection that even real firearms do not presently enjoy—states are specifically prohibited from banning sales, under 15 USC §5001. The government is authorized to study the criminal misuse of toy guns and the effectiveness of the marking systems in police combat situations. The initial study was due in 1989.

Airsoft devices, known as "toy gaming guns" are often precise replicas of popular firearms and virtually identical at a quick glance, so care must be taken to avoid giving the impression they are real (people have been shot for brandishing "nearly" guns). Airsoft is sometimes used with protective gear, for playing "tag." No specific rules applying to them are known at this time.

Non-Guns

No consistent legal status for non-guns has surfaced in the state. These include gun drawings, pointed-finger guns, gun-t-shirts, gun bumper stickers and slogans, twig guns, gun speech and the notorious brandished chicken leg. These are used primarily by schools to threaten, harass and intimidate students, and also for expulsions, suspensions, reprimands, 'demerits, derision, scorn, and reportedly in some cases, anti-rights bigotry directed at the public and letters to parents. Up until the 1970s, many high schools had shooting ranges on campus and kids brought guns to school for competition, got varsity letters in marksmanship, went to ROTC or hunting after class, and even brought guns and ammo for show and tell. Today we find a system that has vilified these vital exemplars of freedom out of the school experience.

WHO CAN BEAR ARMS IN VIRGINIA?

An adult in Virginia may have a gun except:

1–A person convicted of a felony may not possess, transport or carry a firearm. This is a class 6 felony under §18.2-308.2. A convicted felon may be able to get permission to possess a gun from the circuit court with jurisdiction in which the person lives. This may be granted, sometimes for long guns only, to allow a person to hunt for food. However, removal of some or all state prohibitions may not remove the federal bans against a felon, but the state order to restore rights may be useful when working with the Bureau of Alcohol, Tobacco, Firearms and explosives in restoring federal rights.

2–Anyone serving a term of imprisonment in any correctional or detention facility may not possess firearms or ammunition. Violation is a class 6 felony, see §53.1-203.

3–A person who has been acquitted of specified crimes by reason of insanity and committed to a mental health facility may not possess or transport a firearm. Violation is a class 1 misdemeanor under §18.2-308.1:1. A provision for regaining rights under this section was enhanced in 2008.

4–A person who has been judged legally incompetent or mentally incapacitated may not purchase, possess or transport a firearm. A violation is a class 1 misdemeanor under §18.2-308.1:2.

5–A person who has been involuntarily admitted to certain mental health institutions or programs may not purchase, possess or transport a firearm. A violation is a class 1 misdemeanor, §18.2-308.1:3. A provision for regaining rights under this section was enhanced in 2008, and also requires, under §37.2-814, that the person be informed and agree that if voluntarily admitted the right to have or buy firearms is removed. The court must, under §37.2-819, send confidential notice to the state criminal database (CCRE) of the gun restrictions, to be used only to determine the person's eligibility to have, buy or transfer a firearm. The eligibility, but no medical information, must be sent to the federal NICS background check system.

6–A person who is under a protective or restraining order, or an order against stalking, may neither purchase nor transport a firearm. If the person has a CCW permit they must surrender it to the court that issued the order for the duration. A violation is a class 1 misdemeanor under §18.2-308.1:4.

7–A person who has been convicted of two drug-related misdemeanors in a 3-year period may neither purchase nor transport a firearm, under §18.2-308.1:5. This inability is removed five years after the second misdemeanor if there are no further drug convictions.

8–Specified violent juveniles, and a person under 29, who as a juvenile over 14 committed certain specified offenses that would have been felonies if the person was an adult, may not possess or transport a firearm, or carry one concealed. Violation of this law, §18.2-308.2, is a class 6 felony.

9–Foreign nationals (aliens) may not possess, transport or carry concealed assault weapons, a class 6 felony under §18.2-308.2:01. *Illegal* aliens cannot legally possess guns at all.

10–Bag-limit disarmament: A hunter who has reached the daily or season limit may help other hunters but his firearm must be unloaded. A legal hunter who has reached his limit prior to the hunt may help other hunters but may not possess a firearm. Violation is a class 3 misdemeanor under §29.1-521.

11–Added in 2003, anyone in possession of Title I or II controlled substances faces a class 6 felony and mandatory two-year sentence under §18.2-308.4.

12–Added in 2004, bail bondsmen who want to carry must comply with special training and use regulations of the Criminal Justice Services Board, including up to 24 hours of annual training (§9.1-185.2). A discharge while on duty must be reported to the board in 24 hours (§9.1-186.9).

A court petition process exists for restoring the right to bear arms if it is lost to any of the items except number 2 above, and number 7 includes an automatic restoration of rights. The proper authorities and military forces may be exempt from some of these restrictions. The individual statutes have specific details.

The Federal Prohibited Possessor List

A person may also be banned from gun possession under federal laws designed to keep weapons out of the hands of criminals. These are listed in Section 8 of the Firearms Transaction Record, Form 4473, which must be completed when you buy a gun from a federally licensed dealer. Federal law prohibits having, shipping, transporting or receiving a gun by anyone who:

- Is charged with or has been convicted of a crime which carries more than a one-year sentence (except two-year state misdemeanors);
- Is a fugitive from justice;
- Unlawfully uses or is addicted to marijuana, a depressant, a stimulant or a narcotic drug;
- Is mentally defective;
- Is mentally incompetent;
- Is committed to a mental institution;
- Has been dishonorably discharged from the armed forces;
- Has renounced U.S. citizenship;
- Is an illegal alien;
- Is under a court order restraining harassment, stalking or threatening of an intimate partner or partner's child;
- Has been convicted of a misdemeanor domestic-violence offense as described by federal law (for more on this recent addition to federal law see Chapter 7).

In filling out a Firearm Transaction Record form (required for every gun purchase from a dealer) you state that you are not in any of these categories. It's a five-year federal felony to make false statements on a Firearms Transaction Record form, and it's illegal to knowingly provide a firearm to a prohibited possessor.

Under §18.2-308.2:1, it is a class 6 felony to transfer a handgun to a person you know has been acquitted of a crime by reason of insanity, a person under 18-years old, or to a person who has been convicted of a felony.

Landlord Rental Agreements

A landlord cannot prohibit or restrict your tenancy in any public housing for lawful possession of any firearms. Under §55-248.9, any such provision in a lease is unenforceable, and if a landlord brings suit against a tenant on such grounds the tenant may recover actual damages and attorneys fees from the landlord.

Special License Plates

Special Virginia license plates are available from the motor vehicles department, under §46.2-749.6, to supporters of the National Rifle Association. It should be noted that a resident who wishes to take advantage of transporting firearms to and from shooting ranges "unloaded and securely wrapped," as allowed by law, should be a "regularly enrolled member of a target shooting organization" under §18.2-308. The NRA qualifies as such an organization.

JUVENILES

The law for parents to remember nowadays is that, any time your child goes shooting with you or without you, the child must carry written permission from you to receive or have a gun or go shooting, even if you're with your child. That's the net effect of a feel-good Clinton-era federal law, 18 USC §922(x).

State law sets no minimum age at which a child can have or use a firearm under adult supervision. This is a choice made by parents or legal guardians of the minor, who have a legal obligation to act in a responsible manner. Virginia prohibits anyone under the age of 18 from possessing a handgun or "assault firearm" unless accompanied by an adult, under code §18.2-308.7. Violation is a class 1 misdemeanor and a handgun used in violation must be forfeited. This does not apply in the home or on the property of the minor, the minor's parents, grandparents or legal guardian. Also exempt are minors legally hunting or enroute to hunt with an unloaded weapon, minors on someone else's property with written permission from the landowner and prior permission from a parent or guardian, and minors serving in the armed forces or National Guard.

Selling or giving a handgun to a minor is a class 6 felony under §18.2-309. This does not apply to family members or for a sporting event or activity.

One of the few cases where a juvenile may be taken into immediate police custody is for possession of a weapon on school property (§16.1-246). Using a firearm in a serious offense is a factor for transferring a juvenile to adult court (§16.1-269.1). A juvenile can lose driving privileges or be denied a driver's license for various periods of time for certain weapon violations (§16.1-278.9). Provisions for serious juvenile offenders, which includes illegal use of firearms, are found in §16.1-285.1. A juvenile who causes damage by shooting must make at least partial restitution to pay for any harm done, under §16.1-278.8.

Child Safety Law

It is a class 3 misdemeanor to recklessly leave a loaded firearm unsecured and accessible to a child under 14 years of age.

It is a class 1 misdemeanor to allow a child under 12 to use a firearm except under the supervision of an adult. An adult is defined as: 1–a parent or guardian who is supervising the child, or, 2–a person over 21 years old, supervising the child with permission from the parent or guardian. See §18.2-56.2.

Federal Regulation of Juveniles

Federal law (18 USC §922(x) generally prohibits people under 18 from having handguns or matching ammunition, or providing these to juveniles, with some exceptions and requirements: While carrying *written consent* from a parent or guardian (who is not prohibited from possessing a firearm themselves), a minor may have a handgun:

> 1–in the course of employment; 2–in legitimate ranching or farming; 3–for target practice; 4–for hunting; 5–for a class in the safe and lawful use of a handgun; 6–for transport, unloaded in a locked case, directly to and from such activities.

An exception exists for a minor who uses a handgun against an intruder, at home or in another home where the minor is an invited guest. If a handgun or ammunition is legally transferred to a minor, who then commits an offense with the firearm, the firearm must be returned to its lawful owner after due process. Minors may inherit title (but not possession) of a handgun. Violation of this law carries fines and a one-year jail term.

Gun-Free-School-Zone Laws

Like most states, Virginia has strict prohibitions about guns and schools. For federal school-zones law, see Chapter 7.

Deliberately discharging a firearm upon the buildings and grounds of any public, private or religious elementary, middle or high school is a class 4 felony. Shooting upon public property within 1,000 feet of such schools is a class 4 felony, except for lawful hunting. See §18.2-280. This statute excludes: 1– justifiable or excusable acts in protection of life or property; 2– school-sponsored programs; 3–proper authorities; 4–any act otherwise specifically authorized by law.

Merely having a gun on the property of a public or private elementary, middle or high school is a class 6 felony under §18.2-308.1, with narrow exceptions described below. School buses are included, as is property used exclusively for school-sponsored functions while the function is taking place. Possession of other types of weapons such as knives, stun weapons, tasers, brass knuckles or blackjacks is punishable as a class 1 misdemeanor.

Exceptions include unloaded firearms in a "closed container" in a motor vehicle, and unloaded rifles and shotguns in the firearm rack of a motor vehicle. The closed container in this case must be a locked vehicle trunk. Also allowed are weapons in a school-sanctioned program. With regard to knives, exceptions are made for pocket knives with a folding blade less than three inches long, food utensils as long as they're used that way, blades used for business purposes, knives in vehicles, or as part of school activities or approved programs, and for the proper authorities.

With a valid concealed-handgun permit, a handgun can be loaded as long as it remains concealed in your vehicle while on school property. If you are going to get out of the vehicle, the gun must be left concealed in the car. Once you are on school property you cannot put the gun in the trunk, because as soon as you step out of the car with the gun you would be in felony violation of the law. If you plan to get out of the car, you should conceal the handgun before you arrive at the school. Remember these two things and you should be OK: the handgun is concealed at all times and it never leaves the vehicle with you.

Under §22.1-277.07, written to comply with the 1994 federal gun ban for schools, a student may be expelled for a year or more for bringing a gun, destructive device, pneumatic gun or silencer onto school property. This is at the discretion of local school officials, under guidelines they may create. Schools cannot ban Junior Reserve Officer Training Corps (JROTC) programs on campus from conducting marksmanship programs, these programs can include pneumatic guns, and administrators must cooperate in running such marksmanship programs.

In 2004, school divisions were given authority to develop their own disciplinary policies banning guns on school property, buses and activities, see §22.1-277.07:1. School boards, under §22.1-277.2:1 may require students who have been charged with (regardless of whether they are convicted of) weapon violations, to attend alternative education. The family gets notice and there is an opportunity for a hearing. Gun incident reports, which must be made to school principals under §22.1-279.3:1, must include notification to parents, the feds, and centralized state files available to the public.

Although specific exceptions exist in state law for unloaded firearms in the trunk, unloaded long guns in a gun rack, and loaded and concealed carry for permit holders on school grounds, *students* in any of those circumstances could be charged with an offense and expelled if the school has created a gun ban of its own (§22.1-277.07).

Any county, city or town may prohibit any shooting, hunting or carrying loaded firearms while hunting, within 100 yards of a school, as a class 4 misdemeanor under §29.1-527.

Before admitting a student to a public school, the school board must require the parent or guardian to provide a sworn statement indicating whether the student has ever been expelled from a public or private school for a firearm offense. Making a false statement is a class 3 misdemeanor under §22.1-3.2. The document becomes part of the student's permanent record. In addition, the superintendent of a school division is notified by the authorities, as soon as possible by phone, when a juvenile is charged with a serious gun crime (§16.1-260), and in writing within 15 days, by the court clerk, when a juvenile is found delinquent or guilty of a serious firearm offense (§16.1-305.1).

A report must be made for all incidents involving shooting a person on a school bus, school property or a school-sponsored activity, or illegal carrying of firearms or explosives onto a school bus, property or activity, to the office of the principal, under §22.1-280.1. All such reports must be submitted to the school's division superintendent. The superintendents are required to file annual firearm incident reports to the Dept. of Education and the public. A division superintendent who knowingly fails to comply and make others comply faces sanctions described in §22.1-65.

Protection of juvenile criminal information is relaxed in student cases where firearm and certain other offenses are involved, and school staff are provided with limited immunity under §8.01-47, so police and school principals can share information and make reports required by §22.1-280.1. Under §16.1-301 police may release names of juveniles charged with serious gun offenses to the school principal, and must timely report any findings of not guilty, or where cases are dismissed, withdrawn, nolle prosequi, withdrawn at intake or handled informally without charges. A judge may release the name of a juvenile over 14, if charged with a weapon-related offense that would be a felony for an adult, see §16.1-309.1.

A juvenile who uses a gun to knowingly attack a teacher or other school personnel faces a mandatory minimum six-month sentence of confinement, as required by §18.2-57.

Introduced in 1999, every school must now have written emergency plans for dealing with a long list of natural and instigated disasters, including criminal attacks and threats with firearms and other weapons, see §22.1-278.1.

HOW DO YOU OBTAIN FIREARMS?

Guns and ammunition may be bought or sold between private residents of this state under the same conditions as any other private sale of merchandise, provided you comply with all other laws (you can't sell prohibited weapons, or knowingly sell to prohibited possessors or minors, the one-handgun-a-month rule applies for handguns, etc.). Temporary loan or rental of a gun from a state resident is allowed for any lawful sporting purpose.

Sale *and delivery* of firearms by a private resident to *any non-resident* is prohibited by federal law. Such sales are allowed, but delivery must take place through licensed dealers in the two people's states—it's a violation for the non-resident to transport the firearm interstate. Additional details are found in this chapter under *Transport and Shipping* and in *Out-of-State Purchases.*

If you are going to deal in guns (or for that matter, import, manufacture or ship firearms in interstate or foreign commerce), you need a license from the Bureau of Alcohol, Tobacco, Firearms and Explosives. Federal and state authorities may exercise a degree of judgment in determining when multiple firearm sales by a private individual constitute "dealing" in firearms, which is a felony without a license. Federal regulations provide some guidance on the matter. A dealer is:

> "A person who devotes time, attention, and labor to dealing in firearms as a regular course of trade or business with the principle objective of livelihood and profit through the repetitive purchase and resale of firearms, but such a term shall not include a person who makes occasional sales, exchanges, or purchases of firearms for the enhancement of a personal collection or for a hobby, or who sells all or part of his personal collection of firearms." (CFR §178.11)

Enacted in 2000, Virginia's dealers must now also pass a special background check to transfer firearms, under §18.2-308.2:3. Federally licensed dealers of firearms and ammunition are spread across the state. Firearms may be paid for in the same ways as any other retail merchandise. You may sell a gun you own to any dealer in the state willing to buy it from you.

The state police accumulate numerous firearms in the course of duty. After 60 days (§52-11.5), guns unclaimed by their rightful owners and not needed as evidence are taken over by the state. The police can retain any firearms they can use, and can destroy the rest by any means they choose. Prior to destruction they must publish notice on a newspaper and on a website.

In-State Purchase

To purchase a handgun and matching ammunition you must be at least 21 years old. Your request to purchase the handgun from a dealer, under §18.2-308.2:2, is made on the SP-65 form and reported to State Police, who must conduct a criminal-history background check, required by Virginia law. The form must contain only: your written consent to conduct the check; your name, birth date, gender, race, citizenship, and social security number (optional, and it must be safeguarded under §59.1-443.2) and/or any other identification number; the number of firearms by category intended to be sold, rented, traded, or transferred; and answers to these questions:

- Have you been convicted of a felony (or found guilty or adjudicated delinquent as a juvenile at least 14 years of age at the time, of an act that would be a felony if committed by an adult);

- Are you under a court order restraining the harassing, stalking, or threatening of your child or intimate partner, or partner's child, or are you subject to a protective order;

- Do you have any history of mental disability in Virginia or elsewhere that prohibits you from buying, having or transporting firearms.

A waiting period of up to 15 days applies in some other states, but Virginia uses an instant-check system, described below.

To buy a rifle or shotgun and matching ammunition you must be at least 18 years old. The Virginia instant background check, described below, is required for long guns as well as handguns. Some ammunition may be used in either a handgun or a rifle. This type of ammo can be sold to a person between the ages of 18 and 21 only if the dealer is satisfied it will be used in a rifle and not a handgun.

For all firearm purchases from a licensed dealer you must show government-issued photo-identification that is more than 30-days old, with your name, address, date of birth and signature. A driver's license (or state ID card issued under §46.2-345 and §46.2-348 in place of a driver's license) is the usual form of ID expected by most dealers. Obtaining such ID under false pretenses for the purpose of obtaining firearms is a class 4 felony.

An additional second form of identification is required to establish you as a Virginia resident. Although many definitions of residency may exist, for the purpose of obtaining firearms under §18.2-308.2:2, the second ID can be a:

> 1–lease; 2–utility or telephone bill; 3–voter registration card; 4–bank check; 5–passport; 6–automobile registration; 7–hunting or fishing license; 8–receipt of currently paid personal property or real estate tax; 9–other document acceptable to the Dept. of Criminal Justice Services; 10–Any other form of ID acceptable by the Bureau of Alcohol, Tobacco, Firearms and Explosives under ATF Rule 79-7 (allowing for a combination of documents which, as a group, include the necessary detail they may lack individually).

Members of the military can establish residency by showing their military picture ID and a copy of their permanent orders.

When you buy firearms from a licensed dealer you must fill out a federal Firearms Transaction Record, form 4473. There are no duplicate copies made of this form and the original is filed by the dealer. When a dealer goes out of business, the records are sent to a federal repository. The form requires personal identification information, identification of the gun and its serial number, and your signature. By signing the form you are stating that you are not ineligible to obtain firearms under federal law. Licensed dealers keep copies of this form available.

In addition to the federal form, Virginia requires you to fill out a Virginia Firearm Transaction Record, SP-65. The Virginia form is similar to the federal form with the addition of information establishing Virginia residency and a place for indicating if you've purchased a handgun from any source in the last 30 days. A false answer is perjury, a felony, which would revoke all your rights to own, have or use firearms. A person who has a valid permit to carry a concealed handgun may purchase more than one handgun a month by showing the permit to the dealer.

A copy of the Virginia form, without any information about the firearm purchased, is mailed to the Dept. of State Police. The State Police are prohibited from keeping the transaction record for more than 30 days but dealers are required under §54.1-4201 to keep the form for at least two years. The form is subject to local law enforcement inspection as part of a bona fide criminal investigation. In the case of multiple handgun purchases within a 30-day period, the State Police may keep the transaction record for up to 12 months.

A standard informational notice is often posted on the premises of licensed dealers, containing basic details on the laws governing purchase, possession and use of firearms, with copies available to customers.

In 2007, to prevent abusive entrapment schemes perpetrated by people such as New York's mayor Bloomberg, it became a class 6 felony for anyone but a law enforcement officer to try to entice a dealer to sell a firearm to anyone but the actual buyer (a so-called *straw purchase*—attempting to get a gun for anyone who can't legally obtain it themselves). Aiding or abetting such an effort is also a class 6 felony. The *actual buyer* is defined as the person who signs the official forms. §18.2-308.2:2.

As long as all other laws are complied with, a non-resident may temporarily borrow or rent a firearm for any lawful sporting purposes from a dealer. A dealer must conduct a background check before the transfer. You may own any number of firearms and any amount of ammunition.

Instant Background Check

Code of Virginia §52-4.4 establishes a toll-free number for conducting instant background checks. The service is available from 8 a.m. to 10 p.m. seven days a week. Dealers are required to obtain a background check before transferring any firearm to an eligible person. The request for the check must be made on the official SP-65 state form, which are serially numbered and issued in controlled batches to Virginia dealers only. A two-dollar fee for the background check is collected by the dealer and forwarded to the State Police.

The State Police must respond to background requests while the dealer is still on the phone, or by return call without delay. If it appears that the applicant has a criminal record or is otherwise ineligible, the police have until the end of the dealer's next business day to respond. Police don't have to respond on, and the "next business day" does not include Dec. 25.

The Virginia system automatically checks six different databases to determine if you are ineligible to purchase a firearm: the National Crime Information Center (NCIC); the Virginia Central Criminal Records Exchange (CCRE); the Virginia Criminal Information Network (VCIN); the Interstate Identification Index (III); the Virginia database of mental incompetency, the protective orders database (contained in VCIN), the Virginia calendar file on handgun purchases, and the FBI's National Instant Check (NICS), as required by the Brady law. Various laws require the authorities to file and to update information from these databases. For examples see Code of Virginia Title 37.2 and the Brady law. You have the right to inspect the criminal record files if you believe you are in it, and to have inaccurate information corrected, under §9-192.

If the State Police do not respond by the end of the dealer's next business day, the dealer can legally transfer the firearm without further delay (§18.2-308.2:2) but you may find some afraid to do so. The State Police background-check request log, containing your name as the buyer, the dealer, the request date and the official reference number is kept for 12 months.

If the computer system goes down the State Police must estimate the anticipated length of delay and inform the dealer. If the delay will extend past the end of the dealer's next business day then the sale may be concluded immediately.

The 30-Day Rule: Multiple Handgun Purchases

Under most circumstances, law-abiding Virginians who do not possess a valid concealed-handgun permit are restricted by §18.2-308:2.2 to purchasing no more than one handgun in any 30-day period. There is no truth to the rumor about Virginians being required to purchase one handgun a month. If you are not a concealed-handgun-permit holder and you want to purchase more than one handgun in any 30-day period, you must make special application to the Department of State Police who will perform an enhanced background check. This involves contacting local authorities for information that might not be reported at the state level, and any other measures that the State Police deem appropriate.

Applications for multiple handgun purchases may be available at your local police or sheriff's dept. Not all local law enforcement agencies are qualified under state police regulations to provide these forms. If your local police do not have the form, the nearest state police office will. The gun dealer you are working with should know where to get the form in your area.

An application for a multiple handgun purchase lists the number and type of handguns you want to purchase and the intended use of the firearms. Typical intended uses of firearms include purchase for a collection, sporting or competitive use, and personal or business protection. When you meet the State Police requirements, a certificate valid for seven days is issued to you. You must give this certificate to the dealer at the time of purchase and the dealer keeps it on file for a minimum of two years.

Most denials for multiple handgun purchases are due to incomplete information on the request form. Of the people who have applied, 94% had valid reasons and were approved by the State Police. If you are turned down for an incomplete application you may at any time re-apply with the information that was missing. If you are ultimately denied, you may appeal the decision by writing to the Superintendent of State Police. The appeal process requires you to prove your stated requirement for the purchase. It also requires the State Police to show proper cause for the denial.

Another exception to the one-gun-per-30-days restriction is in the case of handguns lost or stolen within 30 days of their purchase. (Replacement of other lost or stolen handguns takes place under the regular multiple-purchase routine.) In this rare case, if you feel it is "essential" to replace it, you may do so without making the special application. To do this, you must provide the gun dealer with evidence of the police report for your lost or stolen property. This is accomplished with a special Lost/Stolen Handgun Report, form SP-194, since a police criminal report is generally not releasable (some departments may allow the report itself to be used). The form is serially numbered to allow tracking and must be given over to the dealer at the time of purchase to prevent re-use. The SP-194 is submitted by the dealer to the State Police with the Virginia Firearms Transaction Record.

A person who trades in a handgun as part of the purchase of another handgun is exempt from the one-gun-per-30-days rule, but may only make one such purchase a day. In 2005, law enforcement officers were exempted from the 30-day rules.

In addition to the Virginia regulations on multiple handgun purchases, the purchase of more than one handgun from the same dealer in a five-day period must be reported to the Bureau of Alcohol, Tobacco, Firearms and Explosives and, under the Brady law, to local authorities as well, before the close of business on the day of the sale.

Out-of-State Purchases

Residents and businesses in Virginia are not prohibited from buying and taking delivery of long guns (rifles and shotguns) from licensed dealers in other states. Licensed dealers, collectors, importers and manufacturers are not prohibited from selling long guns to residents of other states. Such purchases must conform to the local laws of both states and federal laws. Purchase of handguns out of your home state is prohibited by federal law.

Some dealers, concerned with overlapping and often conflicting state and federal gun laws, and afraid of losing their licenses, have been known to refuse sales to residents of other states, even when those sales would be legal.

In any case, to purchase a firearm from an out-of-state dealer, you can always have that dealer transfer the firearm (handgun or long gun) to a Virginia dealer, from whom you can legally make the purchase and take possession with few concerns about the perplexing proprieties of interstate purchases.

Gun Shows

Gun shows are periodically sponsored by national, state and local organizations devoted to the collection, competitive use or other sporting use of firearms. Show promoters must give 30-day advance notice to the State Police before a show is held.

The exhibitor list must be available for inspection by law-enforcement authorities during the show and a complete list must be sent to the authorities, by hand, mail, email or fax, within five days after the show concludes. The list includes the name, residence and business address of the exhibitors. Willful failure to comply is a class 3 misdemeanor under §54.1-4201.1.

One exemption exists to the exhibitor list requirements—it does not apply to any town that had a population of between 1,995 and 2,010 in the 1990 census. This is a roundabout way of saying Hillsville (the only one, at 2,008). Their once-a-year four-day Labor Day gun show and flea market (mostly flea market) is so large—it attracts 2,000+ dealers and 350,000 people—that the decision was made to simply exclude it.

You may buy firearms from an in-state dealer at a gun show the same as you could on their regular retail premises. Out-of-state dealers can display their wares and take orders, but cannot make deliveries to non-licensees at the show. Purchases made from an out-of-state dealer must be transferred to a licensee within this state, from the out-of-state dealer's licensed premises. Non-dealers may exhibit and sell firearms at gun shows, from their personal collection, to anyone who is not a prohibited possessor.

Transport and Shipping
You may ship and transport firearms around the country, but it's illegal to use the U.S. Postal Service to ship handguns, under one of the oldest federal firearms statutes on the books, dating from Feb. 8, 1927. (The oldest federal law still in effect—except for Constitutional provisions—appears to be a firearm forfeiture law for illegal hunting in Yellowstone National Park, passed on May 7, 1894. It's interesting to note that no federal gun laws from the country's first 128 years are still on the books. The very first federal gun laws, in the late 1700s, actually *required* gun possession.) The Post Office says to use registered mail and not identify the package as containing a firearm.

You may have a weapon shipped to a licensed dealer, manufacturer or repair shop and back. However, depending upon the reason for the shipment and the shipper being used, the weapon may have to be shipped from and back to someone with a federal firearms license. You should check with the intended recipient and you must inform the shipping agent in writing before shipping firearms or ammunition.

Any handgun obtained outside Virginia, if shipped to you in Virginia, must go from a licensed dealer where you bought it to a licensed dealer here. Many dealers in the state will act as a "receiving station" for a weapon you buy elsewhere, sometimes for a fee. Taking any gun with you from a private transfer out of state, if it's coming back to your home state, is generally prohibited by federal law.

The only times when you may directly receive an interstate shipment of a gun are: 1–the return of a gun that you sent for repairs, modification or replacement to a licensee in another state and 2–a long gun legally obtained in person from an out-of-state dealer.

Interstate Travel

Personal possession of firearms in other states is subject to the laws of each state you are in. The authorities have been known to hassle, detain or arrest people who are legally traveling with weapons, due to confusion, ignorance, personal bias and for other reasons, even when those reasons are strictly illegal.

Federal law guarantees the right to transport (not the same as carry) a gun in a private vehicle, if you are entitled to have the gun in your home state and at your destination. The gun must be unloaded and locked in the trunk, or in a locked compartment other than the glove compartment or the console, if the vehicle has no trunk. Some states have openly challenged or defied this law, creating a degree of risk for anyone transporting a firearm interstate.

Carrying a firearm (armed and ready) is practically impossible unless you're willing to face misdemeanor or felony criminal charges as you pass through each state. A very helpful book, *The Traveler's Guide to the Firearm Laws of the Fifty States*, summarizes the requirements and restrictions on keeping a gun with you on the road, and is listed in the back of this book.

Article IV of the U.S. Constitution requires the states to respect the laws of all other states. In addition, the 14th Amendment to the Constitution forbids the states from denying any rights that you have as an American citizen. These fundamental requirements are unfortunately frequently ignored by some states. Your constitutional guarantees may be little comfort when a state trooper has you spread eagled for possession of a firearm that was perfectly legal when you were at home.

The bottom line is that the civil right and historical record of law-abiding American citizens traveling with firearms for their own safety has evaporated due to laws and policies at the state level.

People often have no idea what the gun laws are in any state but their own (and rarely enough that), a complete set of the relevant laws is hard to get, understanding the statutes ranges from difficult to nearly impossible, and you can be arrested for making a simple mistake.

The legal risk created by our own government for a family traveling interstate with a personal firearm may be greater than the actual risk of a criminal confrontation. Because of this, the days of traveling armed and being responsible for your own safety and protection have all but ended for people who leave their home state. The proper authorities are generally exempt from these restrictions.

The chilling conclusion is that the Constitution no longer constrains law-making as it used to, and the government has rights to travel that the people do not.

You don't fix a major national problem like this with a book. You fix it by restoring the lost National Right to Carry, also known as the Second Amendment, to the position it always held in America until the last few decades, during which its erosion has been nearly total for interstate travelers.

Readers who bought this book hoping it would somehow enable or empower them to legally travel interstate with a loaded personal firearm must contact their representatives and begin to ask about The Lost National Right to Carry. It has quietly disappeared through incremental attrition at the local level.

Common or Contract Carriers
Federal law allows you to transport firearms and ammunition interstate by "common carriers" (scheduled and chartered airlines, buses, trains, ships, etc.), but you must notify them and comply with their requirements, and possession must be legal at

your destination (see 18USC§922(e), (f), (s) and 49 USC§46505). Although federal law requires written notice from you and a signed receipt from the carrier when you pick up the firearm, verbal communication is often accepted. Call in advance and get precise details and the names of the people you speak with—you wouldn't be the first traveler to miss a departure because of unforeseen technicalities and bureaucratic run-arounds.

For air travel, firearms must be unloaded, cased in a manner that the airline deems appropriate, and may not be possessed by or accessible to you in the "sterile" area anywhere on the gate side of the passenger security checkpoint, including on the aircraft. You may ship your firearms as baggage, which is the usual method, and it's also legal to give custody of firearms to the pilot, captain, conductor or operator for the duration of the trip, though they're not required to take custody.

Airlines must comply with firearms rules found primarily in the Code of Federal Regulations, Title 14, §107 and §108, and, along with other carriers, United States Code, Title 18, section 922, and Title 49. A little-known provision of the Brady law prevents carriers from identifying the outside of your baggage to indicate it contains a firearm, a prime cause for theft in the past.

It's a class 1 misdemeanor to have or transport any type of gun, frame, receiver, muffler, silencer, projectile, ammunition, explosive, stun weapon, missile and more in an airport terminal, and such items are subject to seizure and forfeiture (§18.2-287.01). This doesn't apply to proper authorities, and to airline passengers who lawfully transport firearms or ammunition into or out of terminals, properly checked through as luggage, or to Customs agents for international flights. This 2004 law replaces any other prior state rules on the books.

New rules posted on the Internet by the Transportation Security Administration says that when in airport sterile areas, or onboard an aircraft for which screening is conducted, passengers may not carry these items as accessible property or on their person: BB guns, compressed air guns, guns and firearms, flare pistols, gun lighters, parts of guns and firearms, pellet guns, realistic replicas of firearms, spear guns, starter pistols, stun guns/cattle prods/shocking devices. The rules for private aircraft that are not subject to screening are ambiguous.

LOSS OF RIGHTS

The right to bear arms is not absolute. Gun control—in the true sense—means disarming criminals and is a good idea, a point on which everyone but the criminals agree. The list of people who may not bear arms at all appears earlier in this chapter. A person whose rights are whole may lose those rights, mainly for conviction of a felony. In 2006, the government was prohibited from using any emergency powers to limit the right to keep and bear arms except in specially designated shelters (§44-146.15).

Forfeiture of Rights

Your right to bear arms can be lost. Conviction of any felony removes your civil right to bear firearms under state and federal law. The right to bear arms is forbidden to anyone who is or becomes a prohibited possessor under federal law, as described earlier, or as defined under Code of Virginia §18.2-308.2. A felon may possess a firearm only after petitioning the circuit court in that person's residential district for permission, and by overcoming any federal disability that may also exist. The state court uses its discretion to grant the petition or not.

A misdemeanor domestic violence conviction removes your right to arms under federal law 18 USC §922, and a number of restorations are provided, including expungement, set aside, pardon, civil rights restored, and certain conditions under which the conviction may have been reached.

Recklessly handling a firearm while hunting can revoke your right to hunt with a firearm from one year to life under §18.2-56.1. Violation of any hunting law or regulation can remove certain hunting rights as described in §29.1-529, and a process for appeal is provided.

Seizure and Forfeiture of Weapons

The authorities can take your weapons if they have just cause. Firearms may be seized by a peace officer during an arrest. A search warrant can be issued (§19.2-53) under which weapons may be seized, a warrant for machine guns can be issued under §18.2-296, and a warrant for sawed-off shotguns and sawed-off rifles can be issued per §18.2-306. Any firearm used in a crime, upon conviction, is forfeited to the Commonwealth (§19.2-

386.28 et seq.). A court can order a forfeited weapon destroyed, sold to a licensed dealer, turned over to the state for use by the law enforcement agency that seized it, or disposed of by court order. See § §19.2-386.11 et seq. for the letter of the law. You may be barred from possessing or transporting firearms as a condition of release on bail, see §19.2-123, and bail can be denied in gun-related offenses, see §19.2-120.

If you had no knowledge of events that lead to the seizure, the weapon must be returned to you after due process (in other words, if someone used your firearm without your knowledge). You may petition the court for the return of your personal property provided: 1–you are not otherwise prohibited from possessing the weapon and 2–it is not a prohibited weapon.

All firearms seized, forfeited, found or otherwise held by the State Police and believed to be involved in a crime are tracked through the State Police Criminal Firearms Clearinghouse (see §52-25.1). The information kept includes details on the firearm, how it was obtained, the person from whom it was taken if any, the original place of sale and all subsequent owners if known, and the current disposition of the firearm.

Certain weapons are contraband (or contraband if unregistered) and are subject to seizure by the authorities. Included are stolen weapons, unregistered weapons identified under the National Firearms Act (see Chapter 3), Striker-12 or similar shotguns, defaced weapons and prohibited weapons under state law.

Personal property, including firearms and ammunition, may be seized by BATFE when used or intended to be used or involved in violation of any U.S. laws which the Bureau's agents are empowered to enforce. Acquittal or dismissal of charges allows you to regain any confiscated property, but this may be more difficult than it sounds.

Many state laws specifically require that firearms be seized, forfeited, turned over to the authorities or destroyed if they are involved in a violation.

Restoration of Rights

The state's main conditions for restoring the right to keep and bear arms, if they have been lost due to various convictions, are found in §18.2-308.2, with limited permission for such people to possess stun weapons at home. Other state restoration-of-rights conditions appear where they apply, such as in the hunting laws (§29.1-529).

A person with a truly compelling reason, and sufficient time, money and luck, can conceivably pursue a relief from federal firearms prohibition through the federal courts. Successful examples of this are few. Complete restoration of rights requires clearing both state and federal disabilities. The book *Brady Denial*, available at gunlaws.com, describes the processes for appealing, updating old records, correcting errors (quite common) and other rights-restoration issues.

Federal law (18 USC §925) also provides a method for restoring a person's right to bear arms if it has been lost. This has been useful to some citizens who are responsible community members and whose restrictions were based on decades-old convictions of youth, or other circumstances that pose little threat. The Treasury Dept., responsible for implementing this law, has claimed for many years that they have no budget with which to accomplish this work, Congress has refused to provide any, and the restoration of rights process has basically ground to a halt for anyone whose disability is based on federal charges.

However, BATFE has reportedly recognized the restoration of firearms rights to individuals in Virginia, if the state has granted a complete restoration of civil rights to the person, and the disability was based solely upon a prior state-level restriction.

A pardon from the President would also qualify, and although rare, at least one of the many people pardoned by president Clinton used that to obtain a CCW permit, in Arizona.

Frivolous Lawsuits
In an effort to disarm the public, various groups, including in some cases tax-funded government officials, have initiated enormously expensive junk lawsuits against gun manufacturers, distributors and related businesses—for the non-criminal manufacture and sale of firearms. Destroying the domestic firearms industry is quite a clever tactic, and would have a devastating impact on the civil right of gun ownership. The Defense Dept. testified to Congress on the severe national security threat a weakened or eliminated gun-making industry would have on the nation as a whole. Federal law was amended

in 2005 (P.L. 109-92), to prohibit such frivolous lawsuits, and Congress noted among many things:

"The Second Amendment to the United States Constitution protects the rights of individuals, including those who are not members of a militia or engaged in military service or training, to keep and bear arms." They refer to it as, "a basic constitutional right and civil liberty," and that they are enacting this law, "To preserve a citizen's access to a supply of firearms and ammunition for all lawful purposes, including hunting, self-defense, collecting, and competitive or recreational shooting."

Congress notes that the lawsuits are, "an abuse of the legal system," and, "based on theories without foundation in hundreds of years of the common law and jurisprudence of the United States," and an, "attempt to use the judicial system to circumvent the Legislative branch of government." And finally, they are enacting this law, "To guarantee a citizen's rights, privileges, and immunities, as applied to the States, under the Fourteenth Amendment to the United States Constitution, pursuant to section 5 of that Amendment."

The Congress has now addressed the applicability of the Second Amendment in enacted legislation five times, and in each case it has specifically recognized it as an individual right:

    The Freedman's Bureau Act of 1866
    The Property Requisition Act of 1941
    The Firearm Owner's Protection Act of 1986
    The Protection of Lawful Commerce in Arms Act of 2005
    Disaster Recovery Personal Protection Act of 2006

Congress also required dealers to provide locks with every gun sold, and included immunity for anyone who uses them, from a "qualified civil liability action." They used the same name for this immunity as for the industry immunity, even though they are quite different. If your gun is locked up and useless you are protected from a certain type of liability, from a thief who steals it and criminally misuses it. If your gun is not locked up and is available for immediate use, you have whatever protections you had before the law passed, from a thief's victims. Language was also added to help prevent courts from creatively "finding" any new liabilities.

Grounds for Forfeiture

Note: Beginning in 2004, gun forfeiture requirements were removed from many laws and collated into new statutes at §19.2-386.27-29.* The conditions remain largely the same, and this list is retained for historical reference.

§4.1-318	While involved in and within 100 yards of illegal alcohol manufacture, transport or sale.
§4.1-336	In the immediate vicinity of an illegal alcohol manufacturing operation, with proceeds from the sale of any forfeited firearms going to the Literary Fund.
§15.2-1721	Firearms unclaimed after more than 60 days
§18.2-283.1*	Illegal possession of a weapon in a courthouse
§18.2-287.01	Unauthorized possession in airport terminal buildings
§18.2-295	Failure to show state papers for a machine gun to law enforcement on request
§18.2-308*	Any weapon carried illegally concealed
§18.2-308.1*	Any weapon illegally on school grounds
§18.2-308.1:1	Possession or transportation by any person who has been acquitted of a crime by reason of insanity
§18.2-308.1:2*	Possession or transportation by a person judged mentally incompetent or incapacitated
§18.2-308.1:3*	Possession or transportation by a person involuntarily committed to a mental institution
§18.2-308.1:4*	Purchase or transportation by a person under a restraining or protective order
§18.2-308.1:5	Purchase or transportation by a person convicted of two specified misdemeanor drug offenses in a specified time period, with the disability automatically lifted after five years
§18.2-308.2*	Possession, transportation or carry by certain former juvenile offenders or convicted felons
§18.2-308.2:01*	Certain firearms possessed, transported or carried by foreigners
§18.2-308.2:1*	Firearms possessed intending to provide them to prohibited possessors
§18.2-308.4*	Firearms possessed while in possession of controlled substances
§18.2-308.5*	Firearms with less than 3.7 ounces of metal
§18.2-308.7*	Handguns or certain other weapons possessed by juveniles
§18.2-308.8*	Offenses related to Striker 12 shotguns
§29.1-208	Firearms seized related to hunting violations
§29.1-521.2	Firearms fired in or across a road while hunting
§29.1-524	Firearms used for hunting deer after dark
§29.1-549	Firearms used for hunting deer from a water craft
§29.1-556	Hunting with any weapon not specifically permitted by law
§52-25.1	Sets up a clearinghouse for forfeited guns

Virginia law divides crimes into two categories to help match the punishment to the crime. Felonies are extremely serious; misdemeanors are less serious.

Felonies are divided into *classes* (see Code of Virginia §18.2-10), starting with the most serious, Class 1, through Class 6. Generally, a felony conviction revokes your civil rights, including your right to keep and bear arms, to hold public office and your right to vote, and may include limits on your right to travel, your ability to work, to associate with designated people and other conditions at court discretion.

Misdemeanors are also grouped into classes (see §18.2-11). Class 1 is the most serious charge, diminishing in severity to Class 4.

Punishments are matched to the seriousness of the crime. This runs from a Class 1 felony, which can be punishable by death or life imprisonment, to a Class 4 misdemeanor, which carries a fine of under $250 and no jail sentence. See the Crime and Punishment Chart in Appendix B for the basic penalties for each type of crime.

WHAT DO YOU NEED TO GET A FIREARM?

WHAT DO YOU NEED TO GET A FIREARM FROM A FEDERALLY LICENSED DEALER?

- You must be at least 18 years old for a long gun, 21 years old for a handgun, and not be a "prohibited possessor" under state or federal law;

- You need a government-issued photo ID that establishes your name, address, date of birth and signature, and was issued at least 30 days previously. You need a second ID to verify your place of residence;

- You must file forms with the dealer and pass an instant background check for any disqualifying factors before taking delivery of a firearm;

- If the firearm is a handgun you may not buy it within 30 days of your last handgun purchase if any (a few exceptions exist);

- And if you are not a Virginia resident:

  –It must be legal to have the weapon in your home state, and the transaction must comply with your state's laws;

  –The State Police have up to 10 days to conduct the background check if the request is made by mail (same for a resident but virtually all requests are now made under the instant phone system);

  –You may take possession of a long gun over the counter if you could in your home state;

  –You may not purchase a handgun out of your home state (federal law) but you may have a licensed dealer ship a handgun to your home state for purchase there, if dealers in both states are willing to arrange such a transaction; and

- You must be able to pay for your purchase.

CARRYING FIREARMS 2

Open Carry

Virginians generally have the right to bear arms openly. Unless special conditions apply (and there are quite a few, discussed in this chapter and Chapter 4), it is generally legal to carry a loaded or unloaded gun if it is not concealed from plain sight.

There is a certain pride that Virginia is an open carry state—it reflects our pioneer sense of freedom. Indeed, many states have made it much harder to move a gun from point A to point B than it is here, where people are (or certainly used to be) free to take their firearms around pretty much as they see fit.

But as anyone who has tried it knows, strapping on a six shooter in most metropolitan areas attracts so much attention that it serves as a heavy deterrent. Requiring open carry actually limits the practicality of traveling armed, in a modern society where being inconspicuous is the civilized norm. Unless you're in costume or at a special event, many people just won't wear a gun while out and about these days.

This is less true however in smaller towns and rural areas, where finding people strolling around with sidearms is somehow less poignant, and perhaps a more common sight. At any rate, you do see people from time to time, statewide, going about their affairs, openly bearing arms. Dressing respectfully helps. Some gun-rights activists believe respectful open carry is important for its "inoculation effect," demonstrating publicly that firearm possession is a normal, safe and routine facet of life in a free country. Others think open carry is polarizing, and builds support for more gun control. It's been observed that if you can't or won't exercise a right, then you do not really have it. At least one civil-rights group has issued meeting notices with the line, "Tasteful open carry appreciated."

Guns In Cars

The same rules that apply to carrying a handgun on yourself apply to carrying a handgun in a car. If no attempt is made to conceal the handgun you can have it in your car with few restrictions (mostly related to where you drive to, including schools and other areas that may be restricted). A loaded handgun resting on the seat next to you or on your dashboard is legal, as long as the firearm is not "hidden from common observation." To have a loaded handgun (or unloaded for that matter) hidden from plain sight you must have a concealed-carry permit, described in §18.2-308.

A securely wrapped and unloaded firearm may be carried in a car under the same conditions as it may be carried on your person, as described below (club members to ranges or exhibits, or between your abode and a place of purchase or repair, etc.). To avoid any confusion about how securely wrapped a firearm may be, always use quality cases designed for firearms. A CHP holder can remain in a vehicle on school grounds with a loaded handgun if it is concealed.

Federal law guarantees all citizens the right to transport a firearm unloaded in the trunk of a car, as long as it is legal where you start and at your destination. Chapter 7 has details.

A common question regarding firearms in cars is whether or not you can carry a loaded handgun in your glove compartment without a permit. The short answer is no. The police generally consider a handgun in your glove compartment to be "about your person" (readily accessible) and "hidden from common observation" (concealed). This leaves you subject to arrest, though no specific court case or statute seems definitive on the subject so far. See §18.2-308 for the letter of the law.

There's an irony to the concealed-weapons laws for citizens in Virginia. In one case you may have a loaded handgun in your car within arms reach and be perfectly legal. The same handgun moved further away and in a closed or even locked glove box, even if unloaded, may get you arrested. No one ever said that all the laws make sense, just that they are the laws.

Special Category Firearms

It is a class 1 misdemeanor to carry certain loaded firearms in certain places open to the public. The firearms affected by §18.2-287.4 include any:

> "semi-automatic center-fire rifle or pistol that expels single or multiple projectiles by action of an explosion of a combustible material and is equipped at the time of the offense with a magazine that will hold more than 20 rounds of ammunition or designed by the manufacturer to accommodate a silencer or equipped with a folding stock or a shotgun with a magazine that will hold more than seven rounds of the longest ammunition for which it is chambered"

This law only applies in: 1–cities with populations of 160,000 or more (includes at least Virginia Beach, Chesapeake, Norfolk and Richmond); 2–counties with an Urban-County-Executive form of government (Fairfax only) or those counties or cities surrounded by or adjacent to such a county (Arlington, Loudon and Prince William counties), or any county having a County-Manager-Form form of government (Henrico only). As always it's best to play it safe, but you can see how difficult it has become to know if you are in compliance in Virginia.

The prohibition against carrying those loaded firearms does not apply to: 1–law-enforcement officers or licensed security guards; 2–anyone engaged in lawful hunting; 3–recreational shooting at established ranges or shooting contests, or 4–concealed-handgun-permit holders.

Concealed Weapons

Carrying a concealed firearm (or any other concealed weapon) on yourself without a state-issued permit is generally illegal in Virginia. The law here makes no distinction between loaded or unloaded firearms. See §18.2-308 for the letter of the law. A first offense is a class 1 misdemeanor, a second offense is a class 6 felony. Third and all subsequent offenses are class 5 felonies.

A weapon is considered concealed when it is "hidden from common observation," or when it is disguised to prevent it from being recognized as a weapon. For the concealed weapon to be in violation, it must also be "about your person," which means near enough to be readily accessible, and is a condition that may be open to a degree of interpretation. If you are arrested for a minor infraction you can be strip searched if the authorities believe you have a concealed weapon (§19.2-59.1).

Court cases have reached decisions that indicate it is illegal to carry in a handbag (Schaff 1979), in a gym bag (Hall 1990), under a car floormat (Watson 1993), in a car console (Leith 1994), and in a pocket covered by a duffel bag (Main 1995).

The State Police have posted an interpretation that says a weapon is considered concealed, "at any time it is placed in a location as to be within reach of the person, without the person being required to make an overt act to retrieve such weapon, when such weapon is hidden from common observation," and they include unlocked glove box of a vehicle, under the seat, or on the seat hidden from view without a permit and if no special circumstances apply.

A person may carry a concealed weapon without a permit under the following circumstances:

1–In your own home or the courtyard surrounding your home (technically known as *curtilage*) if any;

2–In your own place of business;

3–When a regular member of a target shooting club is transporting a weapon to or from an established shooting range, if the weapon is unloaded and securely wrapped;

4–When a regular member of a collector's club is transporting a weapon to a bona fide weapons exhibition, if the weapon is unloaded and securely wrapped;

5–When carrying a firearm between your abode and a place of purchase or repair, if it is unloaded and securely wrapped;

6–When engaged in lawful hunting under weather conditions that make temporary protection of the weapon necessary.

A firearm contained in a case designed for firearms will generally satisfy the requirement for *securely wrapped*. By requiring club membership for the carry privileges in state law, the state of Virginia encourages its law-abiding citizens to join organizations where training is readily available.

"Proper authorities" listed in §18.2-308 are generally exempt from permit requirements that restrict the public. In 2008, the Commonwealth's attorneys and retired Capitol police were added to the lengthy list of people whose rights exceed the common citizen, allowing them to carry on or off duty without a permit. In addition, state and local police officers honorably retired with a service-related disability or after at least 15 years of service may carry concealed, while carrying written proof of need, issued by their chief law-enforcement officer. Other state-law exceptions include U.S. mail carriers, prison guards, conservators of the peace (with a few exceptions), employees of the Dept. of Corrections, law enforcement agents of the armed forces or Naval Criminal Investigative Service, federal agents, and the Harbormaster of the City of Hopewell (one of four original east coast ports, where jurisdiction over international arrivals may fall outside regular police domain; it is believed to also include city marina property operated by the private Hopewell Yacht Club; the authority is rarely exercised).

National Police Concealed Carry

Federal law enacted in 2004 (Law Enforcement Officers Safety Act (LEOSA), HR 218, now 18 USC §926B and C) paved the way for specified active- or off-duty officers, and also retired law enforcement officers (RLEOs) to carry concealed nationwide, despite state laws to the contrary. People who can carry under these provisions must qualify periodically and meet other requirements, check with your department for details, and know the rules for states you visit. In 2007, §18.2-308 required police departments to allow retirees, at their own expense, to take part in training necessary to keep their qualification up annually.

THE CONCEALED HANDGUN PERMIT

Carrying a concealed handgun is an awesome responsibility. The legislative battles to establish the concealed-carry permit law were long and hard-fought, and the law is not perfect. It is now up to the citizens to demonstrate intelligent use of this law, to exhibit restraint in all but the most life-threatening situations, and to work hard to make Virginia a better place to live.

Obtaining a permit to carry a concealed handgun used to involve the often arbitrary decisions of officials, who required you to prove a need for the permit. Personal safety, crime deterrence and constitutional guarantees were not enough. In May of 1995, §18.2-308 was amended so any citizen who met basic standards would qualify and could get a permit. A broad array of proper authorities were exempted from the permit law and enjoy uninfringed carry (concealed with no permit), or have special breaks on the taxes, fees, training and other conditions.

Where the previous law called for a discretionary *proven need*, the new law says the government *shall issue* a permit to any qualified applicant. In the first twelve months following the change in the law, approximately 40,000 concealed handgun permits were issued. The permit is valid for five years and may be renewed for additional five-year periods.

In many parts of the country a permit for carrying a concealed weapon is referred to as a CCW. The Virginia concealed-carry permit is by law a concealed *handgun* permit, or CHP. Handguns are the only weapons that can be legally carried with the permit. The following are examples of weapons specifically prohibited from concealed carry under Virginia law:

    1–bowie knives;
    2–switchblades;
    3–ballistic knives;
    4–razors;
    5–slingshots;
    6–spring sticks;
    7–metal knuckles;
    8–blackjacks;
    9–nun chucka;
    10–shuriken;
    11–fighting chains;
    12–any multi-pointed throwing discs or dart;
    13–machetes;
    14–any weapon similar to those listed.

The concealed-carry permit contains your name, address, date of birth, sex, height, weight, color of hair and eyes, and your signature. It is signed by the judge issuing the permit or by the judge's clerk, and includes the issue and expiration dates. You must possess the permit at all times while carrying a concealed handgun and present it with photo-identification to any law enforcement officer when asked.

Statutory limits are set on the taxes, called "fees," that you may be charged by the Court Clerk, State Police and local authorities for a permit. The total tax may not exceed $50 ($100 for non-resident permits, issued under similar conditions), must be accepted in one payment by the person taking your application, is not due until the entire application is accepted, and may be made in any form accepted for other fees or penalties.

Your permit has limits:

1–You cannot carry a concealed handgun into any restaurant or club where alcohol is sold and served for consumption on the premises (but the owner or event sponsor, or their employees, or sworn law enforcement officers, while on duty there, may carry if they have permits; a *club* is defined as a private non-profit organization operated for a national, social, patriotic, political, athletic or similar purpose. A person with a valid permit and a concealed handgun has to switch to open carry, which is not banned, to legally enter such a facility;

2–You cannot carry a concealed handgun on to private property if it is prohibited by the owner;

3–Your concealed-carry permit does not entitle you to carry a handgun in a place where handguns are prohibited by law (and see the special school-grounds limits in Chapter 1). The permit doesn't extend your range of carry (except in state parks and driving to schools), it merely allows you to be discreet where you would otherwise have to carry openly (or unloaded and securely wrapped). See the information in *Prohibited Places* at the end of this chapter.

4–It is a class 1 misdemeanor for a permit holder to carry while intoxicated or on illegal drugs. If convicted, the permit is revoked, and you may not reapply for five years.

Qualifications for a Concealed-Carry Permit

Your local circuit court is required by law to issue your concealed-carry permit if you:

1–Are a legal resident of Virginia, or a member of the U.S. armed forces domiciled in Virginia;

2–Are at least 21 years of age;

3–Can provide proof of demonstrated competence with a handgun by any of these means (no additional proof can be required by the court, and your proof does not expire):

- Completion of any hunter education or safety course approved by the Dept. of Game and Inland Fisheries (or similar agency of another state);

- Completion of any National Rifle Association firearms safety or training course;

- Completion of any firearms safety or training course offered to the public by a law enforcement agency, junior college, college, or private or public organization;

- Completion of any firearms safety or training course at a firearms training school using instructors certified by the NRA or the Dept. of Criminal Justice Services;

- Completion of a law-enforcement firearms safety or training course for security guards, investigators or special deputies;

- Showing evidence of experience with a firearm through participation in organized shooting competition, current military service or an honorable discharge;

- Having been previously licensed to carry a firearm in Virginia, unless the license was revoked for cause;

- Completion of any firearms safety or training course, including an electronic, video or on-line course, conducted by a state-certified or NRA-certified firearms instructor;

- Completion of a police training course for police officers; and

- Completion of any other training the court deems adequate.

Disqualification

The disqualifying factors for a concealed-carry permit are found in §18.2-308. Circuit Courts are required to consult with law enforcement authorities and receive a report from the Central Criminal Records Exchange in order to issue a permit; the CCRE is required to notify the court that issued your permit if you become ineligible because of any disqualifying factor. Each of the disqualifying factors is cause to revoke your permit after it is issued, which the court must do, and promptly notify you of the revocation, and you must surrender it to the court:

1–Acquittal of a crime by reason of insanity, see §18.2-308.1:1;

2–Being deemed legally incompetent or mentally incapacitated, see §18.2-308.1:2;

3–Being involuntarily committed for mental-health reasons, see §18.2-308.1:3;

4–Being placed under a restraining or protective order, see §18.2-308.1:4.

5–Receiving mental-health or substance-abuse treatment in a residential setting within a five-year period prior to the application, see §18.2-308;

6–Having a felony conviction or, at court discretion, a pending felony charge or other specified charge pending, see §18.2-308.2;

7–Having two or more misdemeanor convictions within a five-year period prior to the application (not including traffic violations); if one of the misdemeanors is a class 1 offense denial is automatic, if not, it's at the discretion of the judge;

8–Having a stalking conviction or pending stalking charge;

9–Being dishonorably discharged from any of the Armed Forces of the United States;

10–Being addicted to or a user or distributor of illegal drugs;

11–Being a habitual drunkard, convicted of drunk driving, or convicted of public drunkenness within the last three years;

12–An alien not lawfully admitted to permanent U.S. residence;

13–Being a fugitive from justice;

14–Conviction of any assault, assault and battery, sexual battery, unlawful discharge of a firearm in public or from a vehicle, or brandishing a firearm in the last three years;

15–Conviction of an offense as a juvenile, if the offense would be a felony for an adult;

16–Conviction of possession or distribution of illegal drugs within the past three years;

17–A finding by a court, by a preponderance of the evidence, and based on specific acts of the applicant, that the person is likely to use a weapon unlawfully, negligently, or to endanger others. A Sheriff, Chief of Police or Attorney for the Commonwealth can submit a sworn statement to the court, based on a disqualifying conviction or specific acts described in the statement and personally known to the official, to urge disqualification. Prior to a change in 2005, the officials could disqualify you just by issuing a statement.

A person who has been discharged from the restrictions of incompetency, involuntary commitment or an insanity acquittal must wait five years before applying for a permit.

Concealed-Carry Permit Application

The application requires your name, address, date of birth, sex, height, weight, hair and eye color, signature, and a list of your residences for the last five years. It must be signed by a notary or other official witness, and only the official State Police form may be used. Making a false statement on the application is perjury, a class 5 felony.

Fingerprinting is not required by state law, but many localities took it upon themselves to make such a requirement after the right-to-carry law was passed. In 1997, §18.2-308 was changed to authorize counties or cities to pass an ordinance requiring fingerprinting for a concealed-handgun permit if they wish, and §15.2-915.3 gives them permission under the preemption law (but not for renewals as of 2006 and 2007). If fingerprints are required, you must submit them along with a physical description for use by the FBI through the Central Criminal Records Exchange. The state must pay any FBI fee for fingerprinting from your $50 maximum payment for the permit.

You give the application, along with a certificate of training-course completion, to the circuit court of the city or county where you live. The court works with local sheriffs or police departments and runs a background check through the Virginia Central Criminal Records Exchange. Unless you are determined to be disqualified, the permit must be issued within 45 days of application. If the record check hasn't been completed in the 45 days allowed, a temporary 90-day permit will be issued by the clerk of the court and will be valid until your regular permit is ready. If you are found to be ineligible, then the 90-day temporary permit will be revoked.

After the record check, the State Police must return the fingerprint card to the local agency. The local agency must promptly notify you that you have 21 days to request the return of your card. Cards not claimed within 21 days must be destroyed, as a gesture to prevent the authorities from compiling records on people who have not committed crimes. Digital fingerprints and transmission were approved in 2001, and mandatory destruction of these does not require notification. Fingerprints taken under this program may not be copied, held or used for any other purpose. It's not clear whether this state requirement is binding on federal authorities.

Once issued, the court provides the State Police and local law enforcement agencies with a copy of the order issuing a permit to you. Your application is stored by the court for at least ten years, when it may be destroyed under §17.1-213. If you change your address you must report it to the issuing court within 30 days, and they must issue a new permit.

Application Denials

If you are denied a permit you must be given a reason and you must be told of your rights to appeal, described in §18.2-308 and §17.1-406. Appeal is made to the Court of Appeals or to any judge on the court within 60 days of the denial. The petition of appeal must include a copy of the original application and the circuit court order denying the permit. The decision of the court of appeal is final. If you appeal and win, the taxable cost of the appeal is paid by the Commonwealth.

Beginning in 2006 the State Police are required to run an annual background check on all CHP holders. If a permittee turns up disqualified the permit is revoked and must be surrendered, and carrying a firearm with an invalid permit is a class 6 felony.

Record Keeping

When you've been officially approved as law-abiding, trained and qualified for a concealed-carry permit, the State Police put your name and description in the Virginia Criminal Information Network (VCIN) for access by law enforcement officials for investigative purposes. The chilling effect of being cataloged in the state crime computer, for being certified as an honest person and obtaining a government-authorized permit to bear arms, has deterred most gun-owning residents from applying for the permit. Less than 2% of the public nationwide applies. The wisdom of allocating so much resource for tracking the innocent instead of pursuing criminals is often questioned.

In 1999, the State Police were authorized by law to charge fees to federal agencies (except for the FBI) for access to the VCIN system. According to the Virginia legislative website, 76 federal agencies currently have access to your VCIN information.

CHP Permit Renewals and Replacements

Anyone who has held a resident permit can apply for a new one, and unless you've become disqualified the courts must grant your request. The new permit begins on and is good for five years from the expiration of your current one, if your application is received within 90 to 180 days before the end of your existing permit. A permit renewed in under 90 days will be good for five years from the issue date (meaning you lose a little permit time you've paid for). The same taxes and time frames for new permits apply to renewals. If you move, the originating court must issue a new permit with your new address when you show proof of your new residence and your existing valid permit, for a fee up to $10 (but getting another permit with the changed address is not required). Fingerprints are not required for renewals. Members of the military whose permits expire while they are deployed away from home are granted a 90-day grace period upon their return to reapply, and their permits remain valid during that time.

RECIPROCITY

Virginia has joined the national movement to "license" rights for its residents when they travel outside the state, and to "grant" rights to others who visit the state, by adopting a state-by-state reciprocal-agreement scheme. Concealed-carry permits from other states will be valid in Virginia, whether they recognize ours or not, if there is a way to instantly verify the validity of the permit 24 hours a day. The additional (and unworkable) requirement that the other state have "substantially similar" laws to Virginia was changed in 2001 to the condition that the other state's system be adequate to deny permits to anyone who would be denied under Virginia law.

The State Police are required to work with the Attorney General to determine if any states qualify for reciprocity. The State Police will maintain the list of states they deem qualified and make it available as part of the Virginia Criminal Information Network.

The official State Police reciprocity list is posted on the web, it may not match the list of states some local experts believe are valid under current law, and it recommends you check with the state in question before relying on the reciprocity concept. In 2004, Virginia relaxed its conditions for recognizing other state permits, making more states' permits valid here.

Federal legislation has been introduced to grant some relief, but the idea of federally "allowed" right-to-carry, for government license holders only, has a chilling effect and unlicensed people would have no rights under such plans. The cleanest approach may be a return to the fundamental right, nearly forgotten, that if you have a gun, you're not a criminal, and the gun isn't illegal, then that is not a crime and there are no grounds for arrest or harassment. This has been proposed as the American Historical Rights Protection Act (contact us for a copy).

NOTE: Rumors are swirling about which state has adopted what policy, and relying on a rumor where no rule exists can get you arrested. Viewing the printed statute yourself is a good way to help avoid rumors. Laws may offer less protection when new, before on-the-street police policy is established and well known throughout the law enforcement community. _Do not assume from the information provided below that reciprocity exists, only that the states are looking into the possibilities, and you might want to too._

It would be nice if there was a rock-solid reliable place to call to find out exactly where reciprocity exists, but there is none at the present time. Besides, a complete answer with precisely all the do's and don'ts is more than you can possibly get over the phone. The job of telling you is not the role of the police, the sheriff, the DA, the AG, the library or anyone else. Why, you'd need a book the size of this one for every state you visited.

Reciprocity Lists and Caution

These lists change rapidly and are available through private, commercial and government websites. Most rights organizations have a version posted, and they are linked from our National Directory at gunlaws.com. The accuracy, timeliness, and what it actually means to be on such a list can be hard to tell, and is usually undercut by disclaimers accompanying the lists. Non-resident Virginia licenses are not recognized in at least West Virginia and Florida. It's discouraging to see that in 14 years (1995 to 2009) only 20 states honor the Virginia permit. Info below is from sources believed to be reliable in 2009, and **states can be added or removed at any time without notice.**

Virginia Reciprocity (signed deals with these eleven states to honor each other's carry permits, according to the State Police): Alaska, Florida, Kentucky, Mississippi, North Carolina, Ohio, Pennsylvania, South Carolina, Tennessee, Texas, West Virginia.

Virginia Recognizes Them (states whose permits Virginia will honor, according to the State Police): Arizona, Arkansas, Louisiana, Michigan, Minnesota, Missouri, Montana, New Mexico Oklahoma, Utah, Washington, Wyoming.

They Recognize Virginia (states that will honor your permit, according to the State Police): Arizona, Arkansas, Louisiana, Michigan, Missouri, Montana, New Mexico Oklahoma, Utah.

Get Another State's License (these 21 states issue licenses to qualified non-residents): Arizona, Connecticut, Florida, Idaho, Indiana, Iowa, Maine, Maryland, Massachusetts, Minnesota, Nevada, New Hampshire, New Jersey, North Dakota, Oregon, Pennsylvania, Rhode island, Tennessee, Texas, Utah, Washington.

Freedom to Carry (no permit needed to discreetly exercise the right to keep and bear arms): Alaska, Montana (outside city limits), Texas (in vehicles), Vermont. Check with these states for special conditions that may apply.

These states have passed laws that would allow some bureau within the state (indicated in parenthesis) to cut deals with a bureau in another state, or they have set up other conditions that might lead them to recognize each other's permits—check with them for details:

Arkansas (State Police), Connecticut (Commissioner of State Police), Georgia (County Probate Judge), Louisiana (Deputy Secretary of Public Safety Services), Massachusetts (Chief of Police), Mississippi (Dept. of Public Safety), New Hampshire (Chief of Police), North Dakota (Chief of the Bureau of Criminal Investigation), Pennsylvania (Attorney General), Rhode Island (Attorney General), South Carolina (Law Enforcement Division), Texas (Dept. of Public Safety), Virginia (State Police with Attorney General and Circuit Court), West Virginia (Sheriff).

The different authorities named in this list are a measure of the consistency of the laws from state to state. If, after reading these lists, you get the sense that reciprocity schemes don't solve the problem and unshackle honest citizens, well, you're not alone.

Instead of an uninfringed right to keep and bear arms, your rights as an American have been reduced to a short list of government approved states for licensees only, under the infringement of reciprocity schemes. Enormous police effort that could go directly toward reducing crime is instead being diverted into registering, regulating and tracking the innocent.

A WORD TO THE WISE

Changes may be made to the laws concerning concealed-weapon permits. Sometimes these changes are administrative, sometimes they affect how you carry, and they can make what once was legal illegal, and vice versa. You need to know any changes to ensure you comply with all the current rules to avoid even innocent violations.

Officials may not agree on everything, and how individual law enforcement officers interpret the law may be different from how an attorney interprets it and how you understand it from your own study and training. Unfortunately, the law is not always black and white. The statutes may appear to clearly say one thing but an officer on the scene or a court may interpret it very differently when it addresses the facts of a particular case or when it applies past court precedents.

The elements of this book will undoubtedly change. Remember that you may face serious repercussions for what may be seemingly minor infractions. _The Virginia Gun Owner's Guide is just one tool for helping you on a long road to knowledge, and the road is not perfect._ That road has many turns and pitfalls—you should not rely on a single vehicle for such a complicated route, and be extremely cautious as you travel its course. Take steps to stay current.

Bloomfield Press will be preparing **updates** periodically. To receive free news about updates send us a stamped, self-addressed envelope, or visit our website. The addresses are on page two.

Get on our free email alerts list at gunlaws.com.

WHERE ARE GUNS FORBIDDEN?

PROHIBITED PLACES

In days long gone people would check their firearms before entering where guns were not allowed, such as a place of worship or a courthouse. Today, prohibited places make it necessary to leave your firearm in your car, as risky as that might be, or at home, which also carries some risk. The list has grown with the passage of time, giving rise to the phrase, *infringement creep*.

Some of the restrictions on possession of firearms are found in the *Code of Virginia*. Other prohibitions are found in federal statutes and regulations, agency regulations and codes, and local laws, and the list that follows may not include all of these. A concealed-handgun permit generally does not excuse a person from these restrictions and in fact, a person legally carrying a concealed handgun by permit is under some restrictions that other people are not.

1–*Places of worship*. It is a class 4 misdemeanor to carry any dangerous weapon into a place of worship, without good cause, while a religious meeting is under way, see §18.2-283.

2–*Courthouse*. It is a class 1 misdemeanor to carry weapons or ammunition into a courthouse. Firearm frames, receivers and silencers are also prohibited, see §18.2-283.1.

3–*Schools*. It is a class 6 felony to have a firearm on any public, private or religious elementary, middle or high school, or its grounds, or school bus, or a site used exclusively for a school event, unless it is either part of an activity sanctioned by the school, or if it is unloaded and locked in the trunk of a motor vehicle, see §18.2-308.1 (students are subject to expulsion for firearms in cars even if properly carried, see §22.1-277.01). A CHP holder can remain in a vehicle on school grounds with a loaded handgun if it remains concealed. The federal gun-free school zones law, overturned by the Supreme Court, was reenacted by Congress and can be found in Chapter 7.

4–*Where alcohol is served*. Concealed-carry permitees are prohibited from carrying a concealed firearm into any club or restaurant licensed to sell and serve alcohol, with exceptions for any owner or event sponsor or their employees with permits at such a restaurant or club, and for sworn law-enforcement officers, and certain retired officers (as of 7/1/09), see §18.2-308. Open carry is not prohibited in such places, which means regular CHP holders must switch from discreet to open carry when entering such clubs or restaurants. The legislature has for several years refused efforts to allow CHPs to remain discreet while dining.

5–*Private property.* Concealed-carry permitees cannot carry legally where forbidden by private property owners, see §18.2-308.

6–*Federal facilities.* Guns are generally prohibited in federal facilities (18 USC §930). Knowingly having a gun or other dangerous weapon (except a pocket knife with a blade under 2-1/2 inches) in a federal facility is punishable by a fine and up to one year imprisonment. Exceptions are made for the proper authorities and lawful carrying, "incident to hunting or other lawful purposes." There has been no test case on whether a CHP (or other routine legal carry) will qualify, and federal authorities routinely post this rights restriction without posting the exception, a deplorable practice. You cannot be convicted of this offense unless notice of the law is posted at each public entrance or if you had actual notice of the law (which, it could be argued, you now do). A federal facility is a building (or part), federally leased or owned, where federal employees regularly work.

7–*Airports.* Federal law bans firearm possession on the so-called "sterile" gate side of airport passenger-security checkpoints, with exceptions for the proper authorities. You can check and retrieve firearms as baggage if you do it in accordance with federal and state rules (see Common and Contract Carriers in Chapter 1). Virginia prohibits carry of a firearm, ammunition or other weapons into an air carrier airport terminal, even for permit holders, except as provided above, §18.2-287.01. The Metropolitan Washington Airport Authority, which controls Reagan and Dulles airports, sought jurisdiction anywhere on its property or even adjacent roads and tried to forbid all weapons in any of those places. Thus, driving on the Dulles toll road with a gun in your car (or even a tiny knife), could yield a misdemeanor charge. When our preemption law was strengthened MWAA was eventually forced to obey the law, not claim jurisdiction it does not have, and for now is in compliance with rules that govern all airports in this regard.

8–*Military bases.* Possession of firearms on any military base is subject to control by the commanding officer.

9–*Certain firearms.* Certain high-capacity firearms (21-round magazine capacity or greater in a handgun or long gun, or a firearm designed by the manufacturer for a silencer or that has a folding stock, or a shotgun with an eight-round or greater capacity) cannot be carried loaded in cities with more than 160,000 population, and other conditions apply, see §18.2-287.4. CHP holders and shooting ranges are exempt.

10–*Certain hunting grounds.* The Dept. of Game and Inland Fisheries has regulations prohibiting carrying firearms in certain hunting areas except during hunting season. The authority to prohibit other people from having firearms, except as it pertains to wildlife management, is not clear (see Chapter 6).

11–*Illegal still.* It's illegal to have a firearm anywhere near you while you're involved with an illegal alcohol still or its products, see §4.1-318 & 336.

12–*State Parks and State Forests.* An ongoing struggle with agencies running these areas may succeed in removing bans on carry. As we go to press, both areas seem poised to allow concealed carry with a CHP, and continue to ban open carry, which according to AG Bob McDonnell's opinion they cannot legally do. Check with vcdl.org, which is leading the effort to restore those rights, for the latest info.

13–*National Parks and Wildlife Refuges.* Federal authorities have since 1983 banned all operable firearms in these locations, without apparent delegated authority to do so. In 2008 under enormous pressure from the public and Congress they rescinded the ban but only for concealed carry, under the rules that would apply for concealed carry with a permit in the state. All other carry and possession remains banned (and anti-rights activists are pushing to reinstate the rights denials of the past). By recognizing and yielding to the fact that 48 states have adopted concealed-carry schemes (most of those recently), while ignoring the fact that all 50 states recognize the right to keep and bear arms since they became states, authorities are sanctifying government-licensed permission to the exclusion of constitutional rights, a dangerous precedent. As we go to press, a court just stopped the permit-carry rule from going into effect, which pro-rights groups are now fighting, again.

The prohibited places listed may not apply to the proper authorities in the performance of their duties—peace officers, licensed security guards and bodyguards, members of the military, prison guards, special exempt agents of the government and many more. The federal list alone includes more than 50 different statutes that exempt "special people" from gun laws. An active legislative effort in Virginia in the 1998 and 1999 sessions increased the immunities and privileges various government workers have from the gun laws that control regular citizens.

HOW CAN YOU CARRY A GUN?

HOW CAN YOU CARRY A GUN?

In each of these illustrations the legality depends on where the person is at the moment, and if the person has a government-issued concealed-carry permit.

In the top two examples, the handguns are being carried concealed. Unless you are in your own home or on your courtyard property (known as *curtilage*), or in your own place of business, it is generally illegal to carry a concealed handgun in Virginia without a valid government permit. Even with a permit, you may not carry a firearm into a prohibited place.

In the bottom two pictures, the handguns are being carried openly. It is generally perfectly legal to openly carry a firearm, but open carry is an uncommon practice in Virginia, it may make you the subject of a lot of attention, and the prohibited places list still applies. Many counties and cities have passed laws that outlaw bearing arms depending on the type, time of day, time of year, place and whether or not a firearm is loaded.

As you can see, the right to keep and bear arms has become significantly, (infringed, restricted, encumbered, limited, hampered, diminished, gray, outlawed, pick one) under state law. Many small laws have combined that now supplant the original intention and operation of the Second Amendment in modern-day Virginia.

Much of this has been done in the name of stopping crime. Other efforts appear directed at disarming the public. While efforts at stopping crime have had questionable results, the effect of the gun laws on the law abiding in the state has become acute. The new concealed-carry law has eased the restrictions somewhat, but less than 1% of Virginians have been willing to register with the government for a right-to-carry license.

WHEN CAN YOU CONCEAL A HANDGUN?

- In your own home or on your property immediately around your home (known as *curtilage*);
- In your own place of business;
- If you are a member of a shooting club you may carry a firearm to and from an established range as long as the weapon is unloaded and securely wrapped;
- If you are a member of a collector's club you may carry a firearm to and from a firearm exhibition as long as the weapon is unloaded and securely wrapped;
- When going to and from your home and a place of purchase or repair as long as the weapon is unloaded and securely wrapped;
- When you are hunting in bad weather and it is necessary to protect the weapon;
- With a valid Virginia concealed-carry permit in any places that aren't prohibited by law.

TYPES OF WEAPONS 3

There are weapons and there are weapons. Guns are only one kind of weapon. If a gun is modified in certain ways, it may become a *prohibited weapon*, which may make it a crime to own or possess. In the years from 1994 to 2004, certain firearms and accessories, under the so-called assault-weapon ban, could only be owned if they were made before Sep. 13, 1994 (that ban has ended). The definitions of legal firearms are a moving target, just like the gun laws themselves.

A responsible gun owner needs an understanding of the different types of firearms, and their methods of operation, good selections for personal defense, holstering options, ammunition types, loading and unloading, cleaning and maintenance, accessories, safe storage and more. Many fine books cover these areas. This chapter of *The Virginia Gun Owner's Guide* only covers weapons from the standpoint of those which are illegal, restricted or otherwise specially regulated.

PROHIBITED WEAPONS

In 1934, responding to mob violence spawned by Prohibition, Congress passed the National Firearms Act (NFA), the second major federal law concerning guns since the Constitution (the first was the Militia Act of 1792, which actually required keeping arms). The NFA was an attempt to control what Congress called "gangster-type weapons." Items like machine guns, silencers, short rifles and sawed-off shotguns were put under strict government control and registration. These became known as "NFA weapons."

This gave authorities an edge in the fight against crime. Criminals never registered their weapons, and now simple possession of an unregistered "gangster gun" was a federal offense. Failure to pay the required transfer tax compounded the charge. Other types of personal firearms were unaffected.

Political assassinations in the 1960s led to a public outcry for greater gun controls. In 1968, the federal Gun Control Act was passed, which absorbed the provisions of earlier statutes and added bombs and other destructive devices to the list of strictly controlled weapons. It is generally illegal to make, have, transport, sell or transfer any prohibited weapon without prior government approval and registration. Violation of this is a class 6 felony under state law, and carries federal penalties of up to 10 years in jail and up to a $10,000 fine.

Defaced Deadly Weapons

Removing, altering or destroying the manufacturer's serial number on a gun is a federal felony. Knowingly having a defaced gun is a federal felony. Virginia Code §18.2-311.1 makes it a class 1 misdemeanor to intentionally deface, alter or in any way destroy the serial number, the model number, the name of the maker or any other ID mark of any firearm.

State Prohibited-Weapons List

Under Virginia law certain types of weapons are restricted and must be registered with the Bureau of Alcohol Tobacco and

Firearms. Machine guns must also be registered with the Dept. of State Police. Possession of some other weapons or devices is completely prohibited. The following restrictions and requirements are in addition to federal law.

1–*Explosive materials, devices or firebombs* (§18.2-85): Having, making, transporting, distributing or using is a class 5 felony. Exceptions include use by the military, law enforcement, fire fighters, for scientific research, for educational purposes and for any other lawful purpose.

2–*Hoax bombs* (§18.2-85): Making, placing, sending or using a device in a way that causes another person to believe it is a real bomb, is a class 6 felony.

3–*Machine guns* (§18.2-288 to §18.2-298): The special requirements of Virginia's Uniform Machine Gun Act are discussed in detail, along with the federal requirements for machine gun owners, later in this chapter.

4–*Sawed-off shotguns and rifles* (§18.2-300): Possession or use in a crime is a class 2 felony; other possession or use is a class 4 felony. Exceptions apply to the military, law enforcement or by private persons in compliance with federal NFA weapons laws. Under §18.2-299, firearms less than .225 caliber are excluded.

5–*Plastic firearms* (§18.2-308.5): Firearms designed to evade detection by X-ray machines and metal detectors are illegal. If a firearm does not contain at least 3.7 ounces of metal, its possession, importation, sale, transfer or manufacture would be a class 5 felony. The lightweight Austrian-made Glock, with its polymer frame, created the commotion that lead to passage of this law, for guns that don't exist. A Glock model 21 (.45 cal) uses about 18 ounces of metal, or nearly five times more than is required.

6–*Silencers* (§18.2-308.6): Possession is a class 6 felony. Silencers possessed in compliance with federal NFA weapons laws are not prohibited.

7–*Striker-12 or "Street Sweeper" shotguns* (§18.2-308.8): It is a class 6 felony to possess, sell, transfer or import this type of shotgun. See §18.2-308.8 for a description of Striker-12-type prohibited weapons.

8–*Blackjacks* (§18.2-311): Selling, bartering, having or giving away any blackjacks, metal knuckles, throwing stars, switchblade knives or ballistic knives or similar weapons is a class 4 misdemeanor. Possession of any of these is considered evidence of intent to sell.

9–*Restricted ammunition* (§18.2-308.3): This is ammo designed to defeat bullet-proof vests. See §18.2-308.3 for technical definitions. Use in a crime or attempted crime is a class 5 felony.

A list of weapons which may not be carried concealed, even with a concealed-carry permit, appears in Chapter 2.

Note that the phrase "explosive material" is defined under §18.2-85 to include "gunpowder" (a word usually reserved to connote "black powder," a mixture of sulfur, charcoal and potassium nitrate, which is an explosive) and to "smokeless powder," (a nitrocellulose compound which is a propellant, not an explosive, used in most modern cartridge ammunition). Fire Services Board regulations, and the Fire Prevention Code, under §27-97, regulate the handling, storage and use of "explosives or blasting agents."

Stun Weapons are legal in Virginia, but generally prohibited where firearms are banned. *TASER* is a brand name for only one such device. In 2007 the law re-defined *stun weapon* as "any device that emits a momentary or pulsed output, which is electrical, audible, optical or electromagnetic in nature and which is designed to temporarily incapacitate a person." Stun weapons are regulated under §§18.2-57.02, 18.2-283.1, 18.2-287.01, 18.2-308.1, 18.2-308.2, 19.2-386.28, and 19.2-386.29.

"ILLEGAL" GUNS

(Sometimes also referred to as *NFA weapons,*
prohibited weapons or *destructive devices*)

Frequently but inaccurately termed illegal, these weapons and destructive devices are among those that are legal only if they are pre-registered with the Bureau of Alcohol, Tobacco, Firearms and Explosives.

1–A rifle with a barrel less than 16 inches long;

2–A shotgun with a barrel less than 18 inches long;

3–A modified rifle or shotgun less than 26 inches overall;

4–Machine guns (state registration also required);

5–Silencers of any kind;

6–Firearms over .50 caliber;

7–Street Sweeper, Striker-12 and similar type shotguns (not legal in Virginia even if BATFE-registered; USAS-12 is not banned due to its different design, but as of Mar. 1, 1994, it is reclassified by BATFE as a destructive device and must be registered with them even if owned prior to that date, though the tax is waived if owned prior to the effective date).

Guns with a bore of greater than one-half inch, except regular shotguns, are technically known as destructive devices. Some antique and black-powder firearms have such large bores but are not prohibited, as determined on a case-by-case basis by the Bureau of Alcohol, Tobacco, Firearms and Explosives.

"AFFECTED" WEAPONS

Historical Note: The federal Public Safety and Recreational Firearms Use Protection Act (also called the Crime Bill, also called the assault-weapons ban, which expired on Sep. 13, 2004), allowed citizens to possess certain firearms and accessories only if they were made before Sep. 13, 1994. New products required a date stamp and were off-limits for the public. Having an affected weapon or accessory that had no date stamp was presumption that the item was not affected (that is, it was a pre-crime-bill version) and was OK. This law has now expired, none of these conditions apply any longer, and we can see the value of laws with expiration dates. For the record, the affected weapons (there were about 200) included all firearms, copies or duplicates, in any caliber, known as:

Norinco, Mitchell, and Poly Technologies (Avtomat Kalashnikovs (all models); Action Arms Israeli Military Industries Uzi and Galil; Beretta AR-70 (SC-70); Colt AR-15; Fabrique National FN/FAL, FN/LAR, and FNC; SWD M-10, -11, -11/9, and -12; Steyr AUG; Intratec TEC-9, -DC9 and -22; and revolving cylinder shotguns, such as (or similar to) the Street Sweeper and Striker 12, and, any **rifle** that can accept a detachable magazine and has at least 2 of these features: a folding or telescoping stock; a pistol grip that protrudes conspicuously beneath the action; a bayonet mount; a flash suppressor or threaded barrel for one; and a grenade launcher, and, any **semiautomatic pistol** that can accept a detachable magazine and has at least 2 of these features: a magazine that attaches outside of the pistol grip; a threaded barrel that can accept a barrel extender, flash suppressor, forward handgrip, or silencer; a shroud that is attached to, or partially or completely encircles, the barrel and permits the shooter to hold the firearm with the nontrigger hand without being burned; a manufactured weight of 50 ounces (3-1/8 lbs.) or more when unloaded; and a semiautomatic version of an automatic firearm, and, any **semiautomatic shotgun** that has at least 2 of these features: a folding or telescoping stock; a pistol grip that protrudes conspicuously beneath the action; a fixed magazine capacity in excess of 5 rounds; and an ability to accept a detachable magazine, and, any **magazines**, belts, drums, feed strips and similar devices if they can accept more than 10 rounds of ammunition (fixed tubular devices for a .22 caliber rimfire ammo are not included).

MACHINE GUNS

Under strictly regulated conditions, most private citizens who can own regular firearms can own certain other weapons that would otherwise be prohibited. An example is the machine gun.

Unlike normal firearm possession, the cloak of privacy afforded gun ownership is removed in the case of so-called "NFA weapons" (technically, Title II devices), including full autos, suppressors, "sawed off" long guns, and more—those originally restricted by the National Firearms Act of 1934. The list has grown since that time, through subsequent legislation. For a law-abiding private citizen to obtain an NFA weapon, five conditions must be met. These requirements are designed to keep the weapons out of criminal hands, or to prosecute criminals for possession.

1–The weapon itself must be "available,"—registered in the National Firearms Registry and Transfer Records of the Treasury Dept. This list of arms includes about 193,000 machine guns.

> The registry was closed to full autos on 5/19/86. New registrations since then can only include the other Title II devices. Any full autos made after that date may now only be transferred to proper government agents.

2–Permission to transfer the weapon must be obtained in advance, by filing "ATF Form 4 (5320.4)" available from the BATFE.

3–An FBI background check is performed to locate any criminal record that would disqualify you from possessing the weapon. This is done with a recent 2" x 2" photo of yourself, fingerprints (FBI FD-258 Fingerprint Card) submitted with the application, and signature approval of your local chief law enforcement officer, typically the sheriff or police chief. Corporations are exempt from the photo, fingerprint and CLEO signature requirements.

4–You must pay a $200 transfer tax to the Internal Revenue Service. For some NFA weapons, the transfer tax is $5.00.

5–The previous owner's name in the National Registry is changed to the new owner's name, and a new tax stamp, showing the weapon's serial number, is issued. The original or a copy of this stamp must always accompany the weapon, and permission to take the weapon across state lines must be obtained in advance.

The three ways to legally obtain a machine gun include:

1–A properly licensed dealer (a Class III FFL) can sell a registered machine gun to a qualified private buyer; 2–A legal owner can obtain permission from BATFE to transfer the firearm to a qualified recipient in the same state, and 3-You can inherit one. Any inherited NFA weapon can be transferred interstate directly to the heir, after the registration papers are approved. Special rules for executors of estates that contain NFA weapons are available from BATFE.

With prior approval you can make NFA weapons (except machine guns), such as short rifles, sawed-off shotguns, suppressors, "gadget guns" (technically, "any other weapons" such as pen, cane or wallet guns), etc. The application process is similar to the process for buying such weapons. Unregistered NFA weapons are contraband, and are subject to seizure. Having the unassembled parts needed to make an NFA weapon counts as having one.

The authorities are generally exempt from these provisions. Open trade in automatic weapons in Virginia is allowed between manufacturers and dealers, and includes state and city police, prisons, the state and federal military, the National Guard, museums, educational institutions, and people with special licenses and permits.

The official trade in machine guns is specifically prohibited from becoming a source of commercial supply. Only those machine guns that were in the National Firearms Registry and Transfer Records as of May 19, 1986 may be privately held. This includes about 5,000 machine guns in Virginia. The number available nationally will likely drop, since no new full-autos are being added to the registry, and the existing supply will decrease through attrition. Virginians own about 9,000 NFA weapons in total.

State Controls on Machine Guns

Failing to register a machine gun with the State Police within 24 hours of acquiring it is a class 3 misdemeanor (§18.2-295). The registration is good as long as you own the firearm, the certificate must be kept with the weapon, and it is a class 3 misdemeanor to not have the certificate available for inspection by the proper authorities upon request. A machine gun can be confiscated for failure to show the registration certificate and may be forfeited to the Commonwealth. Failure to notify the State Police when transferring a machine gun is a class 3 misdemeanor. Registration data may not be viewed by the general public.

Under §18.2-290, having a machine gun for an aggressive or offensive purpose is a class 4 felony. Any machine gun is considered to be possessed for aggressive or offensive purposes if: a–it is not registered with the state; b–it is possessed by a criminal; c–it is not at the home or business of its registered owner; or d–if any ammunition or empty shells for it are nearby. If a machine gun is in a room it is presumed to be possessed by each person in the room (§18.2-292).

In contrast however, the law does allow, under §18.2-293.1, "the possession of a machine gun for a purpose manifestly not aggressive or offensive," that covers the sporting and private uses for which law-abiding citizens might own a fully automatic firearm. It is also legal to have a machine gun for scientific purposes or to have one that is non-functional as a memento, provided in either case that the item is registered with the state. Dealers are required to keep a state register (in addition to federal records) of all machine guns they handle, and information on each buyer, under §18.2-294. Having or using a machine gun for a crime of violence is a class 2 felony (§18.2-289).

These Virginia state requirements for machine gun owners are in addition to the federal requirements.

CURIOS, RELICS AND ANTIQUES

Curios and relics are guns that have special value as antiquities, for historical purposes, or other reasons that make it unlikely they will be used currently as weapons. The *Curio and Relic List* is a 60-page document available from the Bureau of Alcohol, Tobacco, Firearms and Explosives. They can also tell you how to apply to obtain curio or relic status for a particular weapon.

Antique firearms, defined as firearms with matchlock, flintlock, percussion cap or similar ignition systems, manufactured in or before 1898, and replicas meeting specific guidelines are exempt from certain federal laws. For complete details contact the Bureau of Alcohol, Tobacco, Firearms and Explosives, and see the technical descriptions in §18.2-308.2:2. Remember, though, if it can fire or readily be made to fire it is a firearm under Virginia state law. State law does exempt antiques from background checks and the one-handgun-per-30-day restraint-of-trade rule.

NEW LEGISLATION

Congress and states nationwide have been considering a variety of selective and categorical firearms bans. You are advised to follow developments and remain keenly aware of any firearms or accessories that were formerly legal and then declared illegal or subjected to new requirements. One such example is the USAS-12 shotgun, described earlier. It's hard to justify, from a constitutional point of view, how a given firearm can be legal one day and outlawed the next. This is often done under the misdirected guise of controlling criminals. Controlling private property the public owns, and catching and prosecuting people for committing crimes regardless of what they use, are different issues, but conflated and confused by politicians, the media and an uninformed public. If politicians go after real criminal misuse of firearms they receive broad public support. When they go after firearms in the public's hands, they meet with fierce resistance. You'd think their choice would be obvious.

WHAT'S WRONG WITH THIS PICTURE?

It is a federal felony to have these weapons and destructive devices unless they are pre-registered with the Bureau of Alcohol, Tobacco, Firearms and Explosives.

- A rifle with a barrel less than 16 inches long
- A shotgun with a barrel less than 18 inches long
- A modified rifle or shotgun less than 26 inches overall
- Street Sweeper, Striker-12 and similar type shotguns (not legal in Virginia even if BATFE-registered; USAS-12 is not prohibited due to its different design, but must be BATFE registered).
- Fully automatic firearms (machine guns, which must also be registered with the State Police)
- Silencers of any kind
- Firearms using fixed ammunition over .50 caliber
- Armor-piercing ammunition
- Explosive, incendiary or poison gas bombs
- Explosive, incendiary or poison gas grenades
- Explosive, incendiary or poison gas mines
- Explosive, incendiary or poison gas rockets with more than 4 ounces of propellant (includes bazooka)
- Missiles with an explosive or incendiary charge greater than 1/4 ounce
- Mortars

Keep in mind that additional weapons may be added to this list in the future.

THERE'S NOTHING WRONG WITH THIS PICTURE!

THERE'S NOTHING WRONG WITH THIS PICTURE!

Practicing the shooting sports outdoors is a natural and wholesome pursuit as long as you comply with the laws.

- The shooters are at a remote location, on private land with the landowner's permission, or at an established shooting range.
- The remote location is outside city limits, violates no county ordinances, and does not cause a noise problem for neighbors.
- The target has a backstop which prevents bullets from causing a potential hazard.
- No wildlife or protected plants are in the line of fire.
- The shooters are using eye and ear protection.
- The sun is shining, they're improving their skills, and they're thoroughly enjoying themselves and their time spent outdoors.

LOCAL LAWS 4

Preemption Law

Virginia has a colorful and growing history of state efforts to control local officials from enacting their own gun laws against the public. This is called *preemption*, and is found beginning in Code of Virginia §15.2-915. Preemption is supposed to provide uniform rules for residents statewide, preventing a patchwork of ordinances people couldn't know or obey as they travel.

On Oct. 1, 1987, state law prohibited local authorities from enacting firearm laws. However, the law had some loopholes and allowed local authorities to pass their own laws at any time, if expressly allowed under other state statutes. Other statutes did exist and made the situation across the Commonwealth very difficult to follow, criminalizing otherwise innocent folks.

Preemption was strengthened in 2002 and again in 2003, when civil-rights activists got wording added that closed loopholes local bureaucrats were wiggling through (dealing with public parks, government buildings and more). In return, localities were granted broad power to adopt workplace rules and conditions of employment relating to firearms.

Then in 2004 the law was made much more airtight, stopping locals from infringing upon the "purchase, possession, transfer, ownership, carrying, storage or transporting of firearms, ammunition, or components or combination thereof other than those expressly authorized by statute." What they can regulate was made more clear, and exceptions were spelled out in detail. Local officials didn't like it but the public relished the freedom.

In 2009, still needing further control, the state added that anyone who wins in court against such local abuses can collect attorney fees, court costs and expenses from the offending party.

Enabling Laws

The laws that authorize local lawmaking are known as *enabling laws*. Within stated limits, local governments have been granted powers to pass certain laws regulating firearms.

- §15.2-915. Enacted to revamp the entire preemption scheme in the state, this removes wide swaths of local authority, clearly delegates others, and awards legal costs if a lawsuit is needed to force localities to comply. It makes the state the sole authority on most firearm matters.

- §15.2-915.2. Allows the governing body of a county or city to adopt laws making it illegal to transport, possess or carry a loaded shotgun or rifle in any vehicle on any public road or highway within the county or city. Unloaded long guns are unaffected. Laws enacted under this statute may carry a fine of up to $100, the Dept. of Game and Inland Fisheries must be notified of any such law for it to be enforceable, and the law does not apply when:

  - Law enforcement or military members are performing their duties, or

  - You reasonably believe the loaded shotgun or rifle is needed for your safety during the conduct of your business or employment. Determining what you "reasonably believe" may depend upon what the police, a judge or a jury thinks is the truth.

- §15.2-915.3. Changed in 1997 to allow counties or cities to require fingerprinting as part of the concealed-handgun permit process. Fingerprinting is not required by state law.

- §15.2-915.4. Allows localities to regulate pneumatic guns and paintball guns. Only parents, guardians and certain trainers can teach minors in the use of pneumatic guns.

- §15.2-916. Allows any locality to control the shooting of all forms of bow and arrow, including crossbow, with an exception for toys.

- §15.2-917. Prohibits holding a shooting range to noise control standards more restrictive than the ones in place when the application to build or operate the range was made, or using eminent domain for that purpose. The effect is to protect ranges from being "zoned" out of business by changing noise ordinances.

- §15.2-918. Allows any locality to control air cannons and similar loud explosive devices designed to repel birds.

- §15.2-1113. Allows municipal corporations to regulate or prohibit: 1–any dangerous, offensive or unhealthful business, trade or enterprise (these and other terms of this law are not specifically defined); 2–transportation of any offensive substance; 3–the manufacture, storage, transportation or possession and use of any explosive or inflammable substance; 4–the use and exhibition of fireworks; and 5–the discharge of firearms. An exemption is required for taking nuisance deer under §29.1-529. Also allows such cities to require safety devices on storage equipment for such items.

- §15.2-1206. Allows the governing body of any county to impose a license tax of up to $25 on a handgun dealer.

- §15.2-1207. Allows counties to require sellers of handguns to report the sale to the clerk of the circuit court. The report may require the name and address of the buyer, the date of purchase, and the number, make and caliber of the handgun. The county may require the report within ten days of the sale, and the court clerk must keep a record of the reports.

- §15.2-1208. The law that had required permits to buy or sell handguns in certain counties since 1944 is repealed, and records from that system must be destroyed by 2004.

- §15.2-1209. Allows a county to prohibit shooting firearms, or bows and arrows as defined in this statute, anywhere it believes is too populated for safety. Counties may not restrict toy bows with a peak draw of under 10 pounds, or taking nuisance deer by firearm or bow under §29.1-529.

- §15.2-1209.1. Allows the governing body of a county to adopt ordinances making it unlawful to have or carry loaded firearms while standing or walking on a public highway in the county if you are not authorized to hunt on private property on both sides of the highway, including a fine of up to $100. Local laws passed under this statute do not apply when: 1–you are in a moving vehicle, or 2–you are acting in defense of people or property. Amended in 2007 to make it clear that possession of firearms for purposes other than hunting is outside the county's jurisdiction (to stop some local officials who tried to use the law to control CHP permitees and others).

- §15.2-1210. Allows the governing body of a county to prohibit hunting within one-half mile of any area the county believes is too heavily populated for safety. Such areas must be precisely described and posted.

- §15.2-1721. Grants power to any county, city or town to destroy perfectly good firearms, in any manner they choose, if they are held by the police and unclaimed after 60 days, provided they give public notice before destruction.

Other restrictions may occur indirectly as a result of zoning ordinances or other laws. In addition, Title 29.1, *Game, Inland Fisheries and Boating*, grant numerous powers to localities for regulating hunting which affect firearms possession and use.

Where Can You Go Shooting

The population density of Virginia makes it difficult to safely shoot outdoors in many areas. In addition, local ordinances may be in effect restricting shooting outdoors, and state prohibitions apply as well. If all the requirements are complied with, shooting is not prohibited on private land provided the shots pose no risk to life or property, and the location is remote enough to avoid complaints about noise. For ranges, the noise limitations in place when an application to build or operate a range was filed, was adopted as a standard in 2005, to keep ranges from being zoned out of existence. Eminent domain protections were added in 2006 (§15.2-917).

For many residents, shooting takes place at established indoor or outdoor shooting ranges which are run by the armed forces, National Guard, commercial operators, private clubs and others. Phone books, gun stores and police officers know where the nearby ranges are. Under a little known federal law (10 USC §4309) any rifle range built at least in part with federal funds may be used by the military, "and by persons capable of bearing arms," a direct recognition of the public's right to arms and need for training. The rules for use are set by whoever controls the range, and the military has first call on booking time there.

Under the federal Civilian Marksmanship Program laws (36 USC §40701) the Army cooperates with civilians to provide practice and instruction in firearms for citizens and for youths in the Boy Scouts, 4-H and similar clubs. For details see the entry in Chapter 7. This program is part of the long historical record of cooperation between the government and the citizens in keeping the population trained in marksmanship and the use of small arms.

COUNTY AND CITY LAWS

Many county or city firearms laws simply duplicate existing state statutes. Duplicate laws are in place primarily to allow a crime to be prosecuted on a local level. Other county or city laws may be of the type authorized by enabling statutes.

Local police or the sheriff's dept. are often the first place a person contacts for gun-law information. However, the police are generally not legal experts, and you have no way to evaluate the quality and correctness of the information you receive—which depends entirely upon who answers the phone. Most important, if you inadvertently violate a law, "the police told me I could do it," may not be much of a defense.

Read the law yourself. Many laws are surprisingly easy to understand. Copies of state and local laws are available at public libraries throughout the Commonwealth. If you do not have easy access to a library, call your local seat of government. Counties and cities generally maintain dedicated law libraries. Just ask one of these for any local firearms-related laws. There may be a small fee to gather, copy and mail the laws to you. These days, most legal authorities post their laws on the Internet, and you can find them using the free National Directory at gunlaws.com.

If for any reason you are unsure about the law, don't take any chances. Contact a lawyer. The National Rifle Association Attorney Referral Program can recommend a local lawyer knowledgeable in firearms law.

LOCAL ORDINANCE SAMPLER

The hurdles gun owners are subjected to by laws at the local level are made abundantly clear by the following partial list of such statutes. The partial list of cities and counties affected by local ordinances gives you an idea of the complexity that has replaced the original concept that the right to keep and bear arms shall not be infringed. The idea that Virginia is a state with the benefit of a preemption law is more of a theory than a practical reality. A similar situation regarding hunting laws can be found in chapter 6.

This is a *partial* list of local laws from 1998. No one has ever determined exactly how many cities, towns and counties have passed gun laws or how many laws that might be. After the list of laws you will find a list of localities where the laws apply.

1–It is unlawful to transport, possess or carry a loaded rifle in any vehicle while on the road from Oct. 1 through Feb. 15.

2–It is unlawful to transport or possess a loaded shotgun or loaded rifle in any vehicle on the road from 1/2 hour after sunset to 1/2 hour before sunrise.

3–It is unlawful to transport or possess a loaded shotgun or loaded rifle on the road from Oct. 1 through Feb. 15.

4–It is unlawful to possess a loaded firearm on the road except when permission to hunt is obtained from landowners on each side.

5–It is unlawful to transport or possess a loaded shotgun or loaded rifle on the road from sundown to sunrise.

6–It is unlawful to transport or possess a loaded firearm on the road in a vehicle.

7–It is unlawful to transport or possess a loaded firearm on the road during deer season.

8–It is unlawful to discharge a firearm from or across any sidewalk, highway or on public land.

9–Minors are restricted as to where and when they may possess firearms.

10–It is unlawful to transport, possess or carry a loaded rifle or shotgun in any vehicle on any public street, road or highway within the boundaries of the road.

11–It is unlawful to carry a concealed weapon without a permit.

12–It is unlawful to furnish firearms or other weapons to minors.

13–It is unlawful to point or brandish a firearm or anything that looks like a firearm.

14–Sale of handguns to minors, drug addicts, habitual drunkards, persons of unsound mind and fugitives from justice is prohibited.

City or County	Ordinance numbers that apply
Albermarle	10
Bath	2
Chesapeake	6, 10
Chesterfield	4
Culpepper	4, 6, 10
Danville	10
Fairfax	9, 12, 14
Fauquier	4, 6, 8, 9, 10
Goochland	5, 9
Greensville	3, 4
James City	10
King George	4, 6
Loudoun	4, 10
Louisa	9
Madison	4, 6, 10
Nelson	4
New Kent	10
Northumberland	9, 10
Orange	4, 7
Petersburg	10
Prince George	9
Prince William	9
Richmond (county)	9
Richmond (city)	9, 10, 11, 12
Roanoke	10
Rockbridge	10
Southampton	1
Stafford	6
Surry	10
Virginia Beach	9, 10, 13
Warren	10
Williamsburg	10

WHAT'S WRONG WITH THIS PICTURE?

WHAT'S WRONG WITH THIS PICTURE?

1–Shooting within city limits is normally prohibited.

2–Shooting in that part of the county might be against the law if the specific county involved has passed such a law.

3–It's illegal to deface signs.

4–Trespassing is illegal.

5–You can't use targets that leave debris.

6–Shooting at wildlife requires a permit or license.

7–The target doesn't have a backstop. The shooter is not controlling the entire trajectory of the bullet.

8–If the shot crosses the road it is illegal.

9–The shooter isn't wearing eye or ear protection.

10–There are no saguaro cacti in Virginia.

DEADLY FORCE and SELF DEFENSE 5

"I got my questionnaire baby,
You know I'm headed off for war,
Well now I'm gonna kill somebody
Don't have to break no kind of law."

- from a traditional blues song

Virginia is one of a handful of states with no statutory laws to define when you can use deadly force in self defense. Although the lack of clearly defined law complicates the issue, the rights of self defense are well established through previous court cases that set *precedents*. A shooting committed in self defense may be viewed as *justifiable* or *excusable* by the courts. The differences are discussed in detail in this chapter. It is the specific circumstances of a shooting that determine whether the shooting is justified or excusable, and if not, which crime has been committed.

Whenever a shooting occurs, a crime has been committed. Either the shooting is legal as a defense against a crime or attempted crime, or else the shooting is neither justified nor excusable, in which case the shooting itself is the crime.

Your civil liability (getting sued) in a shooting case can be a greater risk than the criminal charges that this book covers. You can be charged with both, and your legal protections are less vigorous in civil cases than in criminal ones. With very narrow exceptions, overcoming criminal charges does not protect you from a civil lawsuit—you can be tried twice. Using lethal force is so risky legally it is yet another reason to avoid it if at all possible—for *your own* safety.

USE OF DEADLY PHYSICAL FORCE

A reasonable person hopes it will never be necessary to raise a weapon in self defense. It's smart to always avoid such confrontations. In the unlikely event that you must resort to force to defend yourself, **you are generally required to use as little force as necessary to control a situation. Deadly force can only be used in the most narrowly defined circumstances, and it is highly unlikely that you will ever encounter such circumstances in your life.** You have probably never been near such an event in your life so far. Your own life is permanently changed if you ever kill a person, intentionally or otherwise.

The cover of this books asks, **"When can you shoot?"** The other part of the question is, **"...and expect to be justified in the eyes of the law."** You are only justified when the authorities or a jury determine—after the fact—that your actions were justified. *You never know beforehand.*

An argument can be made against the whole notion of *shoot to kill* on moral and legal grounds. In a true self-defense case, your goal—your intention and mental state—is not to kill, but to protect. *Shoot to stop,* or *shoot to neutralize the threat,* are other ways of saying it. In true self defense, you shoot to live.

No matter how well you understand the law, or how justified you may feel you are in a shooting incident, your fate will probably be determined much later, in a court of law. Establishing all the facts precisely is basically an impossible task and adds to your legal risks.

What were the exact circumstances during the moments of greatest stress, as best you remember them? Were there witnesses, who are they, what will they remember and what will they say to the authorities—each time they're asked—and in a courtroom? What was your relationship to the deceased person? How did you feel at the moment you fired? Did you have any options besides pulling the trigger? Can you look at it differently after the fact? Has there been even one case recently affecting how the law is now interpreted? Was a new law put into place yesterday? How good is your lawyer? How tough is the prosecutor? How convincing are you? Are the police on your side? Does the judge like your face? What will the jury think?

Be smart and never shoot at anyone if there is any way at all to avoid it. Avoiding the use of deadly force is usually a much safer course of action, at least from a legal point of view. You could be on much safer ground if you use a gun to protect yourself *without* actually firing a shot. Even though it's highly unlikely you'll ever need to draw a gun in self defense, the number of crimes prevented by the presence of a citizen's gun—*that isn't fired*—are estimated to be in the millions. And yet, just pulling a gun can subject you to serious penalties. Think of it in reverse—if someone pulled a gun on you, would you want to press charges because they put your life in danger? You must be careful about opening yourself up to such charges.

Still, the law recognizes your right to protect yourself, your loved ones and other people from certain severe criminal acts. In the most extreme incident you may decide it is immediately necessary to use lethal force to survive and deal with the repercussions later. *Shooting at another human being is a last resort, reserved for only if and when innocent life truly depends on it. If it doesn't, don't shoot. If it does, don't miss.*

You are urged to read the actual language of the law about this critical subject, and even then, to avoid using deadly force if at all possible. Read some of the case law cited in this book to get a deeper understanding of the ramifications of using deadly force—and dealing with the legal system after the fact.

The Virginia Gun Owner's Guide is intended to help you on a long journey to competence. Do not rely solely on the information in this book or on any other single source, and recognize that by deciding to prepare to use deadly physical force if it ever becomes necessary you are accepting substantial degrees of risk.

Even with a good understanding of the rules, there may be more to it than meets the eye. As an example, shooting a criminal who is fleeing a crime is very different than shooting a criminal who's committing a crime. You may be justified in shooting at someone in a specific situation, and you might miss and only wound, but if you ever shoot to intentionally wound you'll have an uphill battle in court. The law is strict, complex and not something to take chances with in the heat of the moment if you don't have to.

It's natural to want to know, beforehand, just when it's OK to shoot and be able to claim self defense later. Unfortunately, you will never know for sure until *after* a situation arises. You make your moves whatever they are, and the authorities or a jury decides. The laws and legal precedents don't physically control what you can or can't do—they give the authorities guidelines on how to evaluate what you did after it occurs. **There are extreme legal risks when you choose to use force of any kind.**

Because cases of murder outnumber cases of justifiable homicide, the authorities have a distinct tendency to think of the person holding a smoking gun as the perpetrator, later as the suspect, and finally as the defendant, while the person who gets shot, or was merely threatened with a gun, is the victim and in need of protection. If you ever come close to pulling the trigger, remember there is a possibility you will face a murder charge when it's all over. The effects of the shot last long after the ringing in your ears stops.

DEADLY FORCE PRECEDENTS

Virginia courts have, over the years, established the guidelines that control how a self-defense shooting is interpreted by the authorities. If a court finds that you are in compliance with these principles, you will be acquitted, a free person. If the court finds you in violation, *even if you are not or believe you are not*, you face the penalties of murder. You may languish in jail while the system decides your fate. The legal risk to you in a self-defense shooting can be enormous.

Homicide (the taking of a human life) falls into two categories. The criminal type, which carries severe penalties, includes capital murder, first degree murder, second degree murder and manslaughter. Non-criminal homicides involve cases of self defense and crime prevention, and are called *excusable* homicide and *justifiable* homicide. There is a third type known as civil justification, which covers sanctioned lethal activities such as execution and war.

Normally, *The Virginia Gun Owner's Guide* includes the text of the law so you can read it for yourself. Since there is no "text of the law" on self defense in Virginia, we have included quotations from court decisions that impact this crucial subject. Many more court cases exist than the few selected here as examples, and an effort was made to pick representative or clearly stated cases. Court precedents may change and can be subject to different interpretations. The interpretation that matters the most is the one that takes place when it is you who is on trial for your life. Unfortunately for the average person, court precedents are much harder to keep up with than changes to the statutes (which is not exactly an easy feat in itself).

THE TWELVE PRINCIPLES OF DEADLY FORCE AND SELF DEFENSE

1. *Whenever one person is criminally charged with killing another person Virginia courts presume it is second-degree murder.* Second-degree murder is punishable by 5–20 years in jail and a $100,000 fine. This means the State must only prove that you committed the homicide to make the case for second-degree murder. To increase the charge the prosecutor must prove beyond a reasonable doubt that the special conditions (willful, deliberate, premeditated or other actions) of a first-degree murder were committed.

It is up to the defendant (often referred to as the prisoner or the accused in a self-defense case) to prove that a lesser homicide was committed. The lesser charges are manslaughter, which is still a crime, punishable by 1–10 years in jail and a $2,500 fine, or justifiable or excusable homicide, which are not crimes. This may seem like "guilty until proven innocent" but is a long established standard in Virginia courts.

> When the Commonwealth has proved the commission of a homicide, and has pointed out the accused as the criminal agent, then it may rest its case, and unless the accused shows circumstances of justification, alleviation or excuse, a verdict of murder in the second degree will be warranted. (Boone v. Commonwealth, 1954)

> ...the burden is upon the accused, if he would reduce the offense below murder in the second degree, to show the absence of malice and the

other mitigating circumstances necessary for the purpose. (McDaniels v. Commonwealth, 1883)

2. *In claiming self defense you are admitting that you committed the homicide.* Your claim that your actions were necessary in protecting yourself includes the admission that you committed what the courts will view as a second degree murder charge until shown otherwise. "I shot in self defense," begins with "I shot."

> Self-defense is an affirmative defense,... and in making such a plea defendant implicitly admits that killing was intentional and assumes the burden of introducing evidence of justification or excuse that raises a reasonable doubt in the minds of the jurors. (McGhee v. Commonwealth, 1978)

> If the evidence so offered by the accused is shown to be false, and is insufficient to cause the jury to have a reasonable doubt as to his guilt, the case so made by the Commonwealth is not overcome, and a verdict of second-degree murder is still warranted. (Johnson v. Commonwealth, 1949)

3. *For a shooting to be a justifiable homicide you must be completely free from fault to the tiniest detail.* This is self defense in the truest sense. You are minding your own business and not violating any laws when the unprovoked attack of a stranger compels you to defend yourself (or an innocent third person) with lethal results. The evidence and testimony you present in your defense must raise a "reasonable doubt" in the minds of the jury that your actions were not criminal.

> Justifiable homicide in self-defense occurs where a person, without any fault in provoking or bringing on difficulty, kills another under reasonable apprehension of death or great bodily harm to himself. (Bailey v. Commonwealth, 1958).

> In these several kinds of justifiable homicide, it may be observed, that the slayer is in no kind of fault whatsoever, not even in the minutest degree; and is therefore to be totally acquitted and discharged, with commendation rather than blame. (Dodson v. Commonwealth, 1933)

4. *If you have any fault in the event but tried to retreat until there was nowhere left to go, and only then defended yourself against a perceived deadly threat, it is excusable homicide.*

> Excusable homicide in self-defense occurs where accused, although in some fault in first instance in provoking or bringing on difficulty, retreats as far as possible, when attacked, announces his desire for

peace, and kills adversary from a reasonably apparent necessity to preserve his own life or save himself from great bodily harm. (Bailey v. Commonwealth, 1958)

...if the difficulty is brought about by the accused and he finds that it is necessary to kill his assailant in order to save his own life, such killing is not in the eye of the law excusable. A man cannot go a-gunning for an adversary and kill him on the first appearance of resistance, and rely upon the necessity of the killing as an excuse therefor. (Bell v. Commonwealth, 1986)

But if a sudden fight is brought on, without malice or intention, the accused, if in fault, must retreat as far as he safely can, but, having done so and in good faith abandoned the fight, may kill his adversary, if he cannot in any other way preserve his life or save himself from great bodily harm. (Emphasis retained from the original. Dodson v. Commonwealth, 1933)

5. *You may only respond with the same level of force that is being used against you.* Until a threat reaches truly lethal proportions, responding with a firearm may well be seen as over reaction. Mere physical force, if not likely to cause serious bodily injury, may only be met with physical force, not with deadly force. Whether the threat of deadly force is justifiable (that is, presenting a gun without firing) will depend on the exact circumstances. The entire case may rest on the balance between the illegal force you reasonably believed you faced and the amount of force you responded with in defense.

A person who reasonably apprehends bodily harm by another is privileged to exercise reasonable force to repel the assault. However, the amount of force used to defend oneself must not be excessive and must be reasonable in relation to the perceived threat. (Diffendal v. Commonwealth, 1989)

6. *You may only use deadly force in your defense (or the defense of an innocent third party) during the moment in which there is an illegal threat to your life or limb.* The attacker must have made an overt act that lead you to reasonably believe death or serious bodily harm was immediately imminent. Words and threats alone are never enough. Fear that an attack will come, no matter how great, is never sufficient cause without the overt act of the other person. Once the attack has stopped the justification to shoot evaporates, and shots fired after this point may make you the aggressor and can be interpreted as murder.

...bare fear of injury at the hands of another, in the absence of some overt act indicative of imminent danger at that time, will not justify the taking of human life. (Stoneman v. Commonwealth, 1874)

Words alone are not sufficient provocation to excuse a murder. (Painter v. Commonwealth, 1969)

7. *The judgment of whether you believed that the threat was real must be made from your perspective at the time of the incident.* Your belief in the danger must be real, and you must have grounds for your belief, even if turns out later that the danger was not real. In some states the perspective must be that of a reasonable third person, which switches the judgment to the jury. But the jury in Virginia still must be convinced that you truly believed you were under mortal jeopardy at the moment you acted, leaving you at risk to what they believe.

...where the defendant claims self-defense that it is not necessary that he be actually in danger of his life or of great bodily harm, or that it so appear to the jury, but that the test is whether it reasonably appeared to the defendant at the time that his life was in danger or he was in danger of great bodily harm. (Harper v. Commonwealth, 1955)

...whether danger is reasonably apparent is always to be determined from the viewpoint of the defendant at the time he acted, and it is not essential to the right of self-defense that the danger should in fact exist. (McGhee v. Commonwealth, 1978)

8. *When two people set out to kill each other they commit mutual combat, and neither can claim self defense.* Entering a fight voluntarily is illegal, and defending yourself once in it is not a valid excuse later. Being provoked into a fight is not a defense. The law is watchful for a person who in any way instigates a fight and uses it as an excuse to kill an enemy.

To be mutual it must have been voluntarily and mutually entered into. If this were not so, every fight would be mutual combat without regard to the manner in which it began... One who is assaulted may and usually does defend himself, but the ensuing struggle cannot be accurately described as mutual combat. (Harper v. Commonwealth, 1936)

The general rule is that one cannot provoke an attack, bring on a combat, and then slay his assailant, and claim exemption from the consequences on the ground of self defense... He who provokes a personal encounter, in any case, thereby disables himself from relying on the plea of self defense in justification of a blow which he struck during the encounter. (Sims v. Commonwealth, 1922)

9. *If an innocent third party is killed by a stray shot during mutual combat, each person engaged in the combat is equally guilty.*

The following instruction was given to the jury in a case that was later upheld in the Virginia Supreme Court:

> If you believe from the evidence that two or more men were shooting guns in mutual combat with the intent to kill and as a result of these shootings the deceased, an innocent bystander, was killed, then each is responsible for the death the same as if he had killed the person he intended to kill, unless he was acting in self-defense. (Riddick v. Commonwealth, 1983)

In that case it was never determined who actually fired the fatal shot. It didn't matter who pulled the trigger, everyone engaged in the mutual combat was equally at fault.

In stark contrast to this, in the case of a legitimate self-defense shooting, the person acting in self defense is not *criminally* responsible for an injury or death from a stray bullet. This is no guarantee that you will not be pursued in civil court, even if you are found not guilty.

> If the person committing the homicide acted in self-defense, then he would not be responsible for the death. (Riddick v. Commonwealth, 1983)

10. *If you are not at fault, there is no duty to retreat.* In cases of self defense, where you are not in the smallest part at fault, you are not required to retreat from an attacker. However, defense experts generally agree that if you can leave you should. Avoiding an attack by leaving the scene, if you can safely do so, may be your best course of action.

> If the accused is in no fault whatever, but in discharge of a lawful act, *he need not retreat,* but may repel force by force, *if need be,* to the extent of slaying his adversary. This is *justifiable* homicide in self defense. (Emphasis retained from the original. Dodson v. Commonwealth, 1933)

> Justifiable self-defense arises when the defendant is completely without fault. In such a case, the defendant need not retreat, but is permitted to stand his ground and repel the attack by force, including deadly force, if it is necessary. (Foote v. Commonwealth, 1990; quoting Perkins case, 1947 and McCoy case, 1919)

11. *Deadly force may be used when immediate action is necessary and no other options exist to prevent the commission of violent felonies.* Although the law clearly allows a citizen to act to prevent a crime, this does not make you a freelance police officer, and an act is a violent felony only after a court says so. Because the legal risks are so high, acting to prevent a violent felony must be looked upon as a last resort only. Review the sample scenarios in Chapter 8 for an idea of how complicated crime response can be.

> A distinction is made between such felonies as are attended with force, or any extraordinary degree of atrocity, which in their nature betoken such urgent necessity as will not allow of any delay, and others of a different kind and unaccompanied by violence on the part of the felon. Those only which come within the former description may be prevented by homicide. (Dodson v. Commonwealth, 1933)

12. *Deadly force may be used in the defense of an innocent third person.* You must reasonably believe that the other person is truly innocent, even if it turns out later that this was not true, and all the other conditions of self defense must be met. Force can be used only to the extent that the person being defended could have legally used force. The law is more specific about defense of a person related to you, but encompasses strangers as well.

> And the same justification extends to homicide committed in the mutual and reciprocal defense of such as stand in the relations of husband and wife, parent and child, master and servant... (Dodson v. Commonwealth, 1933)

> The Supreme Court has clearly recognized that one is privileged to use force in defense of family members. <Newbury case, 1950; Green case, 1918; Hodges case, 1892.> We find no Virginia cases, nor have any been cited to us, determining whether and when a person can use force to protect or defend a third person. Generally, however, this privilege is not limited to family members and extends to anyone, even a stranger who is entitled to claim self defense. <citing U.S. Supreme Court and cases from five other states> ...In a majority of jurisdictions, a person asserting a claim of defense of others may do so only where the person to whose aid he or she went would have been legally entitled to defend himself or herself. ...The amount of force which may be used must be reasonable in relation to the harm threatened. (Foster v. Commonwealth 1991)

> ... the jury has a right to consider it, together with the other evidence in the case, to determine whether or not the accused used more drastic

measures than were reasonably necessary to protect his mother from death or serious bodily injury. (Nelson v. Commonwealth 1937)

PRECAUTIONARY NOTE
"Sometimes guilty people go free,
sometimes innocent people do not."

Many factors make relying on the legal argument of self defense a risky business. Yes, your right to self defense is an invaluable and fundamental right. People are indeed often acquitted under justification, but remember that justice is not always served, and people may wonder afterwards if you were guilty and walked. Remember that you are only justified if the authorities or a jury agree, *after the fact,* that you were justified. You get to sweat it out the whole time the case is pursued, which can take years.

Remember that a prosecutor's role is to work hard to convict, regardless of your guilt or innocence, and conviction rates approach 100%. You might hope that's because they only pursue bad apples. Many convictions though come from plea bargains, where regardless of guilt or innocence, you plead to a somewhat lesser charge to avoid the huge cost, humiliation, inconveniences—and risk—of a lengthy trial. Plea bargains help manage the huge case loads and have been called everything from wise to pragmatic, and from expedient to extortion.

The pursuit of high conviction rates may lead to what some would consider dirty lawyer tricks—with your fate on the line. Popular folk wisdom says, "It's better to be tried by twelve than carried by six," but there's another old saying that also has some merit here, "Better a criminal goes free than a lien on your home." It is admittedly a very tough and risky choice.

RELATED LAWS

Brandishing Firearms
It is a class 1 misdemeanor to hold, point or brandish a firearm, or anything that looks like a firearm, or an air- or gas-operated weapon, if it is intentionally done in a way that causes someone to fear they may be shot or injured. This is the typical charge for illegally pointing a gun at a person. If you brandish a firearm on or within 1,000 ft. of school property, the penalty is raised to a class 6 felony (§18.2-282). This law does not apply to using a firearm for legitimate self defense.

Recklessly Handling Firearms
It is a class 1 misdemeanor to recklessly handle a gun in a way that endangers any person or property (see §18.2-56.1). Reckless handling while hunting includes an additional penalty, at the court's discretion, of revoking the privilege of possessing a firearm while hunting for a period ranging from one year to life. The Dept. of Game and Inland Fisheries keeps a list of anyone restricted under this law, and anyone caught hunting and in possession of a firearm while prohibited is subject to a class 1 misdemeanor and an additional five-year restriction on hunting while armed.

Discharging Firearms In Public Places
Willfully firing a gun in any street in any city or town or in any public place is a class 1 misdemeanor; if bodily injury occurs it is a class 6 felony. Willfully firing a gun on school property or on public property within 1,000 feet of school property is a class 4 felony (see §18.2-280). Legally justifiable or excusable shooting in defense of life or property is excluded, as is any act otherwise specifically authorized by law (presumably includes ranges). With regard to school zones, hunting is allowed if it is otherwise lawful, along with programs approved by the school. Firing a gun in or at any occupied building in a way that endangers life is a class 4 felony (see §18.2-279).

Shooting In Streets
Shooting a gun, bow or crossbow in or across any road or in the street of any city or town is a class 4 misdemeanor (see §18.2-286). Authorized shooting ranges and the military are exempt from this requirement. Shooting a gun from a vehicle, creating the risk of death or injury, or causing someone to think they may be killed or injured is a class 5 felony (see §18.2-286.1).

Warning Shots

A warning shot is a bad idea for any number of reasons. It is a violation of several laws and can land you—believing yourself to be innocent—in jail. If there is no justification to shoot in self defense, then there is probably no justification for shooting at all. The shot itself poses a risk to any neighbors within range. A fatality could bring a murder charge against you. Expending a cartridge that may be needed in mortal combat if the situation turns deadly is a questionable strategic move. It also may draw more attention to the shooter than the suspects, who will flee, leaving the "innocent" (or even heroic) shooter to explain to the police what all the commotion was about. A firearm used in such an incident would likely be seized, along with other repercussions to the person firing the shot.

If the situation isn't immediately life or death, don't fire. If you really are locked in mortal combat, don't waste a potentially life-saving shot making scary noises. Firing a warning may serve as evidence that you didn't believe the situation presented an immediately deadly threat, and that you really did fire without justification. Warning shots are an irresponsible instrument of Hollywood (which constantly promotes this dangerous crime), that have little place in the real world.

Wounding a Person Without Justification

A shot fired or actions taken in self defense are only justified if the authorities or a jury, after the fact, say that it was justified. In the event a person's actions are not justified, the possible charges could include:

§18.2-51. Shooting, stabbing, etc. Shooting, stabbing, cutting, wounding or otherwise causing bodily harm to a person with the intent to harm them is illegal. If done with malice it is a class 3 felony. If done without malice it is a class 6 felony.

§18.2-51.2 Aggravated Malicious Wounding. Maliciously shooting, stabbing, cutting, wounding or otherwise causing bodily harm to a person with the intent to harm them, and actually severely harming them, is a class 2 felony.

In the event of a fatality, a charge of murder or manslaughter is possible. The enormous consequences of shooting at a person emphasize the wisdom in holding your fire unless your own life is absolutely on the line.

Booby Traps

Setting a gun or other deadly weapon to be fired by a trip wire or any other remote method is a class 6 felony (see §18.2-281).

Reporting Wounds

Anyone who treats or gives medical aid for a wound he knows or suspects was inflicted by a weapon, unless the wound was self-inflicted, must report the incident to the local Sheriff or Chief of Police. Failure to report is a class 3 misdemeanor (see §54.1-2967).

Threat of Force to Deter Trespass

The issue of stopping trespass is not covered by Virginia statutes. Common law requires that any use of force be reasonable to the situation in which it is used. Deadly force may not be used to stop a criminal trespass therefore, unless the other life-threatening circumstances of self defense or violent-crime prevention exist. Whether the *threat* of deadly force is justified—the presenting of a gun without firing or even without pointing it—is a matter for the authorities or a court to decide, depending on the exact circumstances.

Riot and Unlawful Assembly

A riot occurs, for legal purposes, when three or more people acting together become involved in forceful or violent activities that jeopardize public safety, peace or order. Possession of a firearm during such an event is a class 5 felony. See §18.2-405.

Unlawful assembly occurs when three or more people get together with common intent to do something involving illegal force or violence that may seriously jeopardize public safety, peace or order, if it is enough to make reasonable people fear that threat. Taking part in an unlawful assembly is a class 1 misdemeanor unless you're in possession of a firearm, which makes it a class 5 felony (§18.2-406).

If you are legally bearing arms when a disturbance takes place it could be wise to withdraw from the scene. Involvement, as noted by these two laws, carries an increased legal risk for an armed civilian who might choose to join or who becomes entangled in a melee.

Larceny

Stealing a person's firearm when they're not around is grand larceny regardless of the value of the gun, punishable by up to 20 years in state prison, a fine up to $2,500, or both (§18.2-95).

Exemptions From Paramilitary Activity

It is a class 5 felony to participate in illegal paramilitary activity (§18.2-433.2). This involves training in firearms, explosives and causing injury or death for purposes of civil disorder, as described in §18.2-433.1. Legal activities involving firearms and training are specifically excluded (§18.2-433.3) from any paramilitary restrictions:

Teaching self defense; Practicing self defense; Self defense; Firearms instruction and training intended to teach the safe handling and use of firearms; Any lawful sports involving firearms; Any individual recreational use of firearms; Any individual possession of firearms; Hunting; Target shooting; Collecting; Karate clubs; Self-defense clinics; Any other lawful sports or activities

In addition, individuals or groups involved in any way with the lawful use or display of firearms are exempt from this law.

Bullet-Proof Vests

There is no law against owning or wearing a bullet-proof vest (or as the trade refers to them, bullet-resistant, or ballistic vests). However, it's a class 4 felony to commit crimes of violence or other specified felonies while wearing one (§18.2-287.2).

Lasers

Shining a laser or simulated laser on a peace officer, as defined in §18.2-57.01, is a class 2 misdemeanor.

Use of Force by Teachers

Assault charges do not apply to a teacher, acting in an official capacity, who uses reasonable and necessary force in self defense, defense of others, or to disarm students (§18.2-57).

Keeping Control of Your Firearms

You could face civil lawsuits for negligently letting a minor or other incompetent person get possession of a firearm you own, if it is used to cause injury or damage. This is a volatile area of law controlled more by lawyerly zeal, activist judges and unpredictable court precedents, than by statute. Some legal arguments attempt to spread blame to people other than those who commit criminal acts. It points to the wisdom in controlling access to your firearms at all times.

Disarming an Officer

Knowingly disarming a law enforcement or correctional officer of a firearm or stun weapon is a class 6 felony, under §18.2-57.02. It is a class 1 misdemeanor if the weapon is a chemical irritant or impact weapon.

IF YOU SHOOT A CROOK OUTSIDE YOUR HOUSE
DO YOU HAVE TO DRAG HIM INSIDE?

IF YOU SHOOT A CROOK OUTSIDE YOUR HOUSE DO YOU HAVE TO DRAG HIM INSIDE?

No! Acting on this wide-spread myth is a completely terrible idea. You're talking about tampering with evidence, obstructing justice, interfering with public duties, false reporting and more. If you're involved in a shooting, leave everything at the scene just as it is and call your lawyer, the police and an ambulance.

Don't think for a minute that modern forensics won't detect an altered scene of a crime. At any shooting a crime has been committed. Either the shooting is justified, which means you were in your rights and the victim was acting illegally, or you exceeded your rights in the shooting, regardless of the victim's circumstance. The situation will be investigated to determine the facts, and believe it, the facts will come out. Police tell time-worn jokes about finding "black heel marks on the linoleum." And once you're caught in a lie, your credibility is shot.

If you tamper with the evidence, you have to lie to all the authorities to back it up. Then you have to commit perjury to follow through. Can you pull it off?

If the guy with the mask was shot from the front, armed as he is, the homeowner has a good case for self defense. If the thief was leaving, hands full of loot, there may not have been justification to shoot at all, and this homeowner is in trouble. Either way, he's better off leaving the body where it falls.

Suppose you shoot an armed intruder coming through your window, and the body falls outside the house. You'll have a better time convincing a jury that you were scared to death, than trying to explain how the dead crook in your living room got blood stains on your lawn.

The reason this fable gets so much play is because there is a big difference between a homeowner shooting a crook in the kitchen, and one person shooting another outdoors. Shooting at a stranger outside your house can be murder.

CAN YOU POINT A GUN AT SOMEONE?

No matter how many aces a person is holding, you can't settle the matter with a gun. This also shows how the law can be interpreted in more than one way.

Unless you have solid legal grounds for doing so (and the character here does not), using a gun to put a person in reasonable fear of imminent physical injury is *brandishing a firearm*—a class 1 misdemeanor. *Reckless handling* of a gun in a way that endangers anyone is also a class 1 misdemeanor.

When you go to court, it could be argued that this is actually *attempted murder,* a felony. And if the guy with the gun is angry enough to take back his money, it could become *armed robbery,* a felony punishable by five years to life imprisonment.

By drawing your gun, the other guy may be able to shoot you dead and legally claim self defense. You may never pull a gun to leverage an argument. Merely reaching for a gun is the threat of deadly force and may have legal repercussions.

If someone pointed a gun at you, would you get angry and want to see them arrested? Consider how someone would feel if roles were reversed and it was you who pulled the gun out of some passion other than the will to survive, when it wasn't absolutely necessary to prevent a life-threatening situation.

Despite all this, the law recognizes your right to defend yourself, your loved ones, and other people. These cases, when you *can* point a gun at another person, are described in this chapter.

HUNTING REQUIREMENTS 6

Virginia hunting regulations are complex and highly-detailed. There are more than 180 statewide Game and Inland Fisheries laws. A number of those laws delegate the power to regulate various aspects of hunting to the counties. This chapter is only intended to point you in the right direction.

The main Virginia hunting laws concerning firearms appear in Appendix D. Complete hunting laws are found in Title 29.1 of the Code of Virginia. The laws grant considerable, but not unlimited, regulatory powers to the Dept. of Game and Inland Fisheries (G&IF), and their regulations have the force of law. In 2007 they were required to develop model ordinances for firearm hunting that counties or cities may adopt (§29.1-528).

Hunters need far more information than just the firearms details provided here. For complete hunting regulations and procedures, contact the Virginia Game and Inland Fisheries Dept. at one of the numbers provided in Appendix C. Game and Inland Fisheries is required by law to publish an annual summary of statewide hunting regulations. Called *Hunting & Trapping in Virginia,* it provides all the details on hunting seasons and regulations. A useful overview of County Firearms Ordinances is included. This valuable publication is free of charge from the department.

Hunting licenses are sold by some circuit court clerks and by over 600 authorized agents at sporting goods retailers, hunting shops and bait and tackle stores. A hunting license is required for any person, of any age, who hunts in the state of Virginia with the following exceptions (see §29.1-301):

1–Landowners on their own land, including their parents, spouses, children or grandchildren of any age and their spouses, whether residents or not;

2–Tenants on the land they rent while carrying the landowner's written permission to hunt;

3–Residents 65 years old and over on private property in their county of residence;

4–A stockholder with a 50% or greater interest in a domestic corporation, on that corporation's land, or the stockholder's spouse, children or minor grandchildren whether residents or not;

5–Indians on a reservation or members of Virginia tribes living in Virginia, with a written statement from their proper Indian authority, indicating that they are residents of the reservation or members of the tribe;

6–A resident under 12 years of age if accompanied and directly supervised by a licensed Virginia hunter.

The Virginia Game and Inland Fisheries Department requires mandatory hunter education before receiving a hunting license for anyone 12 to 15 years old, and anyone 16 years or older who never had a hunting license. A new temporary apprentice hunting license was established in 2008 under §29.1-300.4, which substitutes direct adult supervision for the required class.

The Hunter Education Course is free of charge and provides excellent training for all concerned citizens. Virginia accepts all other state and country hunting licenses, and their certifications of hunter education credentials, as compliance with the Virginia hunter education requirement. For more information on a course near you, contact the Virginia Game and Inland Fisheries Dept. in Richmond, or the regional office nearest you. See Appendix C for contact information.

The Hunter Education Program is conducted by over 1,300 volunteers. Instructors follow a uniform outline developed by *Game and Inland Fisheries*. The course must cover at least:

• The safe handling and use of firearms and archery equipment;

• Wildlife conservation and management;

• Hunting laws and applicable rules and regulations;

- Hunting safety ethics and sportsmanship;
- History of hunting and firearms;
- Basic first aid;
- Survival skills.

A certificate is issued by the department upon completing the course. You must present this, or show that you are not required to take the course, to receive a hunting license.

A Virginia hunting license is valid from July 1st or the date it is issued, whichever comes later, to June 30th of the following year, and must be renewed each year. To be considered a resident, you must: 1–have lived in the county or city in which you are applying for a license for six months immediately before applying for your license; 2–be a registered voter in your city or county, or 3–be an active duty member of the U.S. armed forces.

A legal hunter who has reached his daily or season limit while hunting may help other hunters but his firearm must be unloaded. A legal hunter who has reached his limit prior to the hunt may help other hunters but may not possess a firearm. Violation is a class 3 misdemeanor under §29.1-521.

A new set of definitions for firearms, applicable only to the hunting laws, was enacted in 2002, and may be found in §29.1-100. Rules for restoring your hunting rights if they are lost due to an offense are in §29.1-529.

PUBLIC LANDS

The Virginia Dept. of Game and Inland Fisheries annually publishes the *Virginia Hunting Guide*. The guide provides the extensive information on where and when you can hunt in Virginia. Contact addresses and phone numbers for hunting information on public and private lands are included. The guide also contains hunting forecasts for many game species in every area of the state. The *Virginia Hunting Guide* along with *Hunting and Trapping in Virginia*, are publications too useful to be without. They are free and are available for the asking.

National Parks

Hunting is generally prohibited in Virginia's National Parks.

Federal Refuges

Limited hunting is available on the Chincoteague, Presqile, Dismal Swamp, Back Bay and Eastern Shore Federal Refuges. Contact the respective Refuge Manager listed in Appendix C for complete information.

National Forests

In addition to your state hunting license, you need a special permit to hunt in the National Forests. Permits are available where state hunting licenses are sold. Appendix C contains contact addresses and phone numbers for the Forest headquarters and ranger districts in Virginia.

At the federal level, possession of firearms is not prohibited in National Forests and discharge may only be restricted in narrow circumstances. However, state and county hunting laws are enforced in the National Forests. The Dept. of Game and Inland Fisheries has regulations and policies in place that may conflict with basic federal policies, for the stated purpose of wildlife management. For example, the Dept. has a rule against *any* loaded firearms in a motor vehicle at *any* time in the National Forests (not required federally). The Dept. also has a rule prohibiting loaded firearms in National Forests altogether, except while hunting during designated hunting seasons (not required federally).

The basis for this prohibition is Game and Inland Fisheries regulation 325-02-1 §6, which says in part, "It shall be unlawful to have in possession a bow or gun which is not unloaded and cased or dismantled, in the National Forests and on Department-owned lands and on lands managed by the Department under cooperative agreement except during the period when it is lawful to take..." and it goes on to list game animals. The ability to pass a blanket prohibition against firearms does not appear to be granted in the law (§29.1-501). The law only allows the Dept. Board to make regulations "pertaining to the hunting, taking, capture, killing, possession, sale, purchase and transportation of any wild bird, wild animal or inland water fish."

This point is of concern to concealed-carry permit holders, and any other people in Virginia, who are not hunting but have or desire to carry personal firearms while hiking, camping, driving through or otherwise using the National Forests and department-managed lands. Although the regulation does not appear to have a basis, while it remains in place a violator could face legal sanctions. As we go to press, CHPs appear to be exempt.

State Forests

State Forests are owned and managed by the Virginia Dept. of Forestry. With the Dept. of Game and Inland Fisheries they cooperatively manage 250,000 acres of forest land for hunting and fishing. In addition to your state hunting license, you need a special permit to hunt in State Forests. Permits are available from state hunting license agents in the areas surrounding the State Forests. Permits can also be purchased by mail from State Forest offices listed in Appendix C. State and county hunting laws are enforced in the State Forests. Aside from approved hunting, the right to keep and bear arms is denied by the Dept., except for holders of a valid concealed-handgun permit. The Dept. has no apparent authority to ban such possession.

State Parks

State Parks are controlled by the Dept. of Conservation and Recreation. Hunting areas within the State Parks are cooperatively managed with the Dept. of Game and Inland Fisheries. The parks that will be open to hunting is decided yearly. The list of parks open for hunting is available by contacting the Dept. of Conservation and Recreation at the address located in Appendix C. State Park hunting information is also published in the *Virginia Hunting Guide* mentioned earlier.

State and county hunting laws are enforced in the State Parks. The Dept. of Conservation and Recreation has a regulation in place that says loaded firearms are not allowed in State Parks outside of designated hunting areas, with an exception for valid CHP holders. This situation, similar to the one described above for National Forests, is of concern to all law-abiding people whose rights are thus denied. The department has no apparent authority to ban lawful possession for non-hunting purposes.

Wildlife Management Areas

The Dept. of Game and Inland Fisheries owns about 176,000 acres of land grouped into 29 Wildlife Management Areas (WMAs). The land tracts were purchased with proceeds from hunting licenses and are open to public hunting. Hunting seasons and laws generally match those of the surrounding county. There is no additional licensing fee for hunting on WMAs. The *Guide to Hunting in Virginia* contains hunting forecasts and contact points for each WMA. Contact a Game and Inland Fisheries office listed in Appendix C for more WMA information.

Military Areas

Military installations open to civilian hunting include Marine Base MCCDC Quantico, Fort A. P. Hill Military Reservation, the Radford Army Ammunition Plant, and the Fort Pickett Military Reservation. Hunting rules for military installations vary and availability is subject to restrictions due to military operations. Contact the installation in advance at the address listed in Appendix C.

Army Corps of Engineers Land

The U. S. Army Corps of Engineers manages certain lands around the state. Portions of this land are cooperatively managed by the Dept. of Game and Inland Fisheries and are available for hunting. No special permits other than regular hunting licenses are necessary. State and county hunting laws and seasons are observed. The *Virginia Hunting Guide* contains information on Corps of Engineers land. See Appendix C for points of contact.

Corporate Lands

Many Virginia corporations open their lands to public hunting. The *Virginia Hunting Guide* lists about 300,000 acres owned by power and timber companies available to individuals and for lease by clubs. Many, but not all, require the hunter to purchase permits (about $15–$25) from the company. Points of contact are listed in Appendix C.

SOME KEY STATE HUNTING REGULATIONS

Below you'll find the main general rules about the use of firearms while hunting. Remember, hunting regulations are not limited to guns and include archery, falconry, trapping and more. Unless a penalty is specified, hunting violations are class 3 misdemeanors. Note that in 2007, the popular title *game warden* was changed in all Virginia statutes to *conservation police officer*.

* If you are required to have a hunting license, you must carry it with you when you hunt.

* Every hunter or person in a hunting party, in every county designated by the board of Game and Inland Fisheries (and they have designated all counties), must wear a blaze orange hat or blaze orange upper body clothing or display at least 100 square inches of blaze orange material, visible from all around, within arms reach. The blaze orange requirement does not apply: to a hat's brim, to waterfowl hunters, during special muzzle-loading deer season, and for fox hunters on horseback without firearms, and certain other hunters.

* Hunting is banned on Sundays, "a rest day for all species." Exceptions are hunting on licensed shooting preserves, and hunting raccoon until 2:00 a.m. Sunday morning. Lawful possession of a firearm in a hunting area on a Sunday is not a presumption of illegal hunting unless there is evidence to the contrary, see §29.1-521.

* It is illegal to:

    –Intentionally interfere with lawful hunting;

    –Destroy or take down "posted" signs;

    –Destroy, damage or take down any "no hunting" or similar sign;

    –Handle any firearm in a reckless manner and endanger the life, limb or property of another person;

–Kill or cripple any non-migratory game bird or game animal without making a reasonable effort to retrieve the animal;

–Discharge a firearm, crossbow or bow and arrow across or within the right-of-way of any road;

–Shine a light on places that may be used by deer at anytime while in possession of a rifle, shotgun, pistol, crossbow, bow and arrow, or speargun; if this occurs, everyone in the vehicle is considered in violation;

–Hunt deer after dark;

–Hunt under age 12 without supervision by a licensed parent, guardian or person designated by a parent or guardian;

–Shoot a rifle or pistol at birds and animals over state inland waters;

–Carry a loaded rifle or pistol on a boat on inland waters for hunting;

–Shoot waterfowl from a boat propelled by a motor;

–Hunt or trap on private land without the landowner's permission;

–Hunt while under the influence of drugs or alcohol (a class 1 misdemeanor);

–Hunt during a forest fire;

–Shoot or attempt to take any wild bird or animal from any vehicle, except as provided by law (which includes a permit for disabled hunters);

–Use an aircraft to hunt or pursue any animal for hunting;

–Possess a firearm while helping others to hunt, if prior to the hunt you reached certain season limits (§29.1-521);

–Hunt with a fully automatic firearm.

Many hunting regulations concerning the types of firearms allowed, which depends on the game and the season, can be found in §29.1-526 and -528. Hunting with the wrong type of firearm is a class 3 misdemeanor. Some examples are listed below:

- Only shotguns 10 gauge or smaller with barrels at least 18 inches long are allowed.

- Semi-auto and pump shotgun ammo capacity, formerly limited to 3 shells, is now set by regulation by G&IF.

- Shotguns with rifled barrels are permitted in counties where slugs may be used.

- There are no restrictions on shot size except for spring gobbler season when shot may be no larger than number 2 fine shot.

- Rifles may be used for wild animals and birds (except migratory birds and waterfowl) and except where prohibited.

- Rifles used for deer or bear must be .23 caliber or larger.

- Rifles, pistols and revolvers may be used for hunting crows except where prohibited by local laws.

- Pistol and revolver ammunition used for hunting deer and bear must be .23 caliber or larger and have a manufacturer rating of 350 foot-pounds of energy or more.

- Pistols and revolvers firing .22 caliber rim fire ammunition and muzzle-loading pistols may be used where .22 caliber rifles are permitted.

- Muzzle-loading shotguns may be used during the general firearms season.

- Muzzle-loading rifles may be used to hunt during the general firearms season except where prohibited by local law.

- All game birds and animals except deer may be hunted with shotguns from boats.

County Firearm-Hunting Ordinances

Counties and cities have broad power to regulate hunting within their borders. The Dept. of Game and Inland Fisheries pamphlet, *Hunting & Trapping in Virginia* lists 52 ordinances in fifty-five counties or cities. These examples are included to show the type of laws you will encounter on a local level, is *not* a complete list, and may have changed by the time you see this. Counties had tried to use their hunting-law authority to regulate CHP and other gun possession but were stopped in 2007 by §15.2-1209.1

1–Rifles up to .25 caliber may be used to hunt groundhogs from March 1 to September 1 with written permission from the landowner (Halifax county).

2–It shall be unlawful to use a rifle larger than .22 rim fire except that groundhogs may be hunted with a rifle of larger caliber (Appomattox county).

3–It is unlawful to hunt with firearms from the road and within ten feet of the ditch bank (Amelia county).

4–It is against the law to hunt deer with muzzleloading rifles from stands ten feet above the ground (Buckingham, Dinwiddie, Isle of Wight, Lancaster, New Kent and Prince William counties).

5–You cannot shoot a rifle larger than .22 caliber, a muzzleloader larger than .36 caliber, or a shotgun loaded with slugs except from stands at least ten feet above the ground, except for groundhogs in certain areas between March 1 and August 31 (James City County).

6–All rifles, pistols, or shotguns loaded with slugs prohibited for any hunting (Fairfax County).

7–Rifles are not allowed for deer hunting (Chesterfield, Essex, Halifax, Northampton, Prince George, Richmond, and Surry counties).

A Hunter's Pledge

Responsible hunting provides unique challenges and rewards. However, the future of the sport depends on each hunter's behavior and ethics. Therefore, as a hunter, I pledge to:

- Respect the environment and wildlife;
- Respect property and landowners;
- Show consideration for non hunters;
- Hunt safely;
- Know and obey the law;
- Support wildlife and habitat conservation;
- Pass on an ethical hunting tradition;
- Strive to improve my outdoor skills and understanding of wildlife;
- Hunt only with ethical hunters.

By following these principles of conduct each time I go afield, I will give my best to the sport, the public, the environment and myself. The responsibility to hunt ethically is mine; the future of hunting depends on me.

The Hunter's Pledge was created cooperatively by:

International Association of Fish and Wildlife Agencies
Izaak Walton League of America
National Rifle Association
Rocky Mountain Elk Foundation
Tread Lightly! Inc.
Sport Fishing Institute
Times Mirror Magazines Conservation Council
U.S. Dept. of Agriculture Extension Service
Wildlife Management Institute

NOTES ON FEDERAL LAW 7

Although federal laws regulate firearms to a great degree, the same laws prohibit the federal and local governments from encroaching on the right to keep and bear arms. This is seen in the 2nd, 4th 9th and 14th Amendments to the Constitution, and in federal statutory laws, which number about 270.

Dealers of firearms must be licensed by the Bureau of Alcohol, Tobacco, Firearms and Explosives (BATFE). Federal law requires licensed dealers to keep records of each sale, but prohibits using this information in any sort of national registration plan. The information is permanently saved by the dealer and is not centrally recorded by the federal authorities. If a dealer goes out of business the records are sent to a central federal depository for storage (or a state site if approved by the Treasury Dept.). Although federal law prohibits using these records to establish a national firearms registration system, several federal attempts to do so have apparently been made. Reportedly, fingerprints submitted for background checks to the FBI are stored by that agency until the individual reaches 99 years of age.

Paperwork required by the Brady Law is collected by local authorities, but must be destroyed shortly after it is used to conduct background checks, and by law, no records of the checks may be kept. Local authorities are required to certify their compliance with record destruction to the U.S. Attorney General every six months. The Justice Department reports that compliance with this requirement has been quite low.

In theory, there's no central place for anyone to go and see if a given person owns a firearm (except perhaps in the case of those people who have registered for concealed carry, if you assume they all own guns). Firearm ownership in America is traditionally a private matter. For someone to find out if you have a gun they would have to check all the records of all the dealers in the country, a daunting task. As a practical matter, however, authorities are increasingly able to easily determine which people have chosen to own firearms. Only BATFE is authorized to check the records of manufacture, importation and sale of firearms nationally. Local authorities occasionally ask to see a dealer's records, and dealers may feel it's in their best interests to cooperate, even if it isn't required by law. Then, in 2005, the state granted itself authority (§54.1-4201) to examine the federal records of dealers on its own.

The dealer's records allow guns to be *traced,* a very different and important matter. When a gun is involved in a crime, BATFE can find out, from the manufacturer's serial number, which licensed dealer originally received the gun. The dealer can then look through the records and see who purchased the weapon. It's a one-way street—a gun can be linked to a purchaser but owners can't be traced to their guns. One study of successful traces showed that four out of five were of some value to law enforcement authorities.

When President Reagan was shot by John Hinckley Jr., the weapon was traced and in fourteen minutes time, a retail sale to Hinckley was confirmed.

Buying, selling, having, making, transferring and transporting guns is in many cases regulated by federal laws. These regulations are covered in *The Virginia Gun Owner's Guide,* but for the most part, only state penalties are noted. There may be federal penalties as well.

Under the Assimilative Crimes Act, state law controls if there is no federal law covering a situation. It is important to recognize that there can be a question of jurisdiction in some cases.

A long history of federal regulation exists with regard to firearms and other weapons. For an examination of the historical record, see Stephen Halbrook's book, *That Every Man Be Armed*, and the unabridged *Gun Laws of America*, both at gunlaws.com.

The main federal gun laws in effect today include:

- 2nd, 4th and 9th Amendments to the Constitution (1791)
- Fourteenth Amendment to the Constitution (1868)
- National Firearms Act (1934)
- Federal Firearms Act (1938)
- Omnibus Crime Control and Safe Streets Act (1968)
- Gun Control Act (1968)
- Organized Crime Control Act (1970)
- Omnibus Crime Control Act (1986)
- Firearms Owners' Protection Act (1986)
- Brady Handgun Violence Prevention Act (1993)
- Public Safety and Recreational Firearms Use Protection Act (The Crime Bill, 1994)
- Promotion of Rifle Practice and Firearms Safety Act (1996)
- Antiterrorism and Effective Death Penalty Act (1996)
- Omnibus Consolidated Appropriations Act for FY 1997 (Domestic Violence Gun Ban, Gun Free School Zones)
- Omnibus Consolidated & Emergency Supplemental Appropria-tions Act, 1999 (numerous requirements detailed in this chapter)
- Uniting and Strengthening America by Providing Appropriate Tools Required to Intercept and Obstruct Terrorism Act (USA PATRIOT Act); Aviation Security Act (Arm the pilots); Homeland Security Act: (Arm the government) (2001)
- Vision 100--Century of Aviation Reauthorization Act (2003) (Deputize cargo pilots so they may be armed)
- Reauthorize the ban on undetectable firearms (2003)
- Consolidated Appropriations Resolution (2003)
- Law Enforcement Officers Safety Act, LEOSA (2004)
- Protection of Lawful Commerce In Arms Act (2005)
- Disaster Recovery Personal Protection Act (2006)

Additional federal requirements may be found in the Code of Federal Regulations (CFR) and the United States Code (USC).

FEDERAL FIREARMS TRANSPORTATION GUARANTEE

Passed on July 8, 1986 as part of the Firearm Owner's Protection Act, federal law guarantees that a person may legally transport a firearm from one place where its possession is legal to another place where possession is legal, provided it is unloaded and the firearm and ammunition is not readily accessible from the passenger compartment of the vehicle. The law doesn't say it in so many words, but the only non-accessible spot in the average passenger car is the trunk. If a vehicle has no separate compartment for storage, the firearm and ammunition may be in a locked container other than the glove compartment or console.

There have been cases, especially in Eastern states, where local authorities have not complied with this law, creating a degree of risk for people otherwise legally transporting firearms. To avoid any confusion, the text of the federal guarantee is printed here word for word:

Federal Law Number 18 USC § 926A
Interstate transportation of firearms

Notwithstanding any other provision of any law or any rule or regulation of a State or any political subdivision thereof, any person who is not otherwise prohibited by this chapter from transporting, shipping, or receiving a firearm shall be entitled to transport a firearm for any lawful purpose from any place where he may lawfully possess and carry such firearm to any other place where he may lawfully possess and carry such firearm if, during such transportation the firearm is unloaded, and neither the firearm nor any ammunition being transported is readily accessible or is directly accessible from the passenger compartment of such transporting vehicle: Provided, That in the case of a vehicle without a compartment separate from the driver's compartment the firearm or ammunition shall be contained in a locked container other than the glove compartment or console.

Anyone interested in a complete copy of the federal gun laws, with plain English summaries of every law, can get a copy of *Gun Laws of America*, published by Bloomfield Press. See the back section of this book for details.

The Brady Law

Enacted in 1993 as the Brady Handgun Violence Prevention Act, the Brady law in reality turned out to be five things:

1–Centralized federal control over all handgun and long gun retail sales;

2–A $200 million funding mechanism for a national computer system capable of checking out any individual from a single FBI location;

3–The establishment of a national ID card requirement (based on drivers' licenses and social security numbers) for all original firearm purchases;

4–The most thorough commerce tracking system on earth, initially only for retail sales of firearms in America; and

5–A mechanism for preventing known criminals from directly purchasing firearms at retail and paying sales tax.

The widely publicized five-day waiting period was largely a myth, and never existed in most states (Virginia never had one). The effect of the Brady law on crime reduction is essentially unknown, since the hundreds of thousands of criminals reportedly identified by the system (the number is hotly disputed) are on the loose—only minor effort to track or apprehend them has been made. It is a five-year federal felony for criminals and other disqualified persons to attempt to purchase a firearm.

Part 1 of the law, the handgun part, set to expire 60 months after enactment, is described below in small type (it expired Nov. 30, 1998). Brady Part 2, the National Instant Background Check (dubbed NICS by the FBI, who has replaced BATFE to operate the system), controls rifles, shotguns and handguns, and is described as it appears in the federal statute. Complex regulations to implement the new law, which are basically transparent in this state, are not covered (available in their entirety on the FBI and BATFE Internet sites).

The FBI's use of the Brady NICS computer system to record the name and address of every retail gun buyer in America, in apparent violation of long-standing law (strictly forbidden in both the McClure Volkmer Act, 1986, and the Brady law itself), has prompted outcries from the public and Congress, but continued unabated throughout and then after the Clinton administration. In addition, the Justice Dept. under Clinton attempted but failed to levy a tax on the sale of firearms, to benefit the FBI, with no apparent authority to do so (taxes are supposed to originate in Congress). The Bush administration appeared intent on correcting such abuses, but it is distressing to see how politicized administration of the laws has become. States that agree to cooperate with the FBI, as Virginia has done, would have avoided the proposed tax on its licensed dealers.

For updates and detailed analysis of the complex Brady machinations, check our website, gunlaws.com.

The Brady Law, Part 1 (First Five Years, Expired 11/30/98)

The Brady Handgun Violence Prevention Act was signed into law on Nov. 30, 1993. Its provisions for common carriers, reporting multiple handgun sales and license fee increases are among the rules affecting private citizens that took effect immediately. The waiting-period provisions took effect on Feb. 28, 1994, and were set to expire on Nov. 30, 1998.

In addition to the regulation of private citizens described below, the Brady Law: places special requirements on dealers, sets timetables and budgets for the U.S. Attorney General to implement the law, provides funding, sets basic computer system requirements, mandates criminal-history record sharing among authorities, enhances penalties for gun thieves and more. Your federal legislators can send you the full 12-page Brady Law.

The Brady Law refers to a "chief law enforcement officer," defined as the chief of police, the sheriff, an equivalent officer or their designee. The description below refers to such persons as "the authorities." Where the law refers to an individual who is unlicensed under §923 of USC Title 18, this description says "private citizen" or "you." Federally licensed dealers, manufacturers and importers are referred to as "dealers." The act of selling, delivering or transferring is called "transferring." The law defines *handgun* as, "a firearm which has a short stock and is designed to be held and fired by the use of a single hand." A combination of parts which can be assembled into a handgun counts as a handgun.

Under the Brady Law, to legally obtain a handgun from a dealer you must provide:

* A valid picture ID for the dealer to examine;

* A written statement with only the date the statement was made, notice of your intent to obtain a handgun from the dealer, your name, address, date of birth, the type of ID you used and a statement that you are not: 1–under indictment and haven't been convicted of a crime which carries a prison term of more than one year, 2–a fugitive from justice, 3–an unlawful user of or addicted to any controlled substance, 4–an adjudicated mental defective, 5–a person who has been committed to a mental institution, 6–an illegal alien, 7–dishonorably discharged from the armed forces, 8–a person who has renounced U.S. citizenship.

Then, before transferring the handgun to you, the dealer must:

* Within one day, provide notice of the content and send a copy of the statement to the authorities where you live;

* Keep a copy of your statement and evidence that it was sent to the authorities;

* Wait five days during which state offices are open, from the day the dealer gave the authorities notice, and during that time,

* Receive no information from the authorities that your possession of the handgun would violate federal, state or local laws.

The waiting period ends early if the authorities notify the dealer early that you're eligible. The authorities "shall make a reasonable effort" to check your background in local, state and federal records. Long guns are unaffected by the Brady Law until the National Instant Check described below comes on line.

You are excluded from the Brady waiting-period process:

1–If you have a written statement from the authorities, valid for 10 days, that you need a handgun because of a threat to your life or a member of your household's life; or

2–With a handgun permit, in the state which issued it, if the permit is less than five years old and required a background check. The Virginia handgun permit qualifies under the Brady law.

3–In states which have their own handgun background check (Virginia has an instant check, making all Virginia residents exempt from the Brady delay); or

4–If the transfer is already regulated by the National Firearms Act of 1934, as with Class III weapons; or

5–If the dealer has been certified as being in an extremely remote location of a sparsely populated state and there are no telecommunications near the dealer's business premises (written for Alaska, but other localities may qualify).

If a dealer is notified after a transfer that your possession of the handgun is illegal, the dealer must, within one business day, provide any information they have about you to the authorities at the dealer's place of business and at your residence. The information a dealer receives may only be communicated to you, the authorities or by court order. If you are denied a handgun, you may ask the authorities why, and they are required to provide the reason in writing within 20 business days of your request.

Unless the authorities determine that the handgun transfer to you would be illegal, they must, within 20 days of the date of your statement, destroy all records of the process. The authorities are expressly forbidden to convey or use the information in your statement for anything other than what's needed to carry out the Brady process.

The authorities may not be held liable for damages for either allowing an illegal handgun transfer or preventing a legal one. If you are denied a firearm unjustly, you may sue the political entity responsible and get the information corrected or have the transfer approved, and you may collect reasonable attorney's fees.

The Brady Law Part 2—National Instant Check: The Brady Law requires the U.S. Attorney General (AG) to establish a National Instant Criminal Background Check system (NICS) before Nov. 30, 1998 (which they did). With NICS now in effect, the previous process (above, in small type) is eliminated. In order to transfer *any firearm, not just handguns,* with the NICS system is in place, a dealer must verify your identity from a government-issued photo-ID card, contact the system (based in Clarksburg, W. Va., run by the FBI), identify you and either:

- get a unique transfer number back from the system, or

- wait three days during which state offices are open and during which the system provides no notice that the transfer would violate relevant laws.

Virginia has been designated a "Point of Contact" state by the FBI. This means dealers here contact the State Police for all gun sales, as they have done for years. The instant check then automatically includes a check of NICS, and the process is transparent to Virginia's buyers (except when the system is down). In most states, dealers contact the FBI directly.

The NICS system is required to issue the transfer number if the transfer would violate no relevant laws, and it is supposed to immediately destroy all records of approved inquiries except for the identifying number and the date it was issued. The FBI, however, has decided to record the name and address of everyone who buys a gun at retail now that the system is running, and Congress has not stopped them so far. If the transfer is approved, the dealer includes the transfer number in the record of the transaction (on a redesigned version of the 4473 form). The NICS system is bypassed under conditions similar to 2, 4 and 5 listed above (in small type) as exceptions to the Brady process (with number 2 broadened to include "firearms" permit).

A licensed dealer who violates these requirements is subject to a civil fine of up to $5,000 and suspension or revocation of their license, but only if the system is operating and would have shown that the customer would have been ineligible to make a purchase.

It's important to note that the NICS law plainly says you only have to use NICS if it exists and it's running (18 USC §922 (t)(5)), a clause specifically put there by lobbyists who were afraid the system might never be implemented, ending gun sales altogether. But BATFE and the FBI have re-interpreted that clause to mean you can't sell a gun when NICS is down—rewriting the statute from their bureau desks—and dealers are too terrified to follow the law and oppose the government agents. The state police insta-check departments nationwide haven't been willing to stand up for states' rights and force the issue either. So when NICS is off, retail gun sales grind to a halt nationally, and this has occurred scores of times, and even on a regional basis.

If you are denied a firearm under NICS, the law says you may request the reason directly from NICS and it must present you with a written answer within five business days. You may also request the reason from the AG, who must respond "immediately," according to the law. You may provide information to fix any errors in the system, and the AG must immediately consider the information, investigate further, correct any erroneous federal records and notify any federal or state agency that was the source of the errors.

Multiple sales of handguns (two or more from the same dealer in a five day period) have long been reported to the Bureau of Alcohol, Tobacco, Firearms and Explosives, and must now be reported to local authorities as well. Local authorities may not disclose the information, must destroy the records within 20 days from receipt if the transfer is not illegal and must certify every six months to the AG that they are complying with these provisions.

Common or contract carriers (airlines, buses, trains, etc.) may not label your luggage or packages to indicate that they contain firearms. The long-time labeling practice had been responsible for the frequent theft of luggage containing firearms. Federal law requires you to notify the carrier in writing if you are transporting firearms or ammunition, but in actual practice verbal notification is frequently accepted.

Licensing fees for obtaining a new federal firearms license are increased to $200 for three years. The fee for renewing a currently valid license is $90 for three years.

Public Safety and Recreational Firearms Use Protection Act

This law, popularized as the 1994 Crime Bill and sometimes referred to as the assault-weapons ban, affected three areas of existing firearms law: 1–Possession and use of firearms by juveniles; 2–Possession of firearms by people under domestic violence restraining orders; and 3–It created a new class of regulated firearms and accessories. The information on juveniles is found in Chapter 1 since it relates to who can bear arms. The new class of prohibited purchasers (for domestic violence cases) is also in Chapter 1, as part of the list for federal form 4473—the form dealers use with all sales.

Historical Note: The portion of the law that created the legal *assault-weapons* category expired on Sep. 13, 2004. Nothing was actually banned—Americans could still buy, own, sell, trade, have and use any of the millions of affected firearms and accessories.

What the law actually did was to prohibit *manufacturers and importers* from selling newly made goods of that type to the public (and it was a crime for the public to get them). Maybe that is a ban, but not in the sense that was reported. Ten years later, after the end of the ban, there was widespread recognition that it had no effect on crime. The list of affected weapons is preserved for history in Chapter 3. Perhaps more laws should be enacted with expiration dates.

The net effect of the law was to motivate manufacturers to create stockpiles before the law took affect, then to introduce new products that were not affected, and to step up marketing efforts overseas for affected products. Demand and prices skyrocketed for the fixed supply of goods domestically, and then adjusted downward when it became obvious that supplies were still available. When it was over, a normal 15-round magazine for a sidearm dropped from more than $100 to around twenty bucks.

Rifle Practice and Firearms Safety Act (1996)

The Civilian Marksmanship Program, run by the U.S. Army, has served as the federal government's official firearms training, supply and competitions program for U.S. citizens, since 1956. Its history traces back to the late 1800s, when programs were first established to help ensure that the populace could shoot straight, in the event an army had to be raised to defend the country. The program is privatized by this act.

The federal government transfers the responsibility and facilities for training civilians in the use of small arms to a 501(c)(3) non-profit corporation created for this purpose. All law-abiding citizens are eligible to participate, and priority is given to reaching and training youth in the safe, lawful and accurate use of firearms.

Functions formerly performed for this program by the Army are now the responsibility of this new corporation. The Army is required to provide direct support and to take whatever action is necessary to make the program work in its privatized form. The stated program goals are:

1–Teaching marksmanship to U.S. citizens
2–Promoting practice and safety in the use of firearms
3–Conducting matches and competitions
4–Awarding trophies and prizes
5–Procuring supplies and services needed for the program
6–Securing and accounting for all firearms, ammunition and supplies used in the program

7–Giving, lending or selling firearms, ammunition and supplies under the program. Priority must be given to training youths, and reaching as many youths as possible.

Any person who is not a felon, hasn't violated the main federal gun laws, and does not belong to a group that advocates violent overthrow of the U.S. government, may participate in the Civilian Marksmanship Program.

Antiterrorism Act of 1996

A wide variety of gun-law changes were introduced in this 48,728-word act. Eight sections introduce new law, and other sections make 17 amendments to existing federal law. Much of it deals with intentional criminal acts, and so falls outside the scope of *The Virginia Gun Owner's Guide*. Other sections could give rise to unexpected results and are included.

Section 702. Using a firearm in an assault on any person in the U.S. is a federal crime if: 1–the assault involves "conduct transcending national boundaries" (described below) and 2–if any of the following also exist: A–any perpetrator uses the mail or interstate or foreign commerce in committing the crime; B–the offense in any way affects interstate or foreign commerce; C–the victim is anyone in the federal government or the military; D–any structure or property damaged is owned in any part by the federal government, or E–the offense occurs in special U.S. territorial jurisdictions. The maximum penalty in a non-lethal assault with a firearm is 30 years.

Causing a serious risk of injury to anyone, by damaging any structure or property in the U.S., is a federal crime if the conditions described in 1 and 2 above exist. The maximum penalty is 25 years.

Threatening, attempting or conspiring to commit the above acts is a crime, and various penalties are defined.

The phrase "conduct transcending national boundaries" means "conduct occurring outside of the United States in addition to the conduct occurring in the United States." It is not clear what this might include.

The Attorney General is in charge of investigating "federal crimes of terrorism." Such crimes occur when any of a long list of felonies is committed to influence the government by intimidation or coercion, or to retaliate against government actions. An assault involving conduct transcending national boundaries, described in the first part of this law, is one of the felonies.

Section 727. Using or attempting to use deadly force against anyone in the federal government or the military, if the attack is because of the person's government role, is a federal crime (in addition to existing assault and homicide laws). All former personnel are included. Federal penalties for an attack on anyone in this protected class are defined. In the case of such an assault, a gun is considered a gun, even if it jams due to a defective part.

Omnibus Consolidated Appropriation Act for FY 1997
Section 657, Gun-Free School Zone. Congress was stopped in its attempt to exercise police powers at the state level by the U.S. Supreme Court, when the court declared the 1991 Gun-Free School Zone law unconstitutional, in 1995. That law was reenacted, to the surprise of many observers, as an unnoticed add-on to a 2,000-page federal spending bill, in a form essentially identical to the one the Supreme Court overturned.

The law makes it a federal crime to knowingly have a firearm within 1,000 feet of any school. An exemption is granted to anyone willing to register with the government for a specified license to carry the firearm (the VA permit would qualify, and all other school rules still apply), and the prohibition does not apply to: 1–Firearms while on private property that is not part of the school grounds; 2–Any firearm that is unloaded and in a locked container; 3–Any firearm unloaded and locked in a firearms rack on a motor vehicle; 4–Possession of a firearm for use in an approved school program; 5–Possession under a contract with the school; 6–Possession by law enforcement officers in an official capacity; and 7–An unloaded firearm, while crossing school premises to public or private land open to hunting, if crossing the grounds is authorized by the school.

It is also illegal to fire a gun (or attempt to fire a gun), knowingly or with reckless disregard for safety, in a place you know is a school zone, with the following exceptions: 1–On private property that is not part of the school grounds; 2–As part of a program approved by the school; 3–Under contract with the school; 4–By law enforcement acting in an official capacity. Self defense is not mentioned. States are not prohibited from passing their own laws.

America had 121,855 public and private schools as of 1994. In effect, this law criminalizes the actions of nearly anyone who travels in a populated area with a legally possessed firearm, creating millions of federal offenses every day. For a dramatic visual on this problem, see the gun-free zone maps at gunlaws.com. In stark contrast, none of the 6,000 students who brought weapons to school in 1997 were prosecuted. As with its overturned predecessor, its affect on the very real problem of youth violence is unclear, and of course, any firearm used illegally in America, whether it is near a school or not, is already a serious crime with penalties.

Section 658. Misdemeanor Gun Ban for Domestic Violence Offense. Anyone convicted of a state or federal misdemeanor involving the use or attempted use of physical force, or the threatened use of a deadly weapon, among family members (spouse, parent, guardian, cohabiter, or similar) is prohibited from possessing a firearm under federal law. This marks the first time that a misdemeanor offense serves as grounds for denial of the constitutional right to keep and bear arms. The number of people affected is unknown, and no provision is made for the firearms such men and women might already possess. Firearms possession by a prohibited possessor is a five-year federal felony.

A number of narrow conditions may exempt a person from this law, including whether they were represented by an attorney, the type of trial and plea, an expungement or set aside, or a pardon or other restoration of civil rights. Because such offenses are often handled in courts-not-of-record, such a determination may not be possible.

The current congressional practice of placing unrelated laws in larger acts, to get them passed without debate (or unnoticed), has raised concerns among many observers. This law, known as the Lautenberg amendment, is an extreme example.

It caught both firearms-rights advocates and adversaries by surprise. The law is drafted broadly, affecting sworn police officers nationwide, the armed forces, and agencies such as the FBI, CIA, Secret Service, Forest Service and others, most of whom are accustomed to being exempted from such laws. Many of these groups are currently battling to get themselves exempted from the law. They don't believe they should be prevented from defending themselves or others because of prior minor infractions. Some police departments have had to lay off officers who are in violation.

So many problems exist with respect to this legislation that it has raised concerns unlike any recent act of Congress. Indeed, some members reportedly were told before voting that this language had been deleted from the final version, and the vote was held before copies of the 2,000-page act were available for review. Experts close to the issues cite numerous constitutional conflicts, including:

1–It is *ex post facto*—a law passed after the fact to affect your former actions (prohibited by Art. 1, Sec. 9);

2–It impacts the right to keep and bear arms (2nd Amendment);

3–Legally owned property becomes subject to automatic seizure (prohibited by the 4th Amendment);

4–It holds people accountable to a felony without a Grand Jury indictment, represents a second punishment for a single offense creating a double jeopardy, and it requires dispossession of personal property without compensation or due process (all prohibited by the 5th Amendment);

5–It denies your right to be informed of an accusation, and to counsel and a public jury trial because an existing misdemeanor now automatically creates a federal felony (prohibited by the 6th Amendment);

6–Using a misdemeanor (a minor infraction) instead of a felony (a serious crime) to deny civil rights may be cruel and unusual punishment (8th Amendment);

7–Family conflicts, historically an issue at the state level, become federalized (prohibited by the 10th Amendment); and

8–It denies due process, abridges the rights of U.S. citizens by state law, and denies equal protection under the law (violates 14th Amendment guarantees).

Domestic violence does not have a single definition at the state level. Some states' laws require the arrest of at least one party if the police respond to an apparent domestic-violence report. This raises all the issues of judicial process and plea-bargaining after an arrest. A parent who pays a small fine rather than endure a long expensive trial can now face a federal felony; domestic violence pleas have been a standard ploy in divorce proceedings for decades; these charges now deny your right to keep and bear arms, to vote, to hold office and more.

An analogy to cars crystallizes this law's affects. It is as if a former speeding ticket were now grounds for felony arrest if you own a car or gasoline. When a law is scrutinized for constitutionality it is typically held up to a single constitutional provision. The eight constitutional issues in this short piece of legislation may set a record.

Omnibus Consolidated & Emergency Supplemental Appropriations Act, 1999. This 4,000-page budget bill was secretly drafted in committee, rushed to the floor of Congress, voted on two days later, and enacted in October 1998 without any of your representatives actually reading it. It increased federal gun law by almost 6%, with provisions for NICS funding, gun-law enforcement funding, gun safety devices sold at retail, public gun safety training funding, restrictions on aliens, NICS record-keeping and tax prohibitions, shotguns and certain antiques redefined, undetectable gun law reenactment, relief for importers, a pawn shop NICS glitch fix, the Arms Control and Disarmament Agency disbanded with duties moved to the State Dept., and a special ban on using the U.S. global arms control and disarmament agenda against the public. Detailed analysis is available on our website, gunlaws.com.

The USA Patriot Act and the "Arm the Pilots" Law (2001)

Hurriedly enacted as a response to the September 11 attacks, a small part of the huge Patriot Act introduces definitions of terrorism and various gun provisions related to terrorism. Also rushed into law, the Aviation & Transportation Security Act allows pilots to be deputized, so those deputies, whose jurisdiction is solely the flight deck, can be armed. Curiously, there is nothing in current law that prevents pilots from being armed without this bill, it's come down to a plain issue of political pressure, and not law. Pilots are even authorized under existing law to take custody of *your* gun while enroute (though they are not required to do so) in 18 USC §922(e).

Undetectable Firearms Ban Extension, 2003: The ban on these guns, none of which are publicly known to exist, was extended for another ten years, to Dec. 10, 2013.

Arming Cargo Pilots, 2003: Air-cargo pilots, omitted from efforts to arm passenger-plane pilots, may now also be deputized and, as federal officers, be armed against terrorism. Bureaucratic foot-dragging has plagued this effort, the same as for passenger pilots.

Consolidated Appropriations, 2003: Many items, including: Dept. of Agriculture may selectively arm its employees; Judiciary may not tax or add fees to the Brady NICS check and must destroy certain records related to retail gun sales; Federal officers get funding for firearm competitions and awards; reiteration of ban on centralizing certain firearms records; no changes to *Curios or Relics* list; continued denial of relief for people with federal firearms disability except for corporations; no electronic retrieval allowed for out-of-business dealer records; safeguards on using dealer records in police work; $45 million for prosecutions to reduce gun violence; and a renewed ban against advocating or promoting gun control by the Centers for Disease Control.

Congress continues to churn out gun measures, issuing a national concealed-carry law for active, off-duty and retired police in 2004 (enacted as HR 218, now 18 USC §926B and C, known by its acronym LEOSA). That law is summarized in

Chapter 1 and described in detail in *Gun Laws of America*, available at gunlaws.com. The 1994 Crime Bill, with its list of hundreds of restricted weapons, expired in 2004, and frivolous lawsuit protection for the firearms industry passed in 2005 with many civilian conditions attached. In 2006, responding to abusive firearm confiscations in New Orleans following the Katrina hurricane disaster, they passed the Disaster Recovery Personal Protection Act to ban further abuses. Other smaller changes have also been made. Check gunlaws.com update pages for details.

Infringement Creep: Judicial and legislative activity are underway with regard to federal firearms issues on a practically non-stop basis. Despite pronouncements in 1996 about a moratorium on new gun laws, federal gun law grew by more than 13% that year. That's more new federal law in one year than we've seen in almost any *decade*.

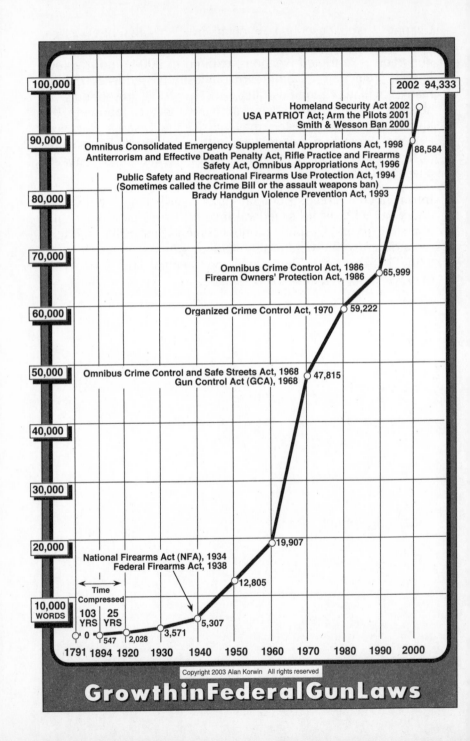

Copyright 2003 Alan Korwin All rights reserved

GrowthinFederalGunLaws

Only two decades in U.S. history—the 1960s and 1970s—saw more gun law enacted by Congress than in 1996 alone. Nearly 10,000 new words of gun law brought the federal total to more than 83,000 words. This represented a 13.43% increase for the year, which, measured by percentage or word count, set records for the federal regulation of the right to keep and bear arms.

Failure to comply with new laws and regulations can have serious consequences to you personally, even if you believe your constitutional rights have been compromised. In fact, many experts have noted that increasing latitudes are being taken by some governmental authorities with respect to constitutional guarantees. Legislative and regulatory changes present serious risks to currently law-abiding people, since what is legal today may not be tomorrow. The entire body of U.S. law is growing at a significant rate and it represents some potential threats to freedoms Americans have always enjoyed. It is prudent to take whatever steps you feel are reasonable to minimize any risks.

New laws may be passed at any time. It is your responsibility to be up-to-date when handling firearms under all circumstances. _This book's contents are guaranteed to age._

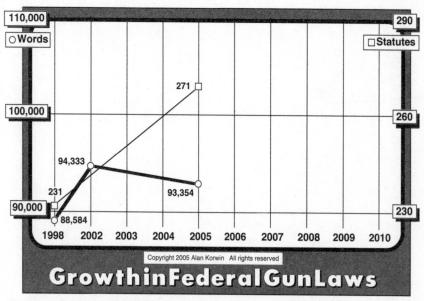

GrowthinFederalGunLaws

The net reduction in words since 2002 results mainly from losses due to codification of the Public Laws since 1995, plus repeals, expirations and amendments. In several cases amendments expanded a law's scope but reduced its word count (e.g., 610 words less in 18 USC §1114). Expiration of the assault-weapon law removed 1,105 words, and the 3,710-word list of approved guns. The increase in numbered statutes is a net gain, accounting for repeals and new enactments. New statutes since 2002 added 4,339 words.

GUN SAFETY

and Self-Defense Training

8

Many fine books and classes exist which teach the current wisdom on gun safety and use. In Virginia, some of the best public classes are given by the Dept. of Game and Inland Fisheries and the National Rifle Association. Advanced firearms and tactical training classes are available from private instructors and schools.

When studying firearm safety (and every gun owner should), you will likely come across the Ten Commandments of Gun Safety. These well-intentioned lists have some serious drawbacks—no two lists are ever the same and there are many more than ten rules to follow for safe gun use. In addition, hunters must learn many rules which don't apply to other shooters. For instance, a hunter should never openly carry game—it makes you an unwitting target of other hunters.

The Commandments of Safety are actually a way of saying, "Here's how people have accidents with guns." Each rule implies a kind of mishap. It's good exercise to look at each rule and read between the lines to find its counterpart—the potential disaster the rule will help you avoid. For example, Rule 1 translates into, "People have accidents with guns which they think are empty." Always keep in mind the prime directive: Take time to be safe instead of forever being sorry.

The federal government has been providing public firearms training opportunities for more than a century, using federal facilities and the military in cooperation with civilian leaders. To get involved with your local Civilian Marksmanship Program, described in detail in Chapter 7, call their office, which is listed in Appendix C.

Federal Laws Support Firearm Training

Although an argument is sometimes made that Americans don't have a right to keep and bear arms (despite clear language in the Constitution and more than two centuries of precedent), federal laws recognize and support an armed populace:

10 USC §4309:   Public can use federally funded rifle ranges.

10 USC §4312:   Public national shooting matches and small arms school are funded and staged, with subsidies for youngsters.

18 USC §922(q): Guns OK at official school training programs.

18 USC §922(x): Handguns and ammunition can be transferred temporarily to juveniles for target practice.

                Juveniles can have handguns and ammunition for a course of instruction in the safe and lawful use of a handgun.

42 USC §3760:   Byrne Grants authorize funds to teach safe gun handling to the public.

36 USC §40701: Civilian marksmanship programs for adults, with special programs for youngsters.

The Gun Owner's Commandments for Safety that follow deal with the routine firearm handling in daily, non-threatening circumstances such as range time, hunting, transporting, cleaning, teaching and similar uses of firearms. The gun safety rules for combat, as in crime prevention and personal safety, are another matter entirely.

If you think there are a lot of safety rules for routine gun handling, wait till you read some books on gun handling in tactical live-or-die situations. In stark contrast to the usual safety rules, the so-called Lovejoy's rules of gun safety include: 1–You must have a gun; 2–Keep your gun loaded and ready to fire at all times; and 3–The first hit counts more than the first shot. Depending on who you ask it is a long list packed with valuable suggestions, e.g., If your shooting stance is good and you have a proper sight picture, you're probably not moving fast enough or using cover correctly.

THE GUN OWNER'S COMMANDMENTS OF SAFETY

1–Treat every gun as if it is loaded until you have personally proven otherwise.

2–Always keep a gun pointed in a safe direction.

3–Don't touch the trigger until you're ready to fire.

4–Be certain of your target and what is beyond it before pulling the trigger.

5–Keep a gun you carry discretely holstered or otherwise concealed unless you're ready to use it.

6–Use but never rely on the safety.

7–Never load a gun until ready to use. Unload a gun immediately after use.

8–Only use ammunition that exactly matches the markings on your gun.

9–Always read and follow manufacturers' instructions carefully.

10–At a shooting range, always keep a gun pointed downrange.

11–Always obey a range officer's commands immediately.

12–Always wear adequate eye and ear protection when shooting.

13–If a gun fails to fire: a) keep it pointed in a safe direction; b) wait thirty seconds in case of a delayed firing; c) unload the gun carefully, avoiding exposure to the breech.

14–Don't climb fences or trees, or jump logs or ditches with a chambered round.

15–Be able to control the direction of the muzzle even if you stumble.

16–Keep the barrel and action clear of obstructions.

17–Avoid carrying ammunition which doesn't match the gun you are carrying.

18–Be aware that customized guns may require ammunition which doesn't match the gun's original markings.

19–Store guns with the action open.

20–Store ammunition and guns separately, and out of reach of children and careless adults.

21–Never pull a gun toward you by the muzzle.

22–Never horseplay with a firearm.

23–Never shoot at a hard flat surface, or at water, to prevent ricochets.

24–Be sure you have an adequate backstop for target shooting.

25–On open terrain with other people present, keep guns pointed upwards, or downwards and away from the people.

26–Never handle a gun you are not familiar with.

27–Learn to operate a gun empty before attempting to load and shoot it.

28–Be cautious transporting a loaded firearm in a vehicle.

29–Never lean a firearm where it may slip and fall.

30–Do not use alcohol or mood-altering drugs when you are handling firearms.

31–When loading or unloading a firearm, always keep the muzzle pointed in a safe direction.

32–Never use a rifle scope instead of a pair of binoculars.

33–Always remember that removing the magazine (sometimes called the clip) from semi-automatic and automatic weapons may still leave a live round, ready to fire, in the chamber.

34–Never rely on one empty cylinder next to the barrel of a revolver as a guarantee of safety, since different revolvers rotate in opposite directions.

35–Never step into a boat holding a loaded firearm.

36–It's difficult to use a gun safely until you become a marksman.

37–It's difficult to handle a gun safely if you need corrective lenses and are not wearing them.

38–Know the effective range and the maximum range of a firearm and the ammunition you are using.

39–Be sure that anyone with access to a firearm kept in a home understands its safe use.

40–Don't fire a large caliber weapon if you cannot control the recoil.

41–Never put your finger in the trigger guard when drawing a gun from a holster.

42–Never put your hand in front of the cylinder of a revolver when firing.

43–Never put your hand in back of the slide of a semiautomatic pistol when firing.

44–Always leave the hammer of a revolver resting over an empty chamber.

45–Never leave ammunition around when cleaning a gun.

46–Clean firearms after they have been used. A dirty gun is not as safe as a clean one.

47–Never fire a blank round directly at a person. Blanks can blind, maim, and at close range, they can kill.

48–Only use firearms in good working condition, and ammunition which is fresh.

49–Accidents don't happen, they are caused, and it's up to you and you alone to prevent them in all cases. Every "accident" which ever happened could have been avoided. Where there are firearms there is a need for caution.

50–Always think first and shoot second.

It is the responsibility of every American to prevent firearms from being instruments of tragedy.

TEACH YOUR CHILDREN WELL

Keeping Children Safe

Choosing to own a firearm—or choosing not to—has serious implications for the safety of your children and family. Your ability to respond in an emergency or not, and a child's dangerous access to a loaded firearm without your approval, should motivate you to take serious precautions for safety where firearms are concerned.

Firearms are dangerous; they're supposed to be dangerous; they wouldn't be very valuable if they weren't dangerous. The same as with power tools, automobiles, medicines, kitchen knives, balconies, swimming pools, electricity and everything else, it is up to responsible adults and their actions to help ensure the safety of those they love and the rest of the community.

In Virginia these are not just good ideas, it's the law. A firearm owner has a direct responsibility to control a child's access to a loaded firearm under Code of Virginia §18.2-56.2.

It is your responsibility to see that your own children, children who might visit you and careless adults are prevented from unauthorized access to any firearms you possess.

A delicate balance exists between keeping a gun immediately ready for response in an emergency, and protecting it from careless adults and children. This is the paradox of home-defense firearms. The more out-of-reach a gun is for safety's sake, the less accessible it is for self defense (also for safety's sake).

Secured Storage

Leaving a loaded gun out *in the open* where careless adults or children could get at it is not being responsible and subjects you to criminal charges if an accident occurs.

Putting a loaded gun in *a hard-to-find spot* may fool some kids (and it's better than doing nothing), but remember how easily you found your folks' stuff when you were a kid.

Putting a gun in *a hard-to-get-to spot* (like the top of a closet) has advantages over hard-to-find spots when small children (like toddlers) are involved. Remember that kids reach an age where they like to climb. And you really have no idea what goes on when the baby-sitter is around.

Hinged *false picture frames*, when done well, provide a readily available firearm that most people will simply never notice. The frame must be in a spot that can't be bumped, and if ever the frame is detected its value is completely and immediately compromised.

Flexible plastic trigger tags warn that a gun is loaded, but they provide a low level of child-proofing since they are typically designed to be removed easily.

Gun locks can be effective in preventing accidents but are completely compromised if a child can get at the key. The location of the key then becomes the paradox factor in keeping the gun at-the-ready yet safe. The closer together you keep the gun and its key the less safety the lock provides.

Combination gun locks eliminate the key problem, but mustn't be forgotten. If written down somewhere handy they too may be discovered. Many are difficult or impossible to operate in the dark. A number of push-button lock designs have been introduced which are made to fit directly into a handgun's mechanism.

Gun safes used properly can prevent accidents and provide reasonable access to personal firearms, but it is an expensive option. Many people with gun collections keep their firearms in a floor-standing safe, for theft and fire protection, simultaneously providing a high degree of accident proofing. Single-gun handgun safes are made for floor or wall mounting and use finger touch buttons that can be operated quickly in the dark. This is an excellent option for keeping a gun available yet highly protected from unauthorized use. Be sure to never let the batteries run down in the electronic models.

A home that doesn't have many visitors and never has kids around has a different challenge than a home with four kids growing up, when it comes to staying safe. Be sure that your home is safe for your kids—safe from those who would do you harm, and safe from the potential for harm your own home holds.

Disabling

Disabling a gun provides a safety margin. The more disabled a gun is the greater the safety, but the more difficult it becomes to bring the gun to bear if it should be needed.

The least disabled condition, and hence the least safe (though better than nothing), is a *safety lever engaged* on a semi-automatic or an appropriate empty chamber on a revolver.

An *unloaded* firearm is disabled in a sense, and incapable of firing, though that reverses completely upon the presence of ammunition. The margin of safety here, for both preventing accidents and providing defense, is as wide as the distance between the gun and its ammunition, very similar to the key and lock relationship.

Removing a firing pin or otherwise disassembling a firearm represents a high degree of disabling, essentially lowering chances of accidents to zero, and removing the possibility of putting the weapon to use in an emergency.

Keeping *no firearm at home* eliminates the ability to respond for safety if necessary, and still leaves a child at risk when visiting friends or when friends visit (especially if the child is not firearms aware).

The bottom line is that there are no perfect solutions, and that life has risks. You trade some for others, and make personal choices that affect everything you do. Be sure you make the hard choices necessary to keep your family safe in your own home.

One Man's Approach

Internationally recognized firearms instructor and author Massad Ayoob believes it's wiser to educate your children than attempting to childproof your gun. For a detailed discussion of this approach to guns and child safety, read his booklet, *Gun-Proof Your Children,* available from Bloomfield Press.

The Eddie Eagle Program

If you look behind all the hot political rhetoric, you'll notice that the main provider of firearms safety training in America is the National Rifle Association, fulfilling a century-old historic tradition that is actually embodied in federal law. Handgun Control, Inc., and the NRA agree that child accidents are tragic and that responsible citizens must take steps to protect youngsters. In response to this well perceived need, the NRA developed its highly acclaimed and widely used Eddie Eagle Safety Program. For teacher lesson plans, class materials, parent kits, video tapes, coloring books, posters and more, contact the NRA, listed in the Appendix.

THE EDDIE EAGLE SAFETY RULES FOR KIDS—

If you find a gun:

STOP!

Don't touch.

Leave the area.

Tell an adult.

HOW WELL DO YOU KNOW YOUR GUN?

Safe and effective use of firearms demands that you understand your weapon thoroughly. This knowledge is best gained through a combination of reading, classes and practice with a qualified instructor. The simple test below will help tell you if you are properly trained in the use of firearms. If you're not sure what all the terms mean, can you be absolutely sure that you're qualified to handle firearms safely?

- ☐ Action
- ☐ Ammunition
- ☐ Automatic
- ☐ Ballistics
- ☐ Barrel
- ☐ Black powder
- ☐ Bolt
- ☐ Bore
- ☐ Break action
- ☐ Breech
- ☐ Buckshot
- ☐ Bullet
- ☐ Butt
- ☐ Caliber
- ☐ Cartridge
- ☐ Case
- ☐ Casing
- ☐ Centerfire
- ☐ Chamber
- ☐ Checkering
- ☐ Choke
- ☐ Clip
- ☐ Cock
- ☐ Comb
- ☐ Cylinder
- ☐ Discharge
- ☐ Dominant eye
- ☐ Effective range
- ☐ Firearm
- ☐ Firing Pin
- ☐ Firing Line

- ☐ Forearm
- ☐ Fouling
- ☐ Frame
- ☐ Gauge
- ☐ Grip
- ☐ Grip panels
- ☐ Grooves
- ☐ Gunpowder
- ☐ Half cock
- ☐ Hammer
- ☐ Handgun
- ☐ Hangfire
- ☐ Hunter orange
- ☐ Ignition
- ☐ Kneeling
- ☐ Lands
- ☐ Lever action
- ☐ Magazine
- ☐ Mainspring
- ☐ Maximum range
- ☐ Misfire
- ☐ Muzzle
- ☐ Muzzleloader
- ☐ Pattern
- ☐ Pistol
- ☐ Powder
- ☐ Primer
- ☐ Projectile
- ☐ Prone
- ☐ Pump action
- ☐ Receiver

- ☐ Repeater
- ☐ Revolver
- ☐ Rifle
- ☐ Rifling
- ☐ Rimfire
- ☐ Safety
- ☐ Sear
- ☐ Semi-automatic
- ☐ Shell
- ☐ Shooting positions
- ☐ Shot
- ☐ Shotgun
- ☐ Sights
- ☐ Sighting-in
- ☐ Sitting
- ☐ Smokeless powder
- ☐ Smoothbore
- ☐ Standing
- ☐ Stock
- ☐ Trigger
- ☐ Trigger guard
- ☐ Unplugged shotgun

CONCEALED-HANDGUN TRAINING

Virginia requires its law-abiding citizens, under §18.2-308, to show the circuit court issuing a handgun-carry permit proof that you have "demonstrated competence" with a handgun. This is described in Chapter 2, and the degree of training is left in large measure up to you.

Even though you can make do with less, it makes sense for you personally to get a high degree of training. Many states expect two full days of training or more to obtain a carry license. Most experts consider this a bare minimum if you're serious about bearing arms.

Some people buy a handgun, a box of ammo, load it up and put it in the night stand. Some will go so far as to run a few rounds through the gun to make sure it works, and then put it in the night stand. This does not constitute a commitment to firearms proficiency. Commitment is an essential element to responsible firearms ownership.

Take the time to get training. The NRA offers firearms training for all levels of experience. Contact them at the phone number in Appendix C and attend one of their excellent courses. The Virginia Dept. of Game and Inland Fisheries' hunter safety course is another good place to start. Their numbers are also in Appendix C. Qualified private trainers are spread all across the state. Whatever training you receive, look at it as a beginning. You must practice frequently throughout your life to keep the needed skills.

Mistakes made with firearms can be tragic. The effect on your life and your loved ones can be devastating. And every mistake made is fuel for the fire of those who seek to deny gun rights. As a gun owner you must rise to a higher level of responsibility.

Here are some sample questions that concealed-carry permit applicants—and all responsible gun owners—probably should know:

Areas of Study:

1–Where are firearms prohibited in Virginia?
(At least seven places in addition to those prohibited by local laws, study chapters 2 and 4)

2–What are the possible penalties for improper display of a weapon in Virginia?
(At least three possible charges could be brought, study chapter 5)

3–What risks exist in drawing a firearm in public?
(Could be used to justify a self-defense claim by another party, accidental discharge, discharge in prohibited area, more, study chapter 5)

4–When does state law justify the use of deadly force?
(Legal precedents set by case law describe justifiable and excusable use of deadly force, study chapter 5)

5–What factors affect the strict legal definitions for justifiable or excusable use of deadly force?
(This is a complex issue frequently subject to debate and interpretation, fact-intensive and specific to the given circumstances, study chapter 5 and 8, and other books, such as In The Gravest Extreme, *by Massad Ayoob)*

6–What responsibility does a person have for firing shots that miss the intended target?
(Severe liabilities and penalties may result from the effect of stray bullets, study chapters 4 and 5)

7–Can you bring a firearm into a bar?
(Special requirements apply to people with concealed-carry permits, study chapter 2)

8–What types of weapons are illegal?
(For federal- and state-law restrictions, study chapter 3)

9–Who can legally bear arms in Virginia?
(Age, background, mental condition and more are taken into account, study chapter 1)

10–Under what circumstances can minors bear arms?
(Study chapters 1 and 4)

11–How can firearms be carried throughout the state?
(Different rules apply for carrying on yourself, in vehicles, while hunting, for minors, in school zones, local ordinances may apply, especially on roads, and more, study chapters 1, 2 and 4)

12–What are the requirements for getting a concealed-carry permit?
(Personal background and demonstrated competency with a handgun are involved, study chapter 2)

13–What do you have to do to ship firearms or carry them with you on a train, plane, or as you travel by car?
(Federal regulations control interstate transit, study chapter 1 and 7)

14–How remote do you have to be to practice target shooting outdoors?
(Land office rules are plentiful, study chapter 4)

15–How much judgment is involved in deciding whether you can use deadly force in a situation?
(No easy answers to this, read everything you can find on the subject, study chapters 5 and 8, get training, and recognize that in using deadly force you accept very definite and substantial legal risks)

16–What are the main rules of firearm safety?
(More than 50 exist, study chapter 8)

17–What types of weapons are suitable for self defense, and what are the best choices for you?
(A very important topic, not covered in this book, you should discuss this at length with your instructor.)

18–How do the various types of firearms operate?
(This topic should be covered by your instructor)

19–What are the options for carrying a concealed handgun?
(This topic should be covered by your instructor)

20–Have any new laws passed that you should know about?
(This requires ongoing information and vigilance. Send Bloomfield Press a self-addressed stamped envelope for news of our next update)

21–Are you mentally prepared to use deadly force?
   *(Mental conditioning for the use of deadly force is a critical
   component, and one that is not easily addressed. Until a
   moment arrives you may never truly know the answer to this
   question.)*

As you can see, your preparation for carrying a concealed
handgun can go well beyond the state-required minimums.
Make the smart choice and exceed the minimum training by
reading extensively, practicing regularly, keeping up on the
important issues, and taking additional training programs.

JUDGMENTAL SHOOTING

All gun owners, and concealed-carry permit holders in
particular, should study issues related to judgmental shooting.
Anyone considering armed response needs an understanding of
the issues involved.

The decision to use deadly force is rarely a clear-cut choice.
Regardless of your familiarity with the laws, your degree of
training, the quality of your judgmental skills and your physical
location and condition at the time of a deadly threat, the
demands placed on you at the critical moment are as intense as
anything you will normally experience in your life, and your
actual performance is an unknown.

Every situation is different. The answers to many questions
relating to deadly force are subject to debate. To be prepared for
armed response you must recognize that such situations are not
black or white, and that your actions, no matter how well
intentioned, will be evaluated by others, probably long after you
act.

The chances that you will come away from a lethal encounter
without any scars—legal, physical or psychological—are small,
and the legal risks are substantial. That's why it's usually best to
practice prevention and avoidance rather than confrontation,
whenever possible.

Most people can think about it this way: You've gotten along this far in life without ever having pulled a weapon on someone, much less having fired it. The odds of that changing once you have a concealed-carry permit are about the same, practically zero.

A concealed handgun may make you feel more secure, but it doesn't change how safe your surroundings actually are, in the places you normally travel, one bit. And it certainly isn't safe to think of a firearm as a license (or a talisman) for walking through potentially dangerous areas you would otherwise avoid like the plague.

Remember that the person holding a gun after a shooting is frequently thought of as the bad guy—the perpetrator—even if it's you and you acted in self defense. The person who is shot often gets a different, more sympathetic name—the victim—and gets the benefit of a prosecutor even if, perhaps, you learn later it's a hardened criminal with a long record.

Maybe your defense will improve if it is indeed a serious repeat offender, but you won't know that until after the fact, and don't count on it. If you ever have to raise a gun to a criminal, you'll find out quickly how good they can be at portraying you as the bad guy and themselves as the helpless innocents, at the mercy of a crazed wacko—you.

Situational Analysis

Think about the deadly force encounters described below, and consider discussing them with your personal firearms-safety trainer:

1–If you are being seriously attacked by a man with a club, is it legal for you to aim for his leg so you can stop the attack without killing him?

2–If you enter your home and find a person looting your possessions are you justified in shooting?

3–If you enter your home and find a person looting your possessions, who runs out the back door as he hears you arrive, can you shoot him to stop him from escaping?

4–If you enter your home and find a person looting your possessions, who turns and whirls toward you when you enter, literally scaring you to death, may you shoot and expect to be justified?

5–If you enter your home and find a stranger in it who charges you with a knife, may you shoot?

6–A stranger in your home has just stabbed your spouse and is about to stab your spouse again. May you shoot the stranger from behind to stop the attack?

7–As you walk past a park at night, you notice a woman tied to a tree and a man tearing off her clothing. May you use deadly force to stop his actions?

8–A police officer is bleeding badly and chasing a man in prison coveralls who runs right past you. May you shoot the fleeing suspect while he is in close range to you?

9–You're in your home at night when a man with a ski mask on comes through an open window in the hallway. May you shoot?

10–You're in your home at night, sleeping, when a noise at the other end of the house awakens you. Taking your revolver you quietly walk over to investigate and notice a short person going through your silverware drawer, 45 feet from where you're standing. The person doesn't notice you. May you shoot ?

11–As you approach your parked car in a dark and remote section of a parking lot, three youthful toughs approach you from three separate directions. You probably can't unlock your vehicle and get in before they reach you and you're carrying a gun. What should you do?

12–From outside a convenience store you observe what clearly appears to be an armed robbery—four people are being held at gun point while the store clerk is putting money into a paper bag. You're armed. What should you do?

13–You're waiting to cross the street in downtown and a beggar asks you for money. He's insistent and begins to insult you when you refuse to ante up. Finally, he gets loud and belligerent and says he'll kill you if you don't give him ten dollars. May you shoot him?

14–You get in your car, roll down the windows, and before you can drive off a man sticks a knife in the window and orders you to get out. Can you shoot him?

15-You get in your car and before you start it a man points a gun at you and tells you to get out. You have a gun in the pocket on the door, another under the seat, and a gun in a holster in your pants. What should you do?

16–Before you get in your car, a man with a gun comes up from behind, demands your car keys, takes them, and while holding you at gun point, starts your car and drives away. Can you shoot at him while he's escaping?

17–You're walking to your car in the mall parking lot after a movie when two armed hoods jump out of a shadow and demand your money. You've got a gun in your back pocket. What should you do?

18–A masked person with a gun stops you on the street, demands and takes your valuables, then flees down the street on foot. You're carrying a concealed handgun. What should you do?

19–A youngster runs right by you down the street and an old lady shouts, "Stop him, he killed my husband!" May you shoot to stop his getaway?

20–You're at work when two ornery-looking dudes amble in. You can smell trouble, so you walk to a good vantage point behind a showcase. Sure enough, they pull guns and announce a stick-up. You and your four employees are armed and there are several customers in the store. What's your move?

21–Your friend and you have been drinking, and now you're arguing over a football bet. You say the spread was six points, he says four. There's $500 hanging in the balance of a five-point game, and it represents your mortgage payment. He pulls a knife and says, "Pay me or I'll slice you up." You've got a gun in your pocket. What should you do?

22–At a gas station, the lines are long, it's hot, and the guy next in line starts getting surly. You're not done pumping and he hits you in the face and tells you to finish up. He shuts off your pump and says he'll kick your butt if you don't move on. Should you pull your gun to put him in his place?

Observations about the situations presented:

1–The Hollywood-promoted idea of *shoot to wound* is incredibly poor in the real world for a host of reasons. If you wing an arm but hit an artery the person can die anyway—there is no such thing as "wounding-level force." Hitting the limb of a moving person may be one of the most difficult shots known, especially in the stressful emotional state where this would occur. If you miss you are jeopardizing your life which is severely threatened in the first place or you would have no justification to shoot at all. It wastes valuable ammunition which may be critical to stopping the lethal attack you face. It's an unlikely case where the justification to use deadly force would be justification to intentionally wound a person. Firing and missing is a different story, but a prosecutor can argue that if the threat wasn't sufficient to use deadly force then there was no justification to shoot at all.

2–Not enough information is provided to make an informed choice.

3–No. The penalty for burglary is jail, not death, and you almost never have justification to shoot to prevent a criminal from escaping. Once the danger to you is over—and it generally is once the criminal is fleeing—your right to use deadly force ends.

4–You need more information to make a responsible choice. Do you always enter your home prepared for mortal combat? Does your story have other holes a prosecutor will notice?

5–It's hard to imagine not being justified in this situation, but stranger things have happened.

6–It's hard to imagine not being justified in this situation, but stranger things have happened. Will the bullet exit the attacker and wound your spouse? In one bizarre case (Arizona 1996), the attacker was actually the husband, wearing a ski mask, and the shooter was the wife's father-in-law—the husband's dad. They didn't even suspect what really happened until they were at the hospital, where the wife learned she was a widow and the shooter realized he had killed his own son.

7–Probably not, since you don't know if the people are consenting adults who like this sort of thing. Even if a crime is being committed, shooting might be viewed as excessive force. A seasoned police officer might cautiously approach the couple, weapon drawn, and with words instead of force determine what's happening, and then make further choices depending on the outcome.

8–Not enough information is provided to make an informed choice. Keep in mind that you do not have the obligation to apprehend criminals that police have.

9–Probably, though a well-trained expert might instead confront the intruder from a secure position and succeed in holding the person for arrest, which is no easy task. The longer you must hold the suspect the greater the risk to you. Armed and from good cover, you might just convince the intruder to leave the way he came.

10–Probably not. The distance and lack of immediate threat will make for a difficult explanation when the police arrive, and if the perpetrator has an accomplice that you didn't notice, the danger to you is severe. If it turns out that the intruder is 11 years old your court defense will be extremely difficult. Remember, you're obligated to not shoot if you don't absolutely have to. A shot would be in conflict with a prime safety rule—clearly identify your target before firing. Has your training prepared you for this?

11–That's a good question, and you should never have parked there in the first place.

12–Call for assistance, go to a defensible position, continue to observe, and recognize that charging into such a volatile situation is incredibly risky for all parties.

13–You are never justified in using deadly force in response to verbal provocation alone, no matter how severe.

14–The prosecutor will make it clear that if you could have stepped on the gas and escaped, the threat to you would have ended, and the need to shoot did not exist. If you were boxed into a parking space, the need to defend yourself would be hard for a prosecutor to refute. These things often come down to the exact circumstances and the quality of the attorneys.

15–Get out quietly and don't provoke someone who has the drop on you. All your guns are no match for a drawn weapon. This is where a real understanding of tactics comes into play.

16–No. Once the threat to you is over, the justification for using lethal force ends.

17–Not enough information is provided to make an informed choice.

18–Anyone crazy enough to rob you at gun point must be considered capable of doing anything, and the smart move is to avoid further confrontation and stay alive. Chasing after him is extremely unwise and risky to you.

19–You don't have enough information. When in doubt, don't shoot.

20–This is where strategy and tactics are critical. If you allow your employees to carry and are prepared for armed defense of your premises you better get plenty of advanced training in gun fighting and self defense. You'll need it to survive, and you'll need it to meet the legal challenges later. If a customer gets shot by one of your own, even if you get the villains, you're in for big time trouble and grief. If no one gets hurt but the criminals, you'll be a hero, though the media might paint you as a wild-eyed vigilante. Either outcome remains burned in memory. Tough choice.

21–Too many killings occur between people who know each other. Your chance of a successful legal defense in a case like this are remote. Would he really have killed you? Probably not. Did you have any other options besides killing him? Probably so. Have you fought like this before? Maybe. What would the witnesses say? Nothing you could count on, and probably all the wrong things. The fact that you have a firearm and can use it doesn't mean you should, the likelihood of absolutely having to use it is small, and using it to settle a bet with a half-soused friend over a point spread may not be the worst thing you can do, but it's close.

22–Cap your tank and move on, you don't need the grief. When you are armed you must be even more reluctant to enter into a conflict than you otherwise might be. Your pride is not worth the price of an armed conflict.

RECOMMENDED READING

Knowledge is power, and the more you have the better off you are likely to be. Everyone concerned with personal safety, and gun owners in particular, should read books on crime avoidance, self defense and the use of deadly force. **If you have a firearm for self defense, decide to read about this critical subject.** A selection of some of the most highly regarded books on these topics appears at the back of *The Virginia Gun Owner's Guide* and are easily available directly from the publisher. If your instructor doesn't include these in your course, get them yourself. The single best book on the subject is probably *In The Gravest Extreme*, by Massad Ayoob.

If you're concerned about preserving your right to keep and bear arms, read up on being effective politically. Too many activists make the mistake of endlessly studying the Bill of Rights and related documents, so that they can win debates. But if you win all your debates you're actually losing. You don't want to win debates, you want to win friends and influence people. Bloomfield Press now carries a line of books with this focus—Getting To Yes, How To Win Friends And Influence People, Confrontational Politics and more, plus the best books on the politics of guns.

You may also choose to obtain a complete copy of the Virginia criminal code, since the laws reproduced in *The Virginia Gun Owner's Guide* are a selected excerpt of gun laws only. Remember that no published edition of the law is complete without the legislation passed during the most recent session of the state congress, and that new federal laws may be passed at any time. An annotated edition of the law, available in major libraries, provides critical info in the form of court case summaries which clarify and expand on the meaning of the actual statutes.

THE NOBLE USES OF FIREARMS

THE NOBLE USES OF FIREARMS

In the great din of the national firearms debate it's easy to lose sight of the noble and respectable place firearms hold and have always held in American life. While some gun use in America is criminal and despicable, other applications appeal to the highest ideals our society cherishes, and are enshrined in and ensured by the statutes on the books:

- Protecting your family in emergencies
- Personal safety and self defense
- Preventing and deterring crimes
- Detaining criminals for arrest
- Guarding our national borders
- Deterring and resisting terrorism
- Preserving our interests abroad
- Helping defend our allies
- Overcoming tyranny
- International trade
- Emergency preparedness
- Obtaining food by hunting
- Commerce and employment
- Historical preservation and study
- Olympic competition
- Collecting
- Sporting pursuits
- Target practice
- Recreational shooting

News reports, by focusing almost exclusively on criminal misuse of firearms, create a false impression that firearms and crime are directly linked, when in fact almost all guns never have any link to crime whatsoever. The media judiciously ignore stories concerning legitimate self defense, which occur almost daily according to the FBI. There is silence on the effect the industry has on jobs in the manufacturing sector, contributions to the tax base, capital and investments, scientific advances, national trade and balance of payments, ballistics, chemistry, metallurgy, physics, and, of course, the enjoyment of millions of decent people who use firearms righteously. <u>Some people associate firearms with crime, fear and danger, or suffer from an irrational hoplophobic condition and want them to go away. Those who associate guns with liberty, freedom, honor, strength and safety understand the irreplaceable role firearms play in our lives.</u>

APPENDIX A
GLOSSARY OF TERMS

Words, when used in the law, often have special meanings you wouldn't expect from simply knowing the English language. For the complete legal description of these and other important terms, see each chapter of the criminal code and other legal texts dealing with language. Often, statutes contain their own definitions. The following plain-English descriptions are provided for your convenience only.

ALCOHOLIC = a person who through use of alcohol has become dangerous to the public or himself; or because of such alcohol use is medically determined to be in need of medical or psychiatric care, treatment, rehabilitation or counseling.

AMMUNITION = Cartridge, pellet, ball, missile or projectile adapted for use in a firearm.

ANTIQUE FIREARM = any firearm manufactured in or before 1898 and any replica of such a firearm not designed for using ammunition which is no longer manufactured in the United States and which is not readily available in the ordinary channels of commercial trade.

ARMOR-PIERCING AMMUNITION = Handgun ammunition designed primarily for penetrating metal or body armor. Referred to as *restricted* ammunition in statute.

ASSAULT FIREARM = Any semi-automatic center-fire rifle or pistol equipped with a magazine which will hold more than twenty rounds of ammunition or accept a silencer or has a folding stock.

BALLISTIC KNIFE = any knife with a detachable blade that is propelled by a spring-operated mechanism.

BATFE = The federal Bureau of Alcohol, Tobacco, Firearms and Explosives, formerly BATF, sometimes referred to as ATF.

CIVIL DISORDER = any public disturbance within the United States or any territorial possessions thereof involving acts of violence by assemblages of three or more persons, which causes an immediate danger of or results in damage or injury to the property or person of any other individual.

CONCEALED HANDGUN = A handgun that can't be seen through ordinary observation or is disguised and unrecognizable as a handgun.

CONVICTED = Found guilty of an offense by a court, even if the sentence is probation, the offender is discharged from community supervision, or the offender is pardoned, unless the pardon is granted for proof of innocence.

CONSERVATOR OF THE PEACE = Anyone duly appointed with legal authority to make arrests. Includes all law enforcement officers, judges, clerks of court, and persons in charge of maintaining order in public areas such as private security guards, ship's captains, game wardens, prison guards, train conductors, airline pilots and bus drivers.

CRIME OF VIOLENCE = Committing or attempting to commit: murder, manslaughter, kidnapping, rape, mayhem, assault.

CRIMINAL INSTRUMENT = Anything which is normally legal but which is put to illegal use.

CULPABLE MENTAL STATE = An accountable state of mind. Specifically and in decreasing order of seriousness: intentionally, knowingly, recklessly or with criminal negligence, in the sense described by law.

CURTILAGE = The land and buildings immediately surrounding a house or dwelling.

DEALER = Anyone licensed as a firearms dealer by the federal government. The federal description of a dealer appears in Chapter 1.

DEADLY FORCE = Physical force which can cause death or serious bodily injury.

DEADLY WEAPON = Anything made or adapted for lethal use or for inflicting serious bodily injury, including a firearm.

EXPLOSIVE DEVICE = Dynamite and all other forms of high explosive. Incendiary, firebomb or similar devices including "Molotov cocktails."

FIREARM = Any weapon that will or is designed to or may readily be converted to expel single or multiple projectiles by the action of an explosion of a combustible material, or the frame or receiver of any such weapon.

FIREARM SHOW = Any gathering, open to the public, not on the premises of a firearm dealer, for the purpose of trading or selling firearms.

FIREARM SILENCER = Any device that can muffle the sound of a firearm.

FELONY = A serious crime, typically carries a prison term of more than one year. A class 1 felony (capital murder) is the most serious, and has a possible sentence of death. A class 6 felony is the least serious, and carries a possible sentence of one year. Felony fines range from $2,500 to $100,000.

GOVERNMENT = The recognized political structure within the state.

HANDGUN = Any pistol or revolver or other firearm, except a machine gun, originally designed, made and intended to fire a projectile by means of an explosion of a combustible material from one or more barrels when held in one hand.

HARM = Loss, disadvantage or injury to a person or someone for whom that person is responsible.

HOAX BOMB = A device that reasonably appears to be an explosive or incendiary device. A device that, by its design, causes alarm or reaction of any type by a public safety agency official or emergency volunteer agency is a hoax bomb.

INDIVIDUAL = A living human being.

INTOXICATED = Having an alcohol concentration of 0.08 or more, or having had enough alcoholic beverages to observably affect manner, disposition, speech, muscular movement, general appearance or behavior.

KNIFE = Any bladed hand instrument that can inflict serious bodily injury or death by cutting or stabbing.

KNUCKLES = A hard substance that can be worn on a fist and can inflict serious bodily injury or death by striking.

LAW = Formal rules by which society attempts to control itself. In Virginia, the law means the Virginia state statutes, the state Constitution, the U.S. Constitution and federal statutes, city ordinances, county commissioners court orders, county ordinances, published court precedents and more. "The law" is a thing too large for any one individual to know.

LAWFULLY ADMITTED FOR PERMANENT RESIDENCE = Lawfully given the privilege of residing permanently in the United States as an immigrant in accordance with the immigration laws.

LAW ENFORCEMENT OFFICER = Any full-time or part-time employee of a police department or sheriff's office who is responsible for the prevention and detection of crime and the enforcement of the penal, traffic or highway laws of this Commonwealth. Also included are agents of the Alcoholic Beverage Control, Virginia Marine Patrol, Department of Game and Inland Fisheries, State Lottery Department and Department of Motor Vehicles when fulfilling their duties.

MACHINE GUN = A firearm capable of shooting more than one shot, without manually reloading, by a single pull of the trigger.

MISDEMEANOR = A crime less serious than a felony. An offense against the law that carries a sentence of imprisonment of up to one year. Misdemeanor fines can run up to $2,500. Misdemeanors are classified as class 1 (most serious) to class 4 (least serious).

MUTATIS MUTANDIS = "When what must be changed has been changed." A legal term used to apply the provisions of one statute to a second statute, once the specifics such as section number have been changed.

PRIMA FACIE = A legal presumption meaning "on the face of it" or "at first sight." Prima facie evidence is presumed to be accurate unless convincing contradicting evidence is presented.

REASONABLE = The admittedly interpretable notion of what is "fair, proper, just, moderate, suitable to the end in view... being synonymous with rational, honest, equitable, fair, suitable, moderate, tolerable." (Black's Law Dictionary)

RESTRICTED AMMUNITION = See armor-piercing ammunition.

SAWED-OFF RIFLE = A rifle with a barrel length less than 16 inches or an overall length of less than 26 inches.

SAWED-OFF SHOTGUN = A smooth bore shotgun with a barrel length less than 18 inches. A rifled barrel shotgun with a length of less than 16 inches and a caliber greater than .225 (federal rules make no distinction as to caliber).

SERIOUS BODILY INJURY = Injury that causes permanent damage to or loss of a limb or organ, or creates a reasonable risk of death or death itself. Also, injury that causes serious and permanent disfigurement or impairment.

SPRING GUN = Any firearm or deadly weapon set to activate or discharge by means of a trip wire or any other remote device.

SPRING STICK = A spring-loaded metal stick activated by pushing a button which rapidly and forcefully telescopes the weapon to several times its original length.

STUN WEAPON = Any device that emits a momentary or pulsed output, which is electrical, audible, optical or electromagnetic in nature and which is designed to temporarily incapacitate a person.

SWITCHBLADE KNIFE = A knife with a blade that comes out of its handle automatically by centrifugal force, by gravity, or by pressing a button or other device on the handle.

UNLAWFUL = Anything that's criminal or a tort.

UNSOUND MIND = The mental condition of someone who has been judged mentally incompetent or mentally ill, who has been found not guilty of a crime by reason of insanity, or who has been diagnosed by a licensed physician as being unable to manage themselves or their personal affairs.

APPENDIX B
Crime and Punishment Chart

EXPLANATIONS

Type of Crime: Illegal activities are divided into these ten categories, to match the punishment to the crime. The category may be affected by how the crime is committed. Felonies are serious crimes, misdemeanors are less serious. Felonies remove the right to keep and bear arms, hold public office, vote, obtain certain types of employment and more.

Jail Term: These are the general ranges for a first offense involving a gun; many crimes have special sentences. A capital felony, in addition to life imprisonment, carries a possible death penalty for first degree murder, which is administered by lethal injection or electrocution. The method of execution is chosen by the prisoner, or if the prisoner refuses to choose, by injection (§53.1-234).

Fines: These are maximums, which may be lowered at court discretion. Fines can be payable immediately or a court may grant permission to pay by a certain date or in installments.

Statute of Limitations: A complex set of rules describes the length of time within which a person may be charged for a crime. The most serious crimes have no time limit for bringing a prosecution. (The limitations are found in Title 19.2.)

Offenses: The chart provides a partial list of offenses in each category, and exceptions often apply.

CRIME AND PUNISHMENT
Felonies

TYPE OF CRIME	PRISON SENTENCE FOR A FIRST OFFENSE	MAXIMUM FINE
Class 1 Felony	**Death or Life in Jail**	**$100,000**
	Capital murder.	
Class 2 Felony	**20 Years to Life**	**$100,000**
	Attempted capital murder, first degree murder, aggravated malicious wounding, armed burglary, use of a machine gun or sawed-off shotgun/rifle in a crime of violence.	
Class 3 Felony	**5–20 Years**	**$100,000**
	Conspiracy to commit capital murder, second degree murder, malicious wounding, burglary, supplying prisoners with weapons, arson of an occupied building.	
Class 4 Felony	**2–10 Years**	**$100,000**
	Malicious discharge of a weapon in an occupied building, Discharge of a firearm within 1000 feet of school property, use of a machine gun for aggressive purposes, possession of a sawed-off shotgun/rifle, shooting at motor vehicles, false statements when attempting to procure a firearm.	
Class 5 Felony	**Up to 10 Years**	**$2,500**
	Manslaughter, possession of explosives, shooting from vehicles to endanger others, possession of plastic firearms, third offense of unlawful concealed weapon, "straw purchases" of a firearm, using restricted ammo in commission of a crime.	
Class 6 Felony	**Up to 5 Years**	**$2,500**
	Shooting in the commission of a felony, hoax explosives, possession of a stolen firearm, possession of a silencer, furnishing firearms to a minor, possession of a firearm on school property, fraudulent ID for a firearms purchase, possession of Striker 12 shotgun, furnishing firearms to felon.	

CRIME AND PUNISHMENT
Misdemeanors

TYPE OF CRIME	JAIL SENTENCE FOR A FIRST OFFENSE	MAXIMUM FINE
Class 1 Misdemeanor	**Up to 1 Year**	**$2,500**

Reckless handling of a firearm, weapons in a courthouse, willful discharge of firearms in public, knowingly allowing access to firearms by children under twelve, brandishing a firearm, carrying a loaded "assault weapon" in a public place, hunting under the influence, first offense of unlawful concealed weapon.

Class 2 Misdemeanor	**Up to 6 Months**	**$1,000**

Deer hunting with a spotlight, hunting out of season, possessing false ID, obtaining criminal history information under false pretenses.

Class 3 Misdemeanor	**None**	**$500**

Trespassing by hunters, hunting under the influence of alcohol, hunting or fishing without a license, hunting with prohibited firearms, recklessly allowing access to firearms by children under fourteen.

Class 4 misdemeanor	**None**	**$250**

Carrying a dangerous weapon in a church, deer hunting from a boat, drinking while driving, spitting in public, selling blackjacks, switchblades or ballistic knives.

THE PROPER AUTHORITIES C

Regulations on guns and their use come from a lot of places. Listed with each authority are the addresses and phones of the nearest offices. All cities are in Virginia unless indicated. You can use the National Directory at gunlaws.com for additional contacts.

Federal Refuges
   Back Bay, Refuge Manager, 4005 Sandpiper Rd, Virginia Beach 23456
   Chincoteague, Refuge Manager, Box 62, Chincoteague 23336
   Dismal Swamp, Refuge Manager, Box 349, Suffolk 23434
   Eastern Shore, Refuge Manager, 5003 Hallett Circle
      Cape Charles 23310
   Presquile, Refuge Manager, Box 620, Hopewell 23860
Army Corps of Engineers 757-441-7500
Attorney General 804-786-2071
Bureau of Alcohol, Tobacco and Firearms 202-566-7591
   Dept. of the Treasury; Washington, DC 20226
Bureau of Indian Affairs 202-343-5116, 7163
   U.S. Dept. of Interior, Washington, DC 20240
Civilian Marksmanship Program 540-775-5204
Corporate Hunting Areas
   Appalachian Power Cooperative Management Areas
      Contact VDGIF, 804-525-7522, Route 6, Box 410, Forest 24551
   Bear Island Timberlands Co., L.P.
      Hunting Permits, PO Box 2119, Ashland 23005
   Smurfit Stone Chesapeake Forest Product Co.
      Eastern VA Region 804-843-5298
         Hunting Permits, 15th and Main Streets, West Point 23181
      Keysville Region 804-736-8505
         Hunting Permits, Box 450, Keysville 23947
      Pocomoke Region, 410-543-8223
         Hunting Permits, Box 300, Pocomoke City, MD 21851
   Glatfelter Pulp Wood Company, PO Box 868, Fredericksburg 22404
   Lester Properties, Forestland Department Manager,
      Post Office Drawer 4991, Martinsville 24115, 276-656-3254

City Governments
Alexandria 703-838-4000
Bedford 540-587-6001
Buena Vista 540-261-6121
Charlottesville 434-970-3333.
Chesapeake 757-382-6345
Clifton Forge 540-863-2501
Colonial Heights 804-520-9265
Covington 540-965-6300
Danville 434-799-5100
Emporia 434-634-3332
Fairfax 703-385-7855
Falls Church 703-248-5001
Franklin 757-562-8504
Fredericksburg 540-372-1010
Galax 276-236-5773
Hampton 757-727-6392
Harrisonburg 540-434-6776
Hopewell 804-541-2249
Lexington 540-462-3700
Lynchburg 434-847-1000
Manassas 703-257-8200
Manassas Park 703-335-8800
Martinsville 276-403-5386
Newport News 757-926-8000
Norfolk 757-664-4000
Norton 276-679-1160
Petersburg 804-733-2301
Poquoson 757-868-7151
Portsmouth 757-393-8000
Radford 540-731-3603
Richmond 804-646-7000
Roanoke 540-853-2000
Salem 540-375-3000
South Boston 434-575-4200
Staunton 540-332-3800
Suffolk 757-514-4000
Virginia Beach 757-385-3111
Waynesboro 540-942-6600
Williamsburg 757-220-6100
Winchester 540-667-1815

County Governments
Accomack 757-787-5700
Albemarle 434-296-5822
Alleghany 540-863-6600
Amelia 804-561-3039
Amherst 434-946-9400
Appomatox 434-352-2637
Arlington 703-228-3000

Augusta 540-245-5600
Bath 540-839-7221
Bedford 540-586-7601
Bland 800-519-3468
Botetourt 540-473-8220
Brunswick 804-848-3107
Buchanan 276-935-6501
Buckingham 434-969-4242
Campbell 434-332-9525
Caroline 804-633-5380
Carroll 276-730-3001
Charlotte 434-542-5117
Chesterfield 804-748-1000
Clarke 540-955-5100
Craig 540-864-5010
Culpeper 540-727-3427
Cumberland 804-492-3625
Dickenson 276-926-1676
Dinwiddie 804-469-4500
Essex 804-443-4331
Fairfax 703-324-2531
Fauquier 540-347-8680
Floyd 540-745-9300
Fluvanna 434-591-1910
Franklin 540-483-3030
Frederick 540-665-5600
Giles 540-921-2525
Gloucester 804-693-4042
Goochland 804-556-5300
Grayson 276-773-2471
Greene 434-985-5201
Greensville 434-348-4205
Halifax 434-476-3300
Hanover 804-365-6000
Henrico (804) 501-4000
Henry 276-634-4601
Highland 540-468-2347
Isle of Wight 757-357-3191
James City 757-253-6728
King and Queen 804-785-5975
King George 540-775-9181
King William 804-769-4927
Lancaster 804-462-5129
Lee 276-346-7714
Loudoun 703-770-0100
Louisa 540-967-0401
Lunenburg 434-696-2142
Madison 540-948-6700
Mathews 804-725-7172
Mecklenburg 434-738-6191

Middlesex 804-758-4330
Montgomery 540-382-6954
Nelson 434-263-7000
New Kent 804-966-9696
Northampton 757-678-0440
Northumberland 804-580-7666
Nottoway 434-645-8696
Orange 540-672-3313
Page 540-743-4142
Patrick 276-694-6094
Pittsylvania 434-432-7700
Powhatan 804-598-5611
Prince Edward 434-392-8837
Prince George 804-722-8600
Prince William 703-792-6000
Pulaski 540-980-7705
Rappahannock 540-675-5330
Richmond County 804-333-3415
Roanoke 540-772-2006

Rockbridge 540-463-4361
Roanoke 703-772-2006
Rockbridge 703-463-4361
Rockingham 703-564-3000
Russell 703-889-8000
Scott 703-386-6521
Shenandoah 703-459-2195
Smyth 703-783-3298
Southampton 757-653-2465
Spotsylvania 703-582-7010
Stafford 703-659-8600
Surry 757-294-5271
Tazwell 703-988-7541
Warren 703-636-4600
Washington 703-676-6202
Westmoreland 804-493-0130
Wise 703-328-2321
Wythe 703-223-6020
York 757-890-2320

Department of Conservation and Recreation 804-786-1712
    203 Governor St. Suite 213, Richmond 23219
Dept. of Forestry Headquarters Office 434-977-6555
    900 Natural Resources Dr # 800, Charlottesville 22903
    Cumberland State Forest 804-492-4121
        Route 1, Box 250, Cumberland 23040
    Appomattox-Buckingham State Forest 804-983-2175
        Route 3, Box 133, Dillwyn 23936
Dept. of Game and Inland Fisheries
    Main Office, Richmond 804-367-1000
        4010 West Broad St., PO Box 11104, Richmond 23230
    Region 1, Williamsburg 804-829-6580
        3801 John Tyler Memorial Hwy, Charles City 23030
    Region 2, 1132 Thomas Jefferson Rd., Forest 24551, 434-525-7522
    Region 3, 1796 Highway Sixteen, Marion 24354, 276-783-4860
    Region 4, PO Box 996, Verona 24482, 540-248-9360
    Region 5, Fredericksburg 540-899-4169
        1320 Belman Rd., Fredericksburg 22401
    Blacksburg District 540-961-8304
        2206 S. Main St. Suite C, Blacksburg 24060
    Farmville District, 107 Foxwood Dr., 23901, 434-392-9645
    Powhatan District 4792 Anderson Hwy., 23139, 804-403-3261
    Chesapeake District 3909 Airline Blvd., 23321, 757-465-6811
Hunters for the Hungry 800-352-4868
Law Libraries
    Fairfax County Law Library 703-246-2170
    Richmond City Law Library 804-646-6500
    Virginia Beach Wahab Law Library 757-427-4419
Legislative Council 804-698-7410, 804-786-9631

Military Areas Open for Hunting
  Fort A. P. Hill 804-633-8300
    USAG Fort A. P. Hill, Attn Wildlife Section, Bowling Green 22427
  Fort Pickett, HQ US Army Garrison 804-292-2618
    Attn: Game check station, Building 420, Fort Pickett 23824
  Marine Base, MCCDC Quantico 703-784-6281
  Radford Army Ammunition Plant, contact Game and Inland Fisheries at
    540-961-8304, VDGIF Blacksburg Field Office, 2206 S. Main St.
    Suite C, Blacksburg 24060
National Forests
  George Washington and Jefferson National Forrests 540-265-6054
National Rifle Association 800-336-7402
  11250 Waples Mill Rd., Fairfax 22030
  Locally, contact the Virginia Shooting Sports Association
Norfolk Clerk of Court 757-664-4380
Secretary of the Commonwealth 804-786-2441
U.S. Forest Service PO Box 96090, Washington, DC 20090
  Forest Headquarters 540-265-6054
    5162 Vallypointe Parkway, Roanoke 24019
  Blacksburg Ranger District 540-552-4641
    110 Southpark Dr., Blacksburg 24060
  Clinch Ranger District, 9416 Darden Dr., Wise 24293, 540-328-2931
  North Field Ranger District 540-885-8028
    Route 6, Box 419, Staunton 24401
  Dry River Ranger District 540-828-2591
    112 North River Rd., Bridgewater 22812
  Glenwood/Pedlar Ranger District 540-291-2189
    PO Box 10, Natural Bridge Station 24579
  James River Ranger District 540-962-2214
    810-A Madison Ave., Covington 24426
  Lee Ranger District, 109 Molineu Rd., Edinburg 22824, 540-984-4101
  Mount Rogers National Recreational Area, 540-783-5196
    Route 1, Box 303, Marion 24354
  New Castle Ranger District 540-864-5195
    Box 246, New Castle 24127
  Pedlar Ranger District 540-261-6105
    2424 Magnolia Ave., Buena Vista 24416
  Warm Springs Ranger District 540-839-2521
    Hwy. 220 South, Route 2, Box 30 Hot Springs 24445
  Wythe Ranger District, 155 Sherwood Forest Rd., Wytheville 24382
    276-228-5551
Virginia Citizens Defense League, Inc. 804-639-0600, 703-372-3285
  757-271-3705, 540-446-5783, PO Box 513, Newington 22122, vcdl.org
Virginia Department of State Police
  Administrative HQ 804-674-2000
  Gun control 804-674-2292
Virginia Shooting Sports Association 800-526-1397, 540-672-5848
  PO Box 1258, Orange 22960, vssa.org
Virginia Wildlife Crimeline 800-237-5712
Virginia Wildlife Federation 804-648-3136

APPENDIX D
THE VIRGINIA GUN LAWS

On the following pages are excerpts from official Virginia state law, formally known as *Code of Virginia*.

Virginia law covers a broad spectrum of subjects but **only gun laws for private citizens are included in this appendix.** A complete copy of the state law is available in major libraries, but keep in mind that those copies are incomplete (and in many instances inaccurate) without the new material from the last legislative session, which this book includes through April 8, 2009, some of which become effective July 1, 2009.

The laws reproduced here are *excerpts.* Only material related to keeping arms and bearing arms has been included. In some cases this means substantial portions of laws may have been edited. **For official legal proceedings do not rely on these excerpts**—obtain unedited texts and competent professional assistance. This version is from the official state website; any errors appearing there at the time of download will be faithfully reproduced here.

How State Law Is Arranged: Each numbered part of the *Code of Virginia* is called a "section," represented by a "§" sign. This makes it easy to refer to any particular statute—just call it by its title and section numbers. For instance, Code of Virginia §18.2-308 is the part about concealed weapons. You say it like this, "Code of Virginia, section eighteen point two dash three oh eight." Has a certain ring to it.

Excerpt from the Constitution of the Commonwealth of Virginia
Article 1, Section 13: MILITIA; STANDING ARMIES;
MILITARY SUBORDINATE TO CIVIL POWER.

That a well regulated militia, composed of the body of the people, trained to arms, is the proper, natural, and safe defense of a free state, therefore, the right of the people to keep and bear arms shall not be infringed; that standing armies, in time of peace, should be avoided as dangerous to liberty; and that in all cases the military should be under strict subordination to, and governed by, the civil power.

Growth in the Gun Laws of Virginia

Total numbered statutes of Virginia gun law: 193

Growth in Virginia gun law, by word count:

1996: 30,154 words; 1997: 30,958 (+2.7%); 1998: 32,317 (+4.4%); 1999: 34,184 (+5.8%); 2000: 36,486 (+6.7%); 2001: 37,242 (+2.1%); 2002: 172 statutes, 38,154 (+2.4%); 2003-5: 190, 44,871, (+17.6%); 2006: 191, 45,494, (+1.4%); 2007: 46,526, (+2.3%); 2008: 193, 47,321, (+1.7%); 2009: 193, 47,391 (+0.1%).

Statutes Affected in the 1997 Legislature: §§15.1-29.15; 18.2-51.1; 18.2-287.2; 29.1-301; 18.2-308; 18.2-308.2:2; 29.1-300.1; 37.1-129; 52-4.4. (9)

1998: §§18.2-31; 18.2-95; 18.2-108.1; 18.2-308; 18.2-308.1:4; 18.2-308.2; 18.2-308.2:2; 29.1-101; 29.1-519; 29.1-521; 29.1-529; 46.2-345; 58.1-638; 59.1-148.3. (14)

1999: §§16.1-260; 16.1-278.8; 16.1-305.1; 16.1-309.1; 18.2-31; 18.2-57; 18.2-95; 18.2-280; 18.2-285; 18.2-308; 18.2-308.1; 18.2-308.2; 18.2-308.4; 18.2-477.2; 19.2-120; 19.2-123; 22.1-277.01; 22.1-278; 22.1-280.1; 29.1-529; 53.1-109.01; 59.1-148.3. (22)

2000: §§15.2-915.1; 15.2-1113; 15.2-1113.1; 15.2-1209; 16.1-278.8; 16.1-278.9; 18.2-10; 18.2-57; 18.2-57.01; 18.2-85; 18.2-308.2:3; 19.2-120; 19.2-123; 22.1-277.01; 22.1-280.1; 29.1-529; 55-248.9; 59.1-148.3. (18)

2001: §§16.1-285.1; 18.2-57.02; 18.2-280; 18.2-308.1; 18.2-308; 18.2-308; 18.2-308; 18.2-308.1:4; 19.2-123; 22.1-278.1; 22.1-278.1; 29.1-301; 29.1-521; 37.1-67.3; 37.1-134.18. (15)

2002: §§15.2-915; 16.1-278.9 §18.2-31; 18.2-308; 18.2-308.1:4; 18.2-308.2; 18.2-308.2:2; 29.1-301; 29.1-530.1; 59.1-148.3. (10)

2003–2005: §§9.1-185.2; 9.1-186.9; 15.2-915; 15.2-915.2; 15.2-915.3; 15.2-915.4; 15.2-917; 15.2-1208; 15.2-1209; 15.2-1209.1; 16.1-260; 16.1-278.8; 16.1-278.9; 16.1-301; 16.1-305.1; 16.1-309.1; 18.2-10; 18.2-46.1; 18.2-53.1; 18.2-57; 18.2-67.3; 18.2-85; 18.2-90; 18.2-154; 18.2-204.1; 18.2-279; 18.2-280; 18.2-282; 18.2-283.1; 18.2-284; 18.2-285; 18.2-287; 18.2-287.01; 18.2-287.4; 18.2-299; 18.2-308; 18.2-308.1; 18.2-308.1:2; 18.2-308.1:3; 18.2-308.1:4; 18.2-308.2; 18.2-308.2:01; 18.2-308.2:1; 18.2-308.2:2; 18.2-308.2:3; 18.2-308.4; 18.2-308.5; 18.2-308.7; 18.2-433.1; 19.2-386.27; 19.2-386.28; 19.2-386.29; 22.1-277.07; 22.1-277.07:1; 22.1-277.2:1; 22.1-279.3:1; 29.1-101; 29.1-301; 29.1-521; 29.1-529; 29.1-530.1; 46.2-345; 52-11.4; 52-11.5; 54.1-4201; 54.1-4201.1; 59.1-148.1; 59.1-148.2; 59.1-148.3; 59.1-148.4; 59.1-443.2. (72)

2006: §§15.2-915.3; 15.2-917; 18.2-308; 44-146.15. (4)

2007: §§3.1-1029 – 65.2-402.1, 15.2-915.3, 15.2-1209.1, 19.2-386.28, 19.2-386.29, 18.2-31, 18.2-46.1, 18.2-57.02, 18.2-136, 18.2-283.1, 18.2-287.01, 18.2-287.4, 18.2-308.2:2, 18.2-308, 18.2-308.1, 18.2-308.2, 29.1-519, 29.1-528, 59.1-148.3 (20+)

2008: §§18.2-10, 18.2-308, 18.2-308.1:1, 18.2-308.1:3, 18.2-308.2, 18.2-308.2:01, 18.2-308.2:1, 18.2-308.2:2, 29.1-300.1, 29.1-300.4, 29.1-301, 37.2-814, 37.2-819, 59.1-443.2 (14)

2009: §§15.2-915, 18.2-308, 59.1-148.3 (3)

Descriptions of the changes are posted at gunlaws.com.

VIRGINIA GUN LAWS • 2009
EXCERPTS FROM THE CODE OF VIRGINIA
<Cross-references and explanatory remarks appear in pointed brackets
and are generally not part of the statutes.>

Title 4.1 Alcoholic Beverage Control Code

§4.1-318. Violations by armed persons; penalty

No person shall unlawfully manufacture, transport or sell any alcoholic beverages, and at the time of the unlawful
manufacturing, transporting, or selling or aiding or assisting in any manner in such act, shall carry on or about his
person, or have on or in any vehicle which he may be using to aid him in any such purpose, or have in his
possession, actual or constructive, at or within 100 yards of any place where any such alcoholic beverages are
being unlawfully manufactured, transported or sold, any dangerous weapon as described in §18.2-308.
Any person convicted of a violation of this section shall be guilty of a Class 6 felony.

§4.1-336. Contraband beverages and other articles subject to forfeiture

All stills and distilling apparatus and materials for the manufacture of alcoholic beverages, all alcoholic beverages and
materials used in their manufacture, all containers in which alcoholic beverages may be found, which are kept,
stored, possessed, or in any manner used in violation of the provisions of this title, and any dangerous weapons as
described in §18.2-308, which may be used, or which may be found upon the person or in any vehicle which such
person is using, to aid such person in the unlawful manufacture, transportation or sale of alcoholic beverages, or
found in the possession of such person, or any horse, mule or other beast of burden, any wagon, automobile, truck
or vehicle of any nature whatsoever which are found in the immediate vicinity of any place where alcoholic
beverages are being unlawfully manufactured and which such animal or vehicle is being used to aid in the
unlawful manufacture, shall be deemed contraband and shall be forfeited to the Commonwealth.
Proceedings for the confiscation of the above property shall be in accordance with §4.1-338 for all such property
except motor vehicles which proceedings shall be in accordance with §4.1-339 through 4.1-348.
Such dangerous weapons seized by any officer charged with the enforcement of this title shall be forfeited to the
Commonwealth upon the conviction of the person owning or possessing such weapons and shall be sold by order
of court and the proceeds of such sale shall be paid into the Literary Fund.

Title 9.1 Commonwealth Public Safety

§9.1-132. Individual's right of access to and review and correction of information

A. Any individual who believes that criminal history record information is being maintained about him by the Central
Criminal Records Exchange (the "Exchange"), or by the arresting law-enforcement agency in the case of offenses
not required to be reported to the Exchange, shall have the right to inspect a copy of his criminal history record
information at the Exchange or the arresting law-enforcement agency, respectively, for the purpose of ascertaining
the completeness and accuracy of the information. The individual's right to access and review shall not extend to
any information or data other than that defined in subdivision 4 of §9.1-101.

C. If an individual believes information maintained about him is inaccurate or incomplete, he may request the agency
having custody or control of the records to purge, modify, or supplement them. Should the agency decline to so
act, or should the individual believe the agency's decision to be otherwise unsatisfactory, the individual may make
written request for review by the Board. The Board or its designee shall, in each case in which it finds prima facie
basis for a complaint, conduct a hearing at which the individual may appear with counsel, present evidence, and
examine and cross-examine witnesses. The Board shall issue written findings and conclusions. Should the record
in question be found to be inaccurate or incomplete, the criminal justice agency maintaining the information shall
purge, modify, or supplement it in accordance with the findings and conclusions of the Board. Notification of
purging, modification, or supplementation of criminal history record information shall be promptly made by the
criminal justice agency maintaining the previously inaccurate information to any individuals or agencies to which
the information in question was communicated, as well as to the individual who is the subject of the records.

§9.1-185.2. Powers of the Criminal Justice Services Board relating to bail bondsmen

The Board shall have full regulatory authority and oversight of property and surety bail bondsmen.
The Board shall adopt regulations that are necessary to ensure respectable, responsible, safe and effective bail
bonding within the Commonwealth. The Board's regulations shall include but not be limited to regulations that

(viii) establish standards for professional conduct, solicitation, collateral received in the course of business, firearms
    training and usage, uniforms and identification, documentation and recordkeeping requirements, reporting
    requirements, and methods of capture for the recovery of bailees;

The Board shall not adopt compulsory, minimum, firearms training standards in excess of 24 hours per year for bail
bondsmen. In adopting its regulations, the Board shall seek the advice of the Private Security Services Advisory
Board established pursuant to §9.1-143.

§9.1-185.11. Firearms, training and usage; standards and requirements

A. If a bail bondsman chooses to carry a firearm in the course of his duties, he shall be required to:

1. First complete basic firearms training, as defined by the Board; and
2. Receive ongoing in-service firearms training, as defined by the Board.

B. In the event a bail bondsman discharges a firearm during the course of his duties, he shall report it to the
    Department within 24 business hours.

§9.1-186.9. Firearms, training and usage; standards and requirements

A. If a bail enforcement agent chooses to carry a firearm, either concealed or visible, in the course of his duties, he
    shall be required to:

1. First complete basic firearms training, as defined by the Board; and
2. Receive ongoing in-service firearms training, as defined by the Board.

B. In the event a bail enforcement agent discharges a firearm during the course of his duties, he shall report it to the
    Department within 24 business hours.

Title 15.2 Counties, Cities and Towns

§15.2-915. Control of firearms; applicability to authorities and local governmental agencies

A. No locality shall adopt or enforce any ordinance, resolution or motion, as permitted by §15.2-1425, and no agent of
    such locality shall take any administrative action, governing the purchase, possession, transfer, ownership,
    carrying, storage or transporting of firearms, ammunition, or components or combination thereof other than those
    expressly authorized by statute. For purposes of this section, a statute that does not refer to firearms, ammunition,
    or components or combination thereof, shall not be construed to provide express authorization.

Nothing in this section shall prohibit a locality from adopting workplace rules relating to terms and conditions of
employment of the workforce. Nothing in this section shall prohibit a law-enforcement officer, as defined in §9.1-
101 from acting within the scope of his duties.

The provisions of this section applicable to a locality shall also apply to any authority or to a local governmental entity,
including a department or agency, but not including any local or regional jail or juvenile detention facility.

B. Any local ordinance, resolution or motion adopted prior to the effective date of this act governing the purchase,
    possession, transfer, ownership, carrying or transporting of firearms, ammunition, or components or combination
    thereof, other than those expressly authorized by statute, is invalid.

C. In addition to any other relief provided, the court may award reasonable attorney fees, expenses, and court costs to
    any person, group, or entity that prevails in an action challenging (i) an ordinance, resolution, or motion as being in
    conflict with this section or (ii) an administrative action taken in bad faith as being in conflict with this section.

§15.2-915.2. Regulation of transportation of a loaded rifle or shotgun

The governing body of any county or city may by ordinance make it unlawful for any person to transport, possess or
carry a loaded shotgun or loaded rifle in any vehicle on any public street, road, or highway within such locality. Any
violation of such ordinance shall be punishable by a fine of not more than $100. Conservation police officers,
sheriffs and all other law-enforcement officers shall enforce the provisions of this section. No ordinance adopted
pursuant to this section shall be enforceable unless the governing body adopting such ordinance so notifies the
Director of the Department of Game and Inland Fisheries by registered mail prior to May 1 of the year in which
such ordinance is to take effect.

The provisions of this section shall not apply to duly authorized law-enforcement officers or military personnel in the
performance of their lawful duties, nor to any person who reasonably believes that a loaded rifle or shotgun is
necessary for his personal safety in the course of his employment or business.

§15.2-915.3. Requiring fingerprinting for concealed handgun permit

Notwithstanding §15.2-915, a county or city may by ordinance require any applicant for a concealed handgun permit
to submit to fingerprinting for the purpose of obtaining the applicant's state or national criminal history record;
however, such ordinance shall not require fingerprinting for the renewal of an existing permit pursuant to
subsection I of §18.2-308.

§15.2-915.4. Counties, cities and towns authorized to regulate use of pneumatic guns

A. A locality may prohibit, by ordinance, the shooting of pneumatic guns in any areas of the locality that are in the
    opinion of the governing body so heavily populated as to make such conduct dangerous to the inhabitants thereof,
    and may require supervision by a parent, guardian, or other adult supervisor approved by a parent or guardian of
    any minor below the age of 16 in all uses of pneumatic guns on private or public property. The ordinance may
    specify that minors above the age of 16 may, with the written consent of a parent or guardian, use a pneumatic

gun at any place designated for such use by the local governing body or on private property with the consent of the owner. The ordinance may specify that any minor, whether permitted by a parent or guardian to use a pneumatic gun or not, shall be responsible for obeying all laws, regulations and restrictions governing such use. Any penalty for a pneumatic gun offense set forth in such an ordinance shall not exceed a Class 3 misdemeanor.
B. No such ordinance authorized by subsection A shall prohibit the use of pneumatic guns at facilities approved for shooting ranges or on other property where firearms may be discharged.
C. Training of minors in the use of pneumatic guns shall be done only under direct supervision of a parent, guardian, Junior Reserve Officers Training Corps instructor, or a certified instructor. Training of minors above the age of 16 may also be done without direct supervision if approved by the minor's instructor, with the permission of and under the responsibility of a parent or guardian, and in compliance with all requirements of this section. Ranges and instructors may be certified by the National Rifle Association, a state or federal agency that has developed a certification program, any service of the Department of Defense, or any person authorized by these authorities to certify ranges and instructors.
D. Commercial or private areas designated for use of pneumatic paintball guns may be established and operated for recreational use. Equipment designed to protect the face and ears shall be provided to participants at such recreational areas, and signs must be posted to warn against entry into the paintball area by persons who are unprotected or unaware that paintball guns are in use.
E. As used in this section, "pneumatic gun" means any implement, designed as a gun, that will expel a BB or a pellet by action of pneumatic pressure. "Pneumatic gun" includes a paintball gun that expels by action of pneumatic pressure plastic balls filled with paint for the purpose of marking the point of impact.

§15.2-916. Prohibiting shooting of compound bows, crossbows, longbows and recurve bows

Any locality may prohibit the shooting of an arrow from a bow in a manner that can be reasonably expected to result in the impact of the arrow upon the property of another without permission from the owner or tenant of such property. For the purposes of this section, "bow" includes all compound bows, crossbows, longbows and recurve bows having a peak draw weight of ten pounds or more. The term "bow" does not include bows which have a peak draw of less than ten pounds or which are designed or intended to be used principally as toys. The term "arrow" means a shaft-like projectile intended to be shot from a bow.

§15.2-917. Applicability of local noise ordinances to certain sport shooting ranges

A. No local ordinance regulating any noise shall subject a sport shooting range to noise control standards more stringent than those in effect at its effective date. The operation or use of a sport shooting range shall not be enjoined on the basis of noise, nor shall any person be subject to action for nuisance or criminal prosecution in any matter relating to noise resulting from the operation of the range, if the range is in compliance with all ordinances relating to noise in effect at the time construction or operation of the range was approved, or at the time any application was submitted for the construction or operation of the range.
B. Any sport shooting range operating or approved for construction within the Commonwealth, which has been condemned through an eminent domain proceeding by any condemning entity, and which relocates to another site within the same locality within two years of the final condemnation order, shall not be subjected to any noise control standard more stringent than those in effect at the effective date of such sport shooting range.
C. For purposes of this section, "sport shooting range" means an area or structure designed for the use of rifles, shotguns, pistols, silhouettes, skeet, trap, black powder, or any other similar sport shooting.
For purposes of this section, "effective date" means the time the construction or operation of the sports shooting range initially was approved, or at the time any application was submitted for the construction or operation of the sports shooting range, whichever is earliest.

§15.2-918. Locality may prohibit or regulate use of air cannons

Any locality may by ordinance prohibit or regulate the use within its jurisdiction of certain devices, including air cannons, carbide cannons, or other loud explosive devices which are designed to produce high intensity sound percussions for the purpose of repelling birds.
Such ordinance may prescribe the degree of sound or the decibel level produced by the cannon or device which is unacceptable in that jurisdiction.
In adopting an ordinance pursuant to the provisions of this section, the governing body may provide that any person who violates the provisions of such ordinance shall be guilty of a Class 3 misdemeanor.

§15.2-1113. Dangerous, etc., business or employment; transportation of offensive substances; explosive or inflammable substances; fireworks

A municipal corporation may regulate or prohibit the conduct of any dangerous, offensive or unhealthful business, trade or employment; the transportation of any offensive substance; the manufacture, storage, transportation, possession and use of any explosive or inflammable substance; and the use and exhibition of fireworks and the discharge of firearms. A municipal corporation may also require the maintenance of safety devices on storage equipment for such substances or items.
Any municipal corporation that regulates or prohibits the discharge of firearms shall provide an exemption for the killing of deer pursuant to §29.1-529. Such exemption shall apply on land of at least five acres that is zoned for agricultural use.

§15.2-1206. Pistols and revolvers; license tax on dealers
The governing body of any county may impose a license tax of not more than $25 on persons engaged in the business of selling pistols and revolvers to the public.

§15.2-1207. Same; reports of sales
The governing body of any county may require sellers of pistols and revolvers to furnish the clerk of the circuit court of the county, within ten days after sale of any such weapon, with the name and address of the purchaser, the date of purchase, and the number, make and caliber of the weapon sold. The clerk shall keep a record of the reports.

§15.2-1208. Same; in certain counties
Chapter 297 of the Acts of 1944, approved March 29, 1944, requiring permits to sell or purchase pistols or revolvers in any county having a density of population of more than 1,000 a square mile, is repealed. Any records or copies thereof that were created pursuant to this section that are in the custody of any county shall be destroyed no later than July 31, 2004. Upon destroying the records, the county shall certify to the circuit court that such destruction has been completed.

§15.2-1209. Prohibiting outdoor shooting of firearms or arrows from bows in certain areas
Any county may prohibit the outdoor shooting of firearms or arrows from bows in any areas of the county which are in the opinion of the governing body so heavily populated as to make such conduct dangerous to the inhabitants thereof.

For purposes of this section, "bow" includes all compound bows, crossbows, longbows and recurve bows having a peak draw weight of 10 pounds or more. The term "bow" does not include bows that have a peak draw of less than 10 pounds or that are designed or intended to be used principally as toys. The term "arrow" means a shaft-like projectile intended to be shot from a bow.

Any county that prohibits the outdoor shooting of firearms or arrows from bows shall provide an exemption for the killing of deer pursuant to §29.1-529. Such exemption for the shooting of firearms shall apply on land of at least five acres that is zoned for agricultural use. Such exemption for the shooting of arrows from bows shall apply on land of at least two acres that is zoned for agricultural use.

§15.2-1209.1. Counties may regulate carrying of loaded firearms on public highways
The governing body of any county is hereby empowered to adopt ordinances making it unlawful for any person to carry or have in his possession, for the purpose of hunting, while on any part of a public highway within such county a loaded firearm when such person is not authorized to hunt on the private property on both sides of the highway along which he is standing or walking; and to provide a penalty for violation of such ordinance not to exceed a fine of $100. The provisions of this section shall not apply to persons carrying loaded firearms in moving vehicles or for purposes other than hunting, or to persons acting at the time in defense of persons or property.

§15.2-1210. Prohibiting hunting in certain areas
Any county may by ordinance prohibit all hunting with firearms or other weapons in, or within one-half mile of, any subdivision or other area of such county which, in the opinion of the governing body, is so heavily populated as to make such hunting dangerous to the inhabitants thereof. Any such ordinance shall clearly describe each area in which hunting is prohibited, and shall further provide that appropriate signs shall be erected designating the boundaries of such area.

§15.2-1721. Disposal of unclaimed firearms or other weapons in possession of sheriff or police
Any locality may destroy unclaimed firearms and other weapons which have been in the possession of law-enforcement agencies for a period of more than sixty days. For the purposes of this section, "unclaimed firearms and other weapons" means any firearm or other weapon belonging to another which has been acquired by a law-enforcement officer pursuant to his duties, which is not needed in any criminal prosecution, which has not been claimed by its rightful owner and which the State Treasurer has indicated will be declined if remitted under the Uniform Disposition of Unclaimed Property Act (§55-210.1 et seq.).

At the discretion of the chief of police, sheriff, or their duly authorized agents, unclaimed firearms and other weapons may be destroyed by any means which renders the firearms and other weapons permanently inoperable. Prior to the destruction of such firearms and other weapons, the chief of police, sheriff, or their duly authorized agents shall comply with the notice provision contained in §15.2-1719.

Title 16.1 Courts Not of Record

§16.1-246. When and how child may be taken into immediate custody
No child may be taken into immediate custody except:

C. 1. When a child has committed a misdemeanor offense involving
(i) shoplifting in violation of §18.2-103
(ii) assault and battery or

(iii) carrying a weapon on school property in violation of §18.2-308.1 and, although the offense was not committed in the presence of the officer who makes the arrest, the arrest is based on probable cause on reasonable complaint of a person who observed the alleged offense;

§16.1-260. Intake; petition; investigation

G. Notwithstanding the provisions of Article 12 (§16.1-299 et seq.) of this chapter, the intake officer shall file a report with the division superintendent of the school division in which any student who is the subject of a petition alleging that such student who is a juvenile has committed an act, wherever committed, which would be a crime if committed by an adult. The report shall notify the division superintendent of the filing of the petition and the nature of the offense, if the violation involves:

1. A firearm offense pursuant to Article 4 (§18.2-279 et seq.), 5 (§18.2-288 et seq.), 6 (§18.2-299 et seq.), or 7 (§18.2-308 et seq.) of Chapter 7 of Title 18.2;

§16.1-269.1. Conditions for transfer to circuit court

A. If a juvenile fourteen years of age or older is charged with an offense which would be a felony if committed by an adult, the court shall, on motion of the attorney for the Commonwealth and prior to a hearing on the merits, hold a transfer hearing and may retain jurisdiction or transfer such juvenile for proper criminal proceedings to the appropriate circuit court having criminal jurisdiction of such offenses if committed by an adult. Any transfer to the appropriate circuit court shall be subject to the following conditions:

4. b. The seriousness and number of alleged offenses, including

(iv) whether the alleged offense involved the use of a firearm or other dangerous weapon by brandishing, threatening, displaying or otherwise employing such weapon.

§16.1-278.8. Delinquent juveniles

B. If the court finds a juvenile delinquent of any of the following offenses, the court shall require the juvenile to make at least partial restitution or reparation for any property damage, for loss caused by the offense, or for actual medical expenses incurred by the victim as a result of the offense: §18.2-51, 18.2-51.1, 18.2-52, 18.2-53, 18.2-55, 18.2-56, 18.2-57, 18.2-57.2, 18.2-121, 18.2-127, 18.2-128, 18.2-137, 18.2-138, 18.2-146, or 18.2-147; or for any violation of a local ordinance adopted pursuant to §15.2-1812.2. The court shall further require the juvenile to participate in a community service project under such conditions as the court prescribes.

§16.1-278.9. Delinquent children; loss of driving privileges for alcohol, firearm and drug offenses; truancy

A. If a court has found facts which would justify a finding that a child at least 13 years of age at the time of the offense is delinquent and such finding involves

(vii) the unlawful use or possession of a handgun or possession of a "streetsweeper" as defined below

the court shall order, in addition to any other penalty that it may impose as provided by law for the offense, that the child be denied a driver's license.

If the offense involves a violation designated under clause (vii), the denial of driving privileges shall be for a period of not less than 30 days, except when the offense involves possession of a concealed handgun or a striker 12, commonly called a "streetsweeper," or any semi-automatic folding stock shotgun of like kind with a spring tension drum magazine capable of holding 12 shotgun shells, in which case the denial of driving privileges shall be for a period of two years unless the offense is committed by a child under the age of 16 years and three months, in which event the child's ability to apply for a driver's license shall be delayed for a period of two years following the date he reaches the age of 16 and three months.

D. If the finding as to such child involves a violation designated under clause (iii), (iv), (v), (vii) or (viii) of subsection A, such child may be referred to appropriate rehabilitative or educational services upon such terms and conditions as the court may set forth.

F. If the finding as to such child involves a violation designated under clause (v), (vi) or (vii) of subsection A, upon fulfillment of the terms and conditions prescribed by the court and after the child's driver's license has been restored, the court shall or, in the event the violation resulted in the injury or death of any person or if the finding involves a violation designated under clause (i) or (ii) of subsection A, may discharge the child and dismiss the proceedings against him. Discharge and dismissal under these provisions shall be without an adjudication of guilt but a record of the proceeding shall be retained for the purpose of applying this section in subsequent proceedings. Failure of the child to fulfill such terms and conditions shall result in an adjudication of guilt. If the finding as to such child involves a violation designated under clause (iii) or (iv) of subsection A, the charge shall not be dismissed pursuant to this subsection but shall be disposed of pursuant to the provisions of this chapter or §18.2-251.

§16.1-285.1. Commitment of serious offenders

A. In the case of a juvenile fourteen years of age or older who has been found guilty of an offense which would be a felony if committed by an adult, and either

(i) the juvenile is on parole for an offense which would be a felony if committed by an adult,

(ii) the juvenile was committed to the state for an offense which would be a felony if committed by an adult within the immediately preceding twelve months or

(iii) the felony offense is punishable by a term of confinement of greater than twenty years if the felony was committed by an adult, or

(iv) the juvenile has been previously adjudicated delinquent for an offense which if committed by an adult would be a felony punishable by a term of confinement of twenty years or more, and the circuit court, or the juvenile or family court, as the case may be, finds that commitment under this section is necessary to meet the rehabilitative needs of the juvenile and would serve the best interests of the community, then the court may order the juvenile committed to the Department of Youth and Family Services for placement in a learning center for the period of time prescribed pursuant to this section.

B. Prior to committing any juvenile pursuant to this section, the court shall consider:

2. The seriousness and number of the present offenses, including:

(iii) whether the offense involved the use of a firearm or other dangerous weapon by brandishing, displaying, threatening with or otherwise employing such weapon;

§16.1-301. Confidentiality of law-enforcement records; disclosures to school principal

B. Notwithstanding any other provision of law, the chief of police or sheriff of a jurisdiction or his designee may disclose, for the protection of the juvenile, his fellow students and school personnel, to the school principal that a juvenile is a suspect in or has been charged with

(i) a violent juvenile felony, as specified in subsections B and C of §16.1-269.1;

(ii) a violation of any of the provisions of Article 1 (§18.2-77 et seq.) of Chapter 5 of Title 18.2; or

(iii) a violation of law involving any weapon as described in subsection A of §18.2-308.

If a chief of police, sheriff or a designee has disclosed to a school principal pursuant to this section that a juvenile is a suspect in or has been charged with a crime listed above, upon a court disposition of a proceeding regarding such crime in which a juvenile is adjudicated delinquent, convicted, found not guilty or the charges are reduced, the chief of police, sheriff or a designee shall, within 15 days of the expiration of the appeal period, if there is no notice of appeal, provide notice of the disposition ordered by the court to the school principal to whom disclosure was made. If the court defers disposition or if charges are withdrawn, dismissed or nolle prosequi, the chief of police, sheriff or a designee shall, within 15 days of such action provide notice of such action to the school principal to whom disclosure was made. If charges are withdrawn in intake or handled informally without a court disposition or if charges are not filed within 90 days of the initial disclosure, the chief of police, sheriff or a designee shall so notify the school principal to whom disclosure was made.

§16.1-305.1. Disclosure of disposition in certain delinquency cases

Upon a court's disposition of a proceeding where a juvenile is charged with a crime listed in subsection G of §16.1-260 in which a juvenile is adjudicated delinquent, convicted, found not guilty or the charges are reduced, the clerk of the court in which the disposition is entered shall, within 15 days of the expiration of the appeal period, if there has been no notice of an appeal, provide written notice of the disposition ordered by the court, including the nature of the offense upon which the disposition was based, to the superintendent of the school division in which the child is enrolled at the time of the disposition or, if he is not then enrolled in school, the division in which he was enrolled at the time of the offense. If the court defers disposition, or the charges are nolle prosequi, withdrawn, or dismissed the clerk shall, within 15 days of such action, provide written notice of such action to the superintendent of the school division in which the child is enrolled at such time or, if he is not then enrolled in school, the division in which he was enrolled at the time of the offense. If charges are withdrawn in intake or handled informally without a court disposition, the intake officer shall, within 15 days of such action, provide written notification of the action to the superintendent of the school division in which the child is enrolled at that time or, if he is not then enrolled in school, the division in which he was enrolled at the time of the offense.

If the child is not enrolled in the school division that receives notification under this section, the superintendent of that division may forward the notification to the superintendent of the school division where the child is enrolled.

A superintendent who receives notification under this section may disclose the information received to anyone to whom he or a principal disclosed that a petition had been filed. Further disclosure of information received under this section by the superintendent to school personnel is authorized only as provided in §22.1-288.2.

§16.1-309.1. Exception as to confidentiality

C. Whenever a juvenile 14 years of age or older is charged with a delinquent act that would be a criminal violation of Article 2 (§18.2-38 et seq.) of Chapter 4 of Title 18.2, a felony involving a weapon, a felony violation of Article 1 (§18.2-247 et seq.) of Chapter 7 of Title 18.2, or an "act of violence" as defined in subsection A of §19.2-297.1 if committed by an adult, the judge may, where consideration of the public interest requires, make the juvenile's name and address available to the public.

Title 17.1 Courts of Record

§17.1-213. Disposition of papers in ended cases

B. The following records for cases ending on or after January 1, 1913, may be destroyed in their entirety at the discretion of the clerk of each circuit court after having been retained for ten years after conclusion:

2. Concealed weapons permit applications;

§17.1-406 Petitions for appeal; cases over which Court of Appeals does not have jurisdiction

A. Any aggrieved party may present a petition for appeal to the Court of Appeals from

(ii) any final decision of a circuit court on an application for a concealed weapons permit pursuant to subsection D of §18.2-308

Title 18.2 Crimes and Offenses Generally

§18.2-10. Punishment for conviction of felony
The authorized punishments for conviction of a felony are:

(a) For Class 1 felonies, death, if the person so convicted was 16 years of age or older at the time of the offense and is not determined to be mentally retarded pursuant to §19.2-264.3:1.1, or imprisonment for life and, subject to subdivision (g), a fine of not more than $100,000. If the person was under 16 years of age at the time of the offense or is determined to be mentally retarded pursuant to §19.2-264.3:1.1, the punishment shall be imprisonment for life and, subject to subdivision (g), a fine of not more than $100,000.

(b) For Class 2 felonies, imprisonment for life or for any term not less than 20 years and, subject to subdivision (g), a fine of not more than $100,000.

(c) For Class 3 felonies, a term of imprisonment of not less than five years nor more than 20 years and, subject to subdivision (g), a fine of not more than $100,000.

(d) For Class 4 felonies, a term of imprisonment of not less than two years nor more than 10 years and, subject to subdivision (g), a fine of not more than $100,000.

(e) For Class 5 felonies, a term of imprisonment of not less than one year nor more than 10 years, or in the discretion of the jury or the court trying the case without a jury, confinement in jail for not more than 12 months and a fine of not more than $2,500, either or both.

(f) For Class 6 felonies, a term of imprisonment of not less than one year nor more than five years, or in the discretion of the jury or the court trying the case without a jury, confinement in jail for not more than 12 months and a fine of not more than $2,500, either or both.

(g) Except as specifically authorized in subdivision (e) or (f), or in Class 1 felonies for which a sentence of death is imposed, the court shall impose either a sentence of imprisonment together with a fine, or imprisonment only. However, if the defendant is not a natural person, the court shall impose only a fine.

For any felony offense committed

(i) on or after January 1, 1995, the court may, and

(ii) on or after July 1, 2000, shall, except in cases in which the court orders a suspended term of confinement of at least six months, impose an additional term of not less than six months nor more than three years, which shall be suspended conditioned upon successful completion of a period of post-release supervision pursuant to §19.2-295.2 and compliance with such other terms as the sentencing court may require. However, such additional term may only be imposed when the sentence includes an active term of incarceration in a correctional facility.

For a felony offense prohibiting proximity to children as described in subsection A of §18.2-370.2, the sentencing court is authorized to impose the punishment set forth in that section in addition to any other penalty provided by law.

§18.2-11. Punishment for conviction of misdemeanor
The authorized punishments for conviction of a misdemeanor are:

(a) For Class 1 misdemeanors, confinement in jail for not more than twelve months and a fine of not more than $2,500, either or both.

(b) For Class 2 misdemeanors, confinement in jail for not more than six months and a fine of not more than $1,000, either or both.

(c) For Class 3 misdemeanors, a fine of not more than $500.

(d) For Class 4 misdemeanors, a fine of not more than $250.

§18.2-31. Capital murder defined; punishment
The following offenses shall constitute capital murder, punishable as a Class 1 felony:

1. The willful, deliberate, and premeditated killing of any person in the commission of abduction, as defined in §18.2-48, when such abduction was committed with the intent to extort money or a pecuniary benefit or with the intent to defile the victim of such abduction;

2. The willful, deliberate, and premeditated killing of any person by another for hire;

3. The willful, deliberate, and premeditated killing of any person by a prisoner confined in a state or local correctional facility as defined in §53.1-1, or while in the custody of an employee thereof;

4. The willful, deliberate, and premeditated killing of any person in the commission of robbery or attempted robbery;

5. The willful, deliberate, and premeditated killing of any person in the commission of, or subsequent to, rape or attempted rape, forcible sodomy or attempted forcible sodomy or object sexual penetration;

6. The willful, deliberate, and premeditated killing of a law-enforcement officer as defined in §9-169 (9) or any law-enforcement officer of another state or the United States having the power to arrest for a felony under the laws of such state or the United States, when such killing is for the purpose of interfering with the performance of his official duties;

7. The willful, deliberate, and premeditated killing of more than one person as a part of the same act or transaction;

8. The willful, deliberate, and premeditated killing of more than one person within a three-year period;

9. The willful, deliberate, and premeditated killing of any person in the commission of or attempted commission of a violation of §18.2-248, involving a Schedule I or II controlled substance, when such killing is for the purpose of furthering the commission or attempted commission of such violation;
10. The willful, deliberate, and premeditated killing of any person by another pursuant to the direction or order of one who is engaged in a continuing criminal enterprise as defined in subsection I of §18.2-248;
11. The willful, deliberate and premeditated killing of a pregnant woman by one who knows that the woman is pregnant and has the intent to cause the involuntary termination of the woman's pregnancy without a live birth;
12. The willful, deliberate, and premeditated killing of a person under the age of fourteen by a person age twenty-one or older;
13. The willful, deliberate, and premeditated killing of any person by another in the commission of or attempted commission of an act of terrorism as defined in §18.2-46.4;
14. The willful, deliberate, and premeditated killing of a justice of the Supreme Court, a judge of the Court of Appeals, a judge of a circuit court or district court, a retired judge sitting by designation or under temporary recall, or a substitute judge appointed under §16.1-69.9:1 when the killing is for the purpose of interfering with his official duties as a judge; and
15. The willful, deliberate, and premeditated killing of any witness in a criminal case after a subpoena has been issued for such witness by the court, the clerk or an attorney when the killing is for the purpose of interfering with the person's duties in such case.

If any one or more subsections, sentences, or parts of this section shall be judged unconstitutional or invalid, such adjudication shall not affect, impair, or invalidate the remaining provisions thereof but shall be confined in its operation to the specific provisions so held unconstitutional or invalid.

§18.2-46.1. Definitions
As used in this article unless the context requires otherwise or it is otherwise provided:
"Predicate criminal act" means
(i) an act of violence;
(ii) any violation of §§18.2-42, 18.2-46.3, 18.2-51, 18.2-51.1, 18.2-52, 18.2-53, 18.2-53.1, 18.2-55, 18.2-56.1, 18.2-57, 18.2-57.2, 18.2-59, 18.2-121, 18.2-127, 18.2-128, 18.2-137, 18.2-138, 18.2-146, 18.2-147, subsection H, H 1 or H 2 of §18.2-248, §18.2-248.01, 18.2-255, 18.2-255.2, 18.2-286.1, 18.2-287.4, or 18.2-308.1;
(iii) a second or subsequent felony violation of subsection C of §18.2-248 or of §18.2-248.1;
(iv) any violation of a local ordinance adopted pursuant to §15.2-1812.2; or (v) any substantially similar offense under the laws of another state or territory of the United States, the District of Columbia, or the United States.

§18.2-51. Shooting, stabbing, etc., with intent to maim, kill, etc.
If any person maliciously shoot, stab, cut, or wound any person or by any means cause him bodily injury, with the intent to maim, disfigure, disable, or kill, he shall, except where it is otherwise provided, be guilty of a Class 3 felony. If such act be done unlawfully but not maliciously, with the intent aforesaid, the offender shall be guilty of a Class 6 felony.

§18.2-51.2. Aggravated malicious wounding; penalty
If any person maliciously shoots, stabs, cuts or wounds any other person, or by any means causes bodily injury, with the intent to maim, disfigure, disable or kill, he shall be guilty of a Class 2 felony if the victim is thereby severely injured and is caused to suffer permanent and significant physical impairment.

§18.2-53.1. Use or display of firearm in committing felony
It shall be unlawful for any person to use or attempt to use any pistol, shotgun, rifle, or other firearm or display such weapon in a threatening manner while committing or attempting to commit murder, rape, forcible sodomy, inanimate or animate object sexual penetration as defined in §18.2-67.2, robbery, carjacking, burglary, malicious wounding as defined in §18.2-51, malicious bodily injury to a law-enforcement officer as defined in §18.2-51.1, aggravated malicious wounding as defined in §18.2-51.2, malicious wounding by mob as defined in §18.2-41 or abduction. Violation of this section shall constitute a separate and distinct felony and any person found guilty thereof shall be sentenced to a mandatory minimum term of imprisonment of three years for a first conviction, and to a mandatory minimum term of five years for a second or subsequent conviction under the provisions of this section. Such punishment shall be separate and apart from, and shall be made to run consecutively with, any punishment received for the commission of the primary felony.

§18.2-56.1. Reckless handling of firearms; reckless handling while hunting
A. It shall be unlawful for any person to handle recklessly any firearm so as to endanger the life, limb or property of any person. Any person violating this section shall be guilty of a Class 1 misdemeanor.
B. If this section is violated while the person is engaged in hunting, trapping or pursuing game, the trial judge may, in addition to the penalty imposed by the jury or the court trying the case without a jury, revoke such person's hunting or trapping license or privilege to hunt or trap while possessing a firearm for a period of one year to life.
C. Upon a revocation pursuant to subsection B hereof, the clerk of the court in which the case is tried pursuant to this section shall forthwith send to the Department of Game and Inland Fisheries
(i) such person's revoked hunting or trapping license or notice that such person's privilege to hunt or trap while in possession of a firearm has been revoked and
(ii) a notice of the length of revocation imposed. The Department shall keep a list which shall be furnished upon request to any law-enforcement officer, Commonwealth's attorney or court in this Commonwealth, and such list

shall contain the names and addresses of all persons whose license or privilege to hunt or trap while in possession of a firearm has been revoked and the court which took such action.

D. If any person whose license to hunt and trap, or whose privilege to hunt and trap while in possession of a firearm, has been revoked pursuant to this section, thereafter hunts or traps while in possession of a firearm, he shall be guilty of a Class 1 misdemeanor, and, in addition to any penalty imposed by the jury or the court trying the case without a jury, the trial judge may revoke such person's hunting or trapping license, or privilege to hunt or trap while in possession of a firearm, for an additional period not to exceed five years. The clerk of the court shall notify the Department of Game and Inland Fisheries as is provided in subsection C herein.

§18.2-56.2. Allowing access to firearms by children; penalty

A. It shall be unlawful for any person to recklessly leave a loaded, unsecured firearm in such a manner as to endanger the life or limb of any child under the age of fourteen. Any person violating the provisions of this subsection shall be guilty of a Class 3 misdemeanor.

B. It shall be unlawful for any person knowingly to authorize a child under the age of twelve to use a firearm except when the child is under the supervision of an adult. Any person violating this subsection shall be guilty of a Class 1 misdemeanor. For purposes of this subsection, "adult" shall mean a parent, guardian, person standing in loco parentis to the child or a person twenty-one years or over who has the permission of the parent, guardian, or person standing in loco parentis to supervise the child in the use of a firearm.

§18.2-57. Assault and battery

D. In addition, if any person commits a battery against another knowing or having reason to know that such other person is a full-time or part-time teacher, principal, assistant principal, or guidance counselor of any public or private elementary or secondary school and is engaged in the performance of his duties as such, he shall be guilty of a Class 1 misdemeanor and the sentence of such person upon conviction shall include a sentence of 15 days in jail, two days of which shall be a mandatory minimum term of confinement. However, if the offense is committed by use of a firearm or other weapon prohibited on school property pursuant to §18.2-308.1, the person shall serve a mandatory minimum sentence of confinement of six months.

F. "Simple assault" or "assault and battery" shall not be construed to include the use of, by any teacher, principal, assistant principal, guidance counselor, or school security officer, in the course and scope of his acting official capacity, any of the following:

(i) incidental, minor or reasonable physical contact or other actions designed to maintain order and control;

(ii) reasonable and necessary force to quell a disturbance or remove a student from the scene of a disturbance that threatens physical injury to persons or damage to property;

(iii) reasonable and necessary force to prevent a student from inflicting physical harm on himself;

(iv) reasonable and necessary force for self-defense or the defense of others; or

(v) reasonable and necessary force to obtain possession of weapons or other dangerous objects or controlled substances or associated paraphernalia that are upon the person of the student or within his control.

In determining whether a person was acting within the exceptions provided in this subsection, due deference shall be given to reasonable judgments that were made by a teacher, principal, assistant principal, guidance counselor, or school security officer, at the time of the event.

§18.2-57.01. Pointing laser at law-enforcement officer unlawful; penalty

If any person, knowing or having reason to know another person is a law-enforcement officer as defined in §18.2-57, a probation or parole officer appointed pursuant to §53.1-143, a correctional officer as defined in §53.1-1, or a person employed by the Department of Corrections directly involved in the care, treatment or supervision of inmates in the custody of the Department engaged in the performance of his public duties as such, intentionally projects at such other person a beam or a point of light from a laser, a laser gun sight, or any device that simulates a laser, shall be guilty of a Class 2 misdemeanor.

§18.2-57.02. Disarming a law-enforcement or correctional officer; penalty

Any person who knows or has reason to know a person is a law-enforcement officer as defined in §18.2-57, a correctional officer as defined in §53.1-1, or a person employed by the Department of Corrections directly involved in the care, treatment or supervision of inmates in the custody of the Department, who is engaged in the performance of his duties as such and, with the intent to impede or prevent any such person from performing his official duties, knowingly and without the person's permission removes a chemical irritant weapon or impact weapon from the possession of the officer or deprives the officer of the use of the weapon is guilty of a Class 1 misdemeanor. However, if the weapon removed or deprived in violation of this section is the officer's firearm or stun weapon as defined in §18.2-308.1, he shall be guilty of a Class 6 felony. A violation of this section shall constitute a separate and distinct offense.

§18.2-58. How punished

If any person commit robbery by partial strangulation, or suffocation, or by striking or beating, or by other violence to the person, or by assault or otherwise putting a person in fear of serious bodily harm, or by the threat or presenting of firearms, or other deadly weapon or instrumentality whatsoever, he shall be guilty of a felony and shall be punished by confinement in a state correctional facility for life or any term not less than five years.

§18.2-58.1. Carjacking; penalty
A. Any person who commits carjacking, as herein defined, shall be guilty of a felony punishable by imprisonment for life or a term not less than fifteen years.
B. As used in this section, "carjacking" means the intentional seizure or seizure of control of a motor vehicle of another with intent to permanently or temporarily deprive another in possession or control of the vehicle of that possession or control by means of partial strangulation, or suffocation, or by striking or beating, or by other violence to the person, or by assault or otherwise putting a person in fear of serious bodily harm, or by the threat or presenting of firearms, or other deadly weapon or instrumentality whatsoever. "Motor vehicle" shall have the same meaning as set forth in §46.2-100.

§18.2-67.3. Aggravated sexual battery
A. An accused shall be guilty of aggravated sexual battery if he or she sexually abuses the complaining witness, and
4. The act is accomplished against the will of the complaining witness by force, threat or intimidation, and
c. The accused uses or threatens to use a dangerous weapon.

§18.2-85. Manufacture, possession, use, etc., of fire bombs or explosive materials or devices; penalties
For the purpose of this section:
"Device" means any instrument, apparatus or contrivance, including its component parts, that is capable of producing or intended to produce an explosion but shall not include fireworks as defined in §27-95.
"Explosive material" means any chemical compound, mechanical mixture or device that is commonly used or can be used for the purpose of producing an explosion and which contains any oxidizing and combustive agents or other ingredients in such proportions, quantities or packaging that an ignition by fire, friction, concussion, percussion, detonation or by any part of the compound or mixture may cause a sudden generation of highly heated gases. These materials include, but are not limited to, gunpowder, powders for blasting, high explosives, blasting materials, fuses (other than electric circuit breakers), detonators, and other detonating agents and smokeless powder.
"Fire bomb" means any container of a flammable material such as gasoline, kerosene, fuel oil, or other chemical compound, having a wick composed of any material or a device or other substance which, if set or ignited, is capable of igniting such flammable material or chemical compound but does not include a similar device commercially manufactured and used solely for the purpose of illumination or cooking.
"Hoax explosive device" means any device which by its design, construction, content or characteristics appears to be or to contain a bomb or other destructive device or explosive but which is an imitation of any such device or explosive.
Any person who
(i) possesses materials with which fire bombs or explosive materials or devices can be made with the intent to manufacture fire bombs or explosive materials or devices or,
(ii) manufactures, transports, distributes, possesses or uses a fire bomb or explosive materials or devices shall be guilty of a Class 5 felony. Any person who constructs, uses, places, sends, or causes to be sent any hoax explosive device so as to intentionally cause another person to believe that such device is a bomb or explosive shall be guilty of a Class 6 felony.
Nothing in this section shall prohibit the authorized manufacture, transportation, distribution, use or possession of any material, substance, or device by a member of the armed forces of the United States, fire fighters or law-enforcement officers, nor shall it prohibit the manufacture, transportation, distribution, use or possession of any material, substance or device to be used solely for scientific research, educational purposes or for any lawful purpose, subject to the provisions of §§27-97 and 27-97.2.

§18.2-89. Burglary; how punished
If any person break and enter the dwelling house of another in the nighttime with intent to commit a felony or any larceny therein, he shall be guilty of burglary, punishable as a Class 3 felony; provided, however, that if such person was armed with a deadly weapon at the time of such entry, he shall be guilty of a Class 2 felony.

§18.2-90. Entering dwelling house, etc., with intent to commit murder, rape, robbery or arson; penalty
If any person in the nighttime enters without breaking or in the daytime breaks and enters or enters and conceals himself in a dwelling house or an adjoining, occupied outhouse or in the nighttime enters without breaking or at any time breaks and enters or enters and conceals himself in any building permanently affixed to realty, or any ship, vessel or river craft or any railroad car, or any automobile, truck or trailer, if such automobile, truck or trailer is used as a dwelling or place of human habitation, with intent to commit murder, rape, robbery or arson in violation of §§18.2-77, 18.2-79 or §18.2-80, he shall be deemed guilty of statutory burglary, which offense shall be a Class 3 felony. However, if such person was armed with a deadly weapon at the time of such entry, he shall be guilty of a Class 2 felony.

§18.2-91. Entering dwelling house, etc., with intent to commit larceny, assault and battery or other felony
If any person commits any of the acts mentioned in §18.2-90 with intent to commit larceny, assault and battery or any felony other than murder, rape or robbery, he shall be guilty of statutory burglary, punishable by confinement

in a state correctional facility for not less than one or more than twenty years or, in the discretion of the jury or the court trying the case without a jury, be confined in jail for a period not exceeding twelve months or fined not more than $2,500, either or both. However, if the person was armed with a deadly weapon at the time of such entry, he shall be guilty of a Class 2 felony.

§18.2-92. Breaking and entering dwelling house with intent to commit other misdemeanor

If any person break and enter a dwelling house while said dwelling is occupied, either in the day or nighttime, with the intent to commit any misdemeanor except assault and battery or trespass, he shall be guilty of a Class 6 felony. However, if the person was armed with a deadly weapon at the time of such entry, he shall be guilty of a Class 2 felony.

§18.2-93. Entering bank, armed, with intent to commit larceny

If any person, armed with a deadly weapon, shall enter any banking house, in the daytime or in the nighttime, with intent to commit larceny of money, bonds, notes, or other evidence of debt therein, he shall be guilty of a Class 2 felony.

§18.2-95. Grand larceny defined; how punished

Any person who
(i) commits larceny from the person of another of money or other thing of value of $5 or more,
(ii) commits simple larceny not from the person of another of goods and chattels of the value of $200 or more, or
(iii) commits simple larceny not from the person of another of any firearm, regardless of the firearm's value, shall be guilty of grand larceny, punishable by imprisonment in a state correctional facility for not less than one nor more than twenty years or, in the discretion of the jury or court trying the case without a jury, be confined in jail for a period not exceeding twelve months or fined not more than $2,500, either or both.

§18.2-108.1. Theft or receipt of stolen firearm

Notwithstanding the provisions of §18.2-108, any person who buys or receives a firearm from another person or aids in concealing a firearm, knowing that the firearm was stolen, shall be guilty of a Class 6 felony and may be proceeded against although the principal offender is not convicted.

§18.2-134. Trespass on posted property

Any person who goes on the lands, waters, ponds, boats or blinds of another, which have been posted in accordance with the provisions of §18.2-134.1, to hunt, fish or trap except with the written consent of or in the presence of the owner or his agent shall be guilty of a Class 1 misdemeanor.

§18.2-136. Right of certain hunters to go on lands of another; carrying firearms or bows and arrows prohibited

Fox hunters and coon hunters, when the chase begins on other lands, may follow their dogs on prohibited lands, and hunters of all other game, when the chase begins on other lands, may go upon prohibited lands to retrieve their dogs, but may not carry firearms or bows and arrows on their persons or hunt any game while thereon. The use of vehicles to retrieve dogs on prohibited lands shall be allowed only with the permission of the landowner or his agent. Any person who goes on prohibited lands to retrieve his dogs pursuant to this section and who willfully refuses to identify himself when requested by the landowner or his agent to do so is guilty of a Class 4 misdemeanor.

§18.2-154. Shooting at or throwing missiles, etc., at train, car, vessel, etc.; penalty

Any person who maliciously shoots at, or maliciously throws any missile at or against, any train or cars on any railroad or other transportation company or any vessel or other watercraft, or any motor vehicle or other vehicles when occupied by one or more persons, whereby the life of any person on such train, car, vessel, or other watercraft, or in such motor vehicle or other vehicle, may be put in peril, is guilty of a Class 4 felony. In the event of the death of any such person, resulting from such malicious shooting or throwing, the person so offending is guilty of murder in the second degree. However, if the homicide is willful, deliberate and premeditated, he is guilty of murder in the first degree.

If any such act is committed unlawfully, but not maliciously, the person so offending is guilty of a Class 6 felony and, in the event of the death of any such person, resulting from such unlawful act, the person so offending is guilty of involuntary manslaughter.

If any person commits a violation of this section by maliciously or unlawfully shooting, with a firearm, at a conspicuously marked law-enforcement, fire or rescue squad vehicle, ambulance or any other emergency medical vehicle, the sentence imposed shall include a mandatory minimum term of imprisonment of one year.

§18.2-204.1. Fraudulent use of birth certificates, drivers' licenses, etc.

A. It shall be unlawful for any person to obtain, possess, sell, or transfer the birth certificate of another for the purpose of establishing a false identity for himself or for another person.

B. It shall be unlawful for any person to obtain, possess, sell, or transfer any document for the purpose of establishing a false status, occupation, membership, license or identity for himself or any other person.

C. Any person who violates the provisions of this section is guilty of a Class 1 misdemeanor, except when the birth certificate or document is obtained, possessed, sold, or transferred with the intent to use such certificate or document to purchase a firearm, in which case a violation of this section shall be punishable as a Class 6 felony.

D. The provisions of this section shall not apply to members of state, federal, county, city or town law-enforcement agencies in the performance of their duties.

§18.2-279. Discharging firearms or missiles within or at building or dwelling house

If any person maliciously discharges a firearm within any building when occupied by one or more persons in such a manner as to endanger the life or lives of such person or persons, or maliciously shoots at, or maliciously throws any missile at or against any dwelling house or other building when occupied by one or more persons, whereby the life or lives of any such person or persons may be put in peril, the person so offending is guilty of a Class 4 felony. In the event of the death of any person, resulting from such malicious shooting or throwing, the person so offending is guilty of murder in the second degree. However, if the homicide is willful, deliberate and premeditated, he is guilty of murder in the first degree.

If any such act be done unlawfully, but not maliciously, the person so offending is guilty of a Class 6 felony; and, in the event of the death of any person resulting from such unlawful shooting or throwing, the person so offending is guilty of involuntary manslaughter. If any person willfully discharges a firearm within or shoots at any school building whether occupied or not, he is guilty of a Class 4 felony.

§18.2-280. Willfully discharging firearms in public places

A. If any person willfully discharges or causes to be discharged any firearm in any street in a city or town, or in any place of public business or place of public gathering, and such conduct results in bodily injury to another person, he shall be guilty of a Class 6 felony. If such conduct does not result in bodily injury to another person, he shall be guilty of Class 1 misdemeanor.

B. If any person willfully discharges or causes to be discharged any firearm upon any public, private or religious elementary, middle or high school, he shall be guilty of a Class 4 felony, unless he is engaged in a program or curriculum sponsored by or conducted with permission of a public, private or religious school.

C. If any person willfully discharges or causes to be discharged any firearm upon any public property within 1,000 feet of the property line of any public, private or religious elementary, middle or high school property he shall be guilty of a Class 4 felony, unless he is engaged in lawful hunting.

D. This section shall not apply to any law-enforcement officer in the performance of his official duties nor to any other person whose said willful act is otherwise justifiable or excusable at law in the protection of his life or property, or is otherwise specifically authorized by law.

E. Nothing in this statute shall preclude the Commonwealth from electing to prosecute under any other applicable provision of law instead of this section.

§18.2-281. Setting spring gun or other deadly weapon

It shall be unlawful for any person to set or fix in any manner any firearm or other deadly weapon so that it may be discharged or activated by a person coming in contact therewith or with any string, wire, spring, or any other contrivance attached thereto or designed to activate such weapon remotely. Any person violating this section shall be guilty of a Class 6 felony.

§18.2-282. Pointing, holding, or brandishing firearm or object similar in appearance; penalty

A. It shall be unlawful for any person to point, hold or brandish any firearm or any air or gas operated weapon or any object similar in appearance, whether capable of being fired or not, in such manner as to reasonably induce fear in the mind of another or hold a firearm or any air or gas operated weapon in a public place in such a manner as to reasonably induce fear in the mind of another of being shot or injured. However, this section shall not apply to any person engaged in excusable or justifiable self-defense. Persons violating the provisions of this section shall be guilty of a Class 1 misdemeanor or, if the violation occurs upon any public, private or religious elementary, middle or high school, including buildings and grounds or upon public property within 1,000 feet of such school property, he shall be guilty of a Class 6 felony.

B. Any police officer in the performance of his duty, in making an arrest under the provisions of this section, shall not be civilly liable in damages for injuries or death resulting to the person being arrested if he had reason to believe that the person being arrested was pointing, holding, or brandishing such firearm or air or gas operated weapon, or object that was similar in appearance, with intent to induce fear in the mind of another.

C. For purposes of this section, the word "firearm" means any weapon that will or is designed to or may readily be converted to expel single or multiple projectiles by the action of an explosion of a combustible material. The word "ammunition," as used herein, shall mean a cartridge, pellet, ball, missile or projectile adapted for use in a firearm.

§18.2-283. Carrying dangerous weapon to place of religious worship

If any person carry any gun, pistol, bowie knife, dagger or other dangerous weapon, without good and sufficient reason, to a place of worship while a meeting for religious purposes is being held at such place he shall be guilty of a Class 4 misdemeanor.

§18.2-283.1. Carrying weapon into courthouse

It shall be unlawful for any person to possess in or transport into any courthouse in this Commonwealth any

i) gun or other weapon designed or intended to propel a missile or projectile of any kind,

ii) frame, receiver, muffler, silencer, missile, projectile or ammunition designed for use with a dangerous weapon and

iii) any other dangerous weapon, including explosives, stun weapons as defined in §18.2-308.1, and those weapons specified in subsection A of §18.2-308. Any such weapon shall be subject to seizure by a law-enforcement officer. A violation of this section is punishable as a Class 1 misdemeanor.

The provisions of this section shall not apply to any police officer, sheriff, law-enforcement agent or official, conservation police officer, conservator of the peace, magistrate, court officer, or judge while in the conduct of such person's official duties.

§18.2-284. Selling or giving toy firearms

No person shall sell, barter, exchange, furnish, or dispose of by purchase, gift or in any other manner any toy gun, pistol, rifle or other toy firearm, if the same shall, by action of an explosion of a combustible material, discharge blank or ball charges. Any person violating the provisions of this section shall be guilty of a Class 4 misdemeanor. Each sale of any of the articles hereinbefore specified to any person shall constitute a separate offense.

Nothing in this section shall be construed as preventing the sale of what are commonly known as cap pistols.

§18.2-285. Hunting with firearms while under influence of intoxicant or narcotic drug; penalty

It shall be unlawful for any person to hunt wildlife with a firearm, bow and arrow, or crossbow in the Commonwealth of Virginia while he is (i) under the influence of alcohol; (ii) under the influence of any narcotic drug or any other self-administered intoxicant or drug of whatsoever nature, or any combination of such drugs, to a degree that impairs his ability to hunt with a firearm, bow and arrow, or crossbow safely; or (iii) under the combined influence of alcohol and any drug or drugs to a degree that impairs his ability to hunt with a firearm, bow and arrow, or crossbow safely. Any person who violates the provisions of this section is guilty of a Class 1 misdemeanor. Conservation police officers, sheriffs and all other law-enforcement officers shall enforce the provisions of this section.

§18.2-286. Shooting in or across road or in street

If any person discharges a firearm, crossbow or bow and arrow in or across any road, or within the right-of-way thereof, or in a street of any city or town, he shall, for each offense, be guilty of a Class 4 misdemeanor.

The provisions of this section shall not apply to firing ranges or shooting matches maintained, and supervised or approved, by law-enforcement officers and military personnel in performance of their lawful duties.

§18.2-286.1. Shooting from vehicles so as to endanger persons; penalty

Any person who, while in or on a motor vehicle, intentionally discharges a firearm so as to create the risk of injury or death to another person or thereby cause another person to have a reasonable apprehension of injury or death shall be guilty of a Class 5 felony. Nothing in this section shall apply to a law-enforcement officer in the performance of his duties.

§18.2-287.01. Carrying weapon in air carrier airport terminal

It shall be unlawful for any person to possess or transport into any air carrier airport terminal in the Commonwealth any

(i) gun or other weapon designed or intended to propel a missile or projectile of any kind,

(ii) frame, receiver, muffler, silencer, missile, projectile or ammunition designed for use with a dangerous weapon, and

(iii) any other dangerous weapon, including explosives, stun weapons as defined in 18.2-308.1, and those weapons specified in subsection A of §18.2-308. Any such weapon shall be subject to seizure by a law-enforcement officer. A violation of this section is punishable as a Class 1 misdemeanor. Any weapon possessed or transported in violation of this section shall be forfeited to the Commonwealth and disposed of as provided in subsection A of §18.2-308.

The provisions of this section shall not apply to any police officer, sheriff, law-enforcement agent or official, or conservation police officer, or conservator of the peace employed by the air carrier airport, nor shall the provisions of this section apply to any passenger of an airline who, to the extent otherwise permitted by law, transports a lawful firearm, weapon, or ammunition into or out of an air carrier airport terminal for the sole purposes, respectively, of

(i) presenting such firearm, weapon, or ammunition to U.S. Customs agents in advance of an international flight, in order to comply with federal law,

(ii) checking such firearm, weapon, or ammunition with his luggage, or

(iii) retrieving such firearm, weapon, or ammunition from the baggage claim area.

Any other statute, rule, regulation, or ordinance specifically addressing the possession or transportation of weapons in any airport in the Commonwealth shall be invalid, and this section shall control.

§18.2-287.1. Transporting a loaded rifle or shotgun

The governing body of any county or city is hereby empowered to adopt ordinances making it unlawful for any person to transport, possess or carry a loaded shotgun or loaded rifle in any vehicle on any public street, road, or highway within such locality. Any violation of such ordinance shall be punishable by a fine of not more than $100. Conservation police officers, sheriffs and all other law-enforcement officers shall enforce the provisions of this section. No ordinance adopted pursuant to this section shall be enforceable unless the governing body adopting such ordinance so notifies the Director of the Department of Game and Inland Fisheries by registered mail prior to May 1 of the year in which such ordinance is to take effect.

The provisions of this section shall not apply to duly authorized law-enforcement officers or military personnel in the performance of their lawful duties, nor to any person who reasonably believes that a loaded rifle or shotgun is necessary for his personal safety in the course of his employment or business.

§18.2-287.01. Carrying weapon in air carrier airport terminal.

It shall be unlawful for any person to possess or transport into any air carrier airport terminal in the Commonwealth any

(i) gun or other weapon designed or intended to propel a missile or projectile of any kind,

(ii) frame, receiver, muffler, silencer, missile, projectile or ammunition designed for use with a dangerous weapon, and

(iii) any other dangerous weapon, including explosives, stun weapons as defined in §18.2-308.1, and those weapons specified in subsection A of § 18.2-308. Any such weapon shall be subject to seizure by a law-enforcement officer. A violation of this section is punishable as a Class 1 misdemeanor. Any weapon possessed or transported in violation of this section shall be forfeited to the Commonwealth and disposed of as provided in subsection A of §18.2-308.

The provisions of this section shall not apply to any police officer, sheriff, law-enforcement agent or official, or conservation police officer, or conservator of the peace employed by the air carrier airport, nor shall the provisions of this section apply to any passenger of an airline who, to the extent otherwise permitted by law, transports a lawful firearm, weapon, or ammunition into or out of an air carrier airport terminal for the sole purposes, respectively, of

(i) presenting such firearm, weapon, or ammunition to U.S. Customs agents in advance of an international flight, in order to comply with federal law,

(ii) checking such firearm, weapon, or ammunition with his luggage, or

(iii) retrieving such firearm, weapon, or ammunition from the baggage claim area.

Any other statute, rule, regulation, or ordinance specifically addressing the possession or transportation of weapons in any airport in the Commonwealth shall be invalid, and this section shall control.

§18.2-287.2. Wearing of body armor while committing a crime; penalty

Any person who, while committing a crime of violence as defined in §18.2-288 (2), or a felony violation of §18.2-248 or subdivision (a) 2 or 3 of §18.2-248.1, has in his possession a firearm or knife and is wearing body armor designed to diminish the effect of the impact of a bullet or projectile shall be guilty of a Class 4 felony.

§18.2-287.4. Carrying loaded firearms in public areas prohibited; penalty

It shall be unlawful for any person to carry a loaded

(a) semi-automatic center-fire rifle or pistol that expels single or multiple projectiles by action of an explosion of a combustible material and is equipped at the time of the offense with a magazine that will hold more than 20 rounds of ammunition or designed by the manufacturer to accommodate a silencer or equipped with a folding stock or

(b) shotgun with a magazine that will hold more than seven rounds of the longest ammunition for which it is chambered on or about his person on any public street, road, alley, sidewalk, public right-of-way, or in any public park or any other place of whatever nature that is open to the public in the Cities of Alexandria, Chesapeake, Fairfax, Falls Church, Newport News, Norfolk, Richmond, or Virginia Beach or in the Counties of Arlington, Fairfax, Henrico, Loudoun, or Prince William.

The provisions of this section shall not apply to law-enforcement officers, licensed security guards, military personnel in the performance of their lawful duties, or any person having a valid concealed handgun permit or to any person actually engaged in lawful hunting or lawful recreational shooting activities at an established shooting range or shooting contest. Any person violating the provisions of this section shall be guilty of a Class 1 misdemeanor.

The exemptions set forth in §18.2-308 shall apply, mutatis mutandis <"with necessary changes made">, to the provisions of this section.

<The following laws, through §18.2-298, are known as the Uniform Machine Gun Act.>

§18.2-288. Definitions

When used in this article:

1. "Machine gun" applies to any weapon which shoots or is designed to shoot automatically more than one shot, without manual reloading, by a single function of the trigger.

2. "Crime of violence" applies to and includes any of the following crimes or an attempt to commit any of the same, namely, murder, manslaughter, kidnapping, rape, mayhem, assault with intent to maim, disable, disfigure or kill, robbery, burglary, housebreaking, breaking and entering and larceny.

3. "Person" applies to and includes firm, partnership, association or corporation.

§18.2-289. Use of machine gun for crime of violence

Possession or use of a machine gun in the perpetration or attempted perpetration of a crime of violence is hereby declared to be a Class 2 felony.

§18.2-290. Use of machine gun for aggressive purpose

Unlawful possession or use of a machine gun for an offensive or aggressive purpose is hereby declared to be a Class 4 felony.

§18.2-291. What constitutes aggressive purpose

Possession or use of a machine gun shall be presumed to be for an offensive or aggressive purpose:

1. When the machine gun is on premises not owned or rented for bona fide permanent residence or business occupancy by the person in whose possession the machine gun may be found;
2. When the machine gun is in the possession of, or used by, a person who has been convicted of a crime of violence in any court of record, state or federal, of the United States of America, its territories or insular possessions;
3. When the machine gun has not been registered as required in §18.2-295; or
4. When empty or loaded shells which have been or are susceptible of use in the machine gun are found in the immediate vicinity thereof.

§18.2-292. Presence prima facie evidence of use

The presence of a machine gun in any room, boat or vehicle shall be prima facie evidence of the possession or use of the machine gun by each person occupying the room, boat, or vehicle where the weapon is found.

§18.2-293. What article does not apply to

The provisions of this article <Uniform Machine Gun Act> shall not be applicable to:

1. The manufacture for, and sale of, machine guns to the armed forces or law-enforcement officers of the United States or of any state or of any political subdivision thereof, or the transportation required for that purpose; and
2. Machine guns and automatic arms issued to the national guard of Virginia by the United States or such arms used by the United States army or navy or in the hands of troops of the national guards of other states or territories of the United States passing through Virginia, or such arms as may be provided for the officers of the State Police or officers of penal institutions.

§18.2-293.1. What article does not prohibit

Nothing contained in this article <Uniform Machine Gun Act> shall prohibit or interfere with:

1. The possession of a machine gun for scientific purposes, or the possession of a machine gun not usable as a weapon and possessed as a curiosity, ornament, or keepsake; and
2. The possession of a machine gun for a purpose manifestly not aggressive or offensive.

Provided, however, that possession of such machine guns shall be subject to the provisions of §18.2-295.

§18.2-294. Manufacturer's and dealer's register; inspection of stock

Every manufacturer or dealer shall keep a register of all machine guns manufactured or handled by him. This register shall show the model and serial number, date of manufacture, sale, loan, gift, delivery or receipt of every machine gun, the name, address, and occupation of the person to whom the machine gun was sold, loaned, given or delivered, or from whom it was received. Upon demand every manufacturer or dealer shall permit any marshal, sheriff or police officer to inspect his entire stock of machine guns, parts, and supplies therefor, and shall produce the register, herein required, for inspection. A violation of any provisions of this section shall be punishable as a Class 3 misdemeanor.

§18.2-295. Registration of machine guns

Every machine gun in this Commonwealth shall be registered with the Department of State Police within twenty-four hours after its acquisition or, in the case of semi-automatic weapons which are converted, modified or otherwise altered to become machine guns, within twenty-four hours of the conversion, modification or alteration. Blanks for registration shall be prepared by the Superintendent of State Police, and furnished upon application. To comply with this section the application as filed shall be notarized and shall show the model and serial number of the gun, the name, address and occupation of the person in possession, and from whom and the purpose for which, the gun was acquired or altered. The Superintendent of State Police shall upon registration required in this section forthwith furnish the registrant with a certificate of registration, which shall be valid as long as the registrant remains the same. Certificates of registration shall be retained by the registrant and produced by him upon demand by any peace officer. Failure to keep or produce such certificate for inspection shall be a Class 3 misdemeanor, and any peace officer, may without warrant, seize the machine gun and apply for its confiscation as provided in §18.2-296. Upon transferring a registered machine gun, the transferor shall forthwith notify the Superintendent in writing, setting forth the date of transfer and name and address of the transferee. Failure to give the required notification shall constitute a Class 3 misdemeanor. Registration data shall not be subject to inspection by the public.

§18.2-296. Search warrants for machine guns

Warrant to search any house or place and seize any machine gun possessed in violation of this article may issue in the same manner and under the same restrictions as provided by law for stolen property, and any court of record, upon application of the attorney for the Commonwealth, a police officer or conservator of the peace, may order any machine gun, thus or otherwise legally seized, to be confiscated and either destroyed or delivered to a peace officer of the Commonwealth or a political subdivision thereof.

§18.2-299. Definitions

When used in this article:

"Sawed-off shotgun" means any weapon, loaded or unloaded, originally designed as a shoulder weapon, utilizing a self-contained cartridge from which a number of ball shot pellets or projectiles may be fired simultaneously from a smooth or rifled bore by a single function of the firing device and which has a barrel length of less than 18 inches for smooth bore weapons and 16 inches for rifled weapons. Weapons of less than .225 caliber shall not be included.

"Sawed-off rifle" means a rifle of any caliber, loaded or unloaded, which expels a projectile by action of an explosion of a combustible material and is designed as a shoulder weapon with a barrel or barrels length of less than 16 inches or which has been modified to an overall length of less than 26 inches.

"Crime of violence" applies to and includes any of the following crimes or an attempt to commit any of the same, namely, murder, manslaughter, kidnapping, rape, mayhem, assault with intent to maim, disable, disfigure or kill, robbery, burglary, housebreaking, breaking and entering and larceny.

"Person" applies to and includes firm, partnership, association or corporation.

§18.2-300. Possession or use of "sawed-off" shotgun or rifle

A. Possession or use of a "sawed-off" shotgun or "sawed-off" rifle in the perpetration or attempted perpetration of a crime of violence is a Class 2 felony.

B. Possession or use of a "sawed-off" shotgun or "sawed-off" rifle for any other purpose, except as permitted by this article and official use by those persons permitted possession by §18.2-303, is a Class 4 felony.

§18.2-303. What article does not apply to

The provisions of this article shall not be applicable to:

1. The manufacture for, and sale of, "sawed-off" shotguns or "sawed-off" rifles to the armed forces or law-enforcement officers of the United States or of any state or of any political subdivision thereof, or the transportation required for that purpose; and
2. "Sawed-off" shotguns, "sawed-off" rifles and automatic arms issued to the National Guard of Virginia by the United States or such arms used by the United States Army or Navy or in the hands of troops of the national guards of other states or territories of the United States passing through Virginia, or such arms as may be provided for the officers of the State Police or officers of penal institutions.

§18.2-303.1. What article does not prohibit

Nothing contained in this article shall prohibit or interfere with the possession of a "sawed-off" shotgun or "sawed-off" rifle for scientific purposes, the possession of a "sawed-off" shotgun or "sawed-off" rifle possessed in compliance with federal law or the possession of a "sawed-off" shotgun or "sawed-off" rifle not usable as a firing weapon and possessed as a curiosity, ornament, or keepsake.

§18.2-304. Manufacturer's and dealer's register; inspection of stock

Every manufacturer or dealer shall keep a register of all "sawed-off" shotguns and "sawed-off" rifles manufactured or handled by him. This register shall show the model and serial number, date of manufacture, sale, loan, gift, delivery or receipt of every "sawed-off" shotgun and "sawed-off" rifle, the name, address, and occupation of the person to whom the "sawed-off" shotgun or "sawed-off" rifle was sold, loaned, given or delivered, or from whom it was received. Upon demand every manufacturer or dealer shall permit any marshal, sheriff or police officer to inspect his entire stock of "sawed-off" shotguns and "sawed-off" rifles, and "sawed-off" shotgun or "sawed-off" rifle barrels, and shall produce the register, herein required, for inspection. A violation of any provision of this section shall be punishable as a Class 3 misdemeanor.

§18.2-306. Search warrants for "sawed-off" shotguns and rifles; confiscation and destruction

Warrant to search any house or place and seize any "sawed-off" shotgun or "sawed-off" rifle possessed in violation of this article may issue in the same manner and under the same restrictions as provided by law for stolen property, and any court of record, upon application of the attorney for the Commonwealth, a police officer or conservator of the peace, may order any "sawed-off" shotgun or "sawed-off" rifle thus or otherwise legally seized, to be confiscated and either destroyed or delivered to a peace officer of the Commonwealth or a political subdivision thereof.

§18.2-308. Personal protection; carrying concealed weapons; when lawful to carry

A. If any person carries about his person, hidden from common observation,

(i) any pistol, revolver, or other weapon designed or intended to propel a missile of any kind by action of an explosion of any combustible material;

(ii) any dirk, bowie knife, switchblade knife, ballistic knife, machete, razor, slingshot, spring stick, metal knucks, or blackjack;

(iii) any flailing instrument consisting of two or more rigid parts connected in such a manner as to allow them to swing freely, which may be known as a nun chahka, nun chuck, nunchaku, shuriken, or fighting chain;

(iv) any disc, of whatever configuration, having at least two points or pointed blades which is designed to be thrown or propelled and which may be known as a throwing star or oriental dart; or

(v) any weapon of like kind as those enumerated in this subsection, he shall be guilty of a Class 1 misdemeanor. A second violation of this section or a conviction under this section subsequent to any conviction under any substantially similar ordinance of any county, city, or town shall be punishable as a Class 6 felony, and a third or subsequent such violation shall be punishable as a Class 5 felony. For the purpose of this section, a weapon shall be deemed to be hidden from common observation when it is observable but is of such deceptive appearance as to disguise the weapon's true nature.

B. This section shall not apply to any person while in his own place of abode or the curtilage thereof.

Except as provided in subsection J1, this section shall not apply to:

1. Any person while in his own place of business;
2. Any law-enforcement officer, wherever such law-enforcement officer may travel in the Commonwealth;
3. Any regularly enrolled member of a target shooting organization who is at, or going to or from, an established shooting range, provided that the weapons are unloaded and securely wrapped while being transported;
4. Any regularly enrolled member of a weapons collecting organization who is at, or going to or from, a bona fide weapons exhibition, provided that the weapons are unloaded and securely wrapped while being transported;
5. Any person carrying such weapons between his place of abode and a place of purchase or repair, provided the weapons are unloaded and securely wrapped while being transported;
6. Any person actually engaged in lawful hunting, as authorized by the Board of Game and Inland Fisheries, under inclement weather conditions necessitating temporary protection of his firearm from those conditions, provided that possession of a handgun while engaged in lawful hunting shall not be construed as hunting with a handgun if the person hunting is carrying a valid concealed handgun permit;
7. Any State Police officer retired from the Department of State Police, any officer retired from the Division of Capitol Police, any local law-enforcement officer, auxiliary police officer or animal control officer retired from a police department or sheriff's office within the Commonwealth, any special agent retired from the State Corporation Commission or the Alcoholic Beverage Control Board, any conservation police officer retired from the Department of Game and Inland Fisheries, and any Virginia Marine Police officer retired from the Law Enforcement Division of the Virginia Marine Resources Commission, other than an officer or agent terminated for cause,

(i) with a service-related disability;
(ii) following at least 15 years of service with any such law-enforcement agency, board or any combination thereof;
(iii) who has reached 55 years of age, or
(iv) who is on long-term leave from such law-enforcement agency or board due to a service-related injury,

provided such officer carries with him written proof of consultation with and favorable review of the need to carry a concealed handgun issued by the chief law-enforcement officer of the last such agency from which the officer retired or the agency that employs the officer or, in the case of special agents, issued by the State Corporation Commission or the Alcoholic Beverage Control Board. A copy of the proof of consultation and favorable review shall be forwarded by the chief or the Board to the Department of State Police for entry into the Virginia Criminal Information Network. The chief law-enforcement officer shall not without cause withhold such written proof if the retired law-enforcement officer otherwise meets the requirements of this section. An officer set forth in clause (iv) of this subdivision who receives written proof of consultation to carry a concealed handgun shall surrender such proof of consultation upon return to work or upon termination of employment with the law-enforcement agency. Notice of the surrender shall be forwarded to the Department of State Police for entry into the Virginia Criminal Information Network. However, if such officer retires on disability because of the service-related injury, and would be eligible under clause (i) of this subdivision for written proof of consultation to carry a concealed handgun, he may retain the previously issued written proof of consultation.

For purposes of applying the reciprocity provisions of subsection P, any person granted the privilege to carry a concealed handgun pursuant to this subdivision, while carrying the proof of consultation and favorable review required, shall be deemed to have been issued a concealed handgun permit.

For purposes of complying with the federal Law Enforcement Officers Safety Act of 2004, a retired law-enforcement officer who receives proof of consultation and review pursuant to this subdivision shall have the opportunity to annually participate, at the retired law-enforcement officer's expense, in the same training and testing to carry firearms as is required of active law-enforcement officers in the Commonwealth. If such retired law-enforcement officer meets the training and qualification standards, the chief law-enforcement officer shall issue the retired officer certification, valid one year from the date of issuance, indicating that the retired officer has met the standards of the agency to carry a firearm;

8. Any State Police officer who is a member of the organized reserve forces of any of the armed services of the United States, national guard, or naval militia, while such officer is called to active military duty, provided such officer carries with him written proof of consultation with and favorable review of the need to carry a concealed handgun issued by the Superintendent of State Police. The proof of consultation and favorable review shall be valid as long as the officer is on active military duty and shall expire when the officer returns to active law-enforcement duty. The issuance of the proof of consultation and favorable review shall be entered into the Virginia Criminal Information Network. The Superintendent of State Police shall not without cause withhold such written proof if the officer is in good standing and is qualified to carry a weapon while on active law-enforcement duty.

For purposes of applying the reciprocity provisions of subsection P, any person granted the privilege to carry a concealed handgun pursuant to this subdivision, while carrying the proof of consultation and favorable review required, shall be deemed to have been issued a concealed handgun permit; and

9. Any attorney for the Commonwealth or assistant attorney for the Commonwealth, wherever such attorney may travel in the Commonwealth.

C. This section shall also not apply to any of the following individuals while in the discharge of their official duties, or while in transit to or from such duties:

1. Carriers of the United States mail;
2. Officers or guards of any state correctional institution;
3. [Repealed.]
4. Conservators of the peace, except that an attorney for the Commonwealth or assistant attorney for the Commonwealth may carry a concealed handgun pursuant to subdivision B 9. However, the following conservators of the peace shall not be permitted to carry a concealed handgun without obtaining a permit as provided in subsection D hereof: (a) notaries public; (b) registrars; (c) drivers, operators or other persons in charge of any motor vehicle carrier of passengers for hire; or (d) commissioners in chancery;
5. Noncustodial employees of the Department of Corrections designated to carry weapons by the Director of the Department of Corrections pursuant to §53.1-29; and
6. Harbormaster of the City of Hopewell.

D. Any person 21 years of age or older may apply in writing to the clerk of the circuit court of the county or city in which he resides, or if he is a member of the United States Armed Forces, the county or city in which he is domiciled, for a permit to carry a concealed handgun. There shall be no requirement regarding the length of time an applicant has been a resident or domiciliary of the county or city. The application shall be made under oath before a notary or other person qualified to take oaths and shall be made only on a form prescribed by the Department of State Police, in consultation with the Supreme Court, requiring only that information necessary to determine eligibility for the permit. The clerk shall enter on the application the date on which the application and all other information required to be submitted by the applicant is received. The court shall consult with either the sheriff or police department of the county or city and receive a report from the Central Criminal Records Exchange. As a condition for issuance of a concealed handgun permit, the applicant shall submit to fingerprinting if required by local ordinance in the county or city where the applicant resides and provide personal descriptive information to be forwarded with the fingerprints through the Central Criminal Records Exchange to the Federal Bureau of Investigation for the purpose of obtaining criminal history record information regarding the applicant, and obtaining fingerprint identification information from federal records pursuant to criminal investigations by state and local law-enforcement agencies. However, no local ordinance shall require an applicant to submit to fingerprinting if the applicant has an existing concealed handgun permit issued pursuant to this section and is applying for a new five-year permit pursuant to subsection I. Where feasible and practical, the local law-enforcement agency may transfer information electronically to the State Police instead of inked fingerprint cards. Upon completion of the criminal history records check, the State Police shall return the fingerprint cards to the submitting local agency or, in the case of scanned fingerprints, destroy the electronic record. The local agency shall then promptly notify the person that he has 21 days from the date of the notice to request return of the fingerprint cards, if any. All fingerprint cards not claimed by the applicant within 21 days of notification by the local agency shall be destroyed. All optically scanned fingerprints shall be destroyed upon completion of the criminal history records check without requiring that the applicant be notified. Fingerprints taken for the purposes described in this section shall not be copied, held or used for any other purposes. The court shall issue the permit and notify the State Police of the issuance of the permit within 45 days of receipt of the completed application unless it is determined that the applicant is disqualified. Any order denying issuance of the permit shall state the basis for the denial of the permit and the applicant's right to and the requirements for perfecting an appeal of such order pursuant to subsection L. An application is deemed complete when all information required to be furnished by the applicant is delivered to and received by the clerk of court before or concomitant with the conduct of a state or national criminal history records check. If the court has not issued the permit or determined that the applicant is disqualified within 45 days of the date of receipt noted on the application, the clerk shall certify on the application that the 45-day period has expired, and send a copy of the certified application to the applicant. The certified application shall serve as a de facto permit, which shall expire 90 days after issuance, and shall be recognized as a valid concealed handgun permit when presented with a valid government-issued photo identification pursuant to subsection H, until the court issues a permit or finds the applicant to be disqualified. If the applicant is found to be disqualified after the de facto permit is issued, the applicant shall surrender the de facto permit to the court and the disqualification shall be deemed a denial of the permit and a revocation of the de facto permit. If the applicant is later found by the court to be disqualified after a permit has been issued, the permit shall be revoked. The clerk of court may withhold from public disclosure the social security number contained in a permit application in response to a request to inspect or copy any such permit application, except that such social security number shall not be withheld from any law-enforcement officer acting in the performance of his official duties.

D1. Whenever any person moves from the address shown on the concealed handgun permit, he shall, within 30 days, notify the issuing court of his change of address. The court shall issue a new concealed handgun permit as provided in subsection H and provide the Department of State Police with the permit information as required in subsection K.

E. The following persons shall be deemed disqualified from obtaining a permit:

1. An individual who is ineligible to possess a firearm pursuant to §18.2-308.1:1, 18.2-308.1:2 or 18.2-308.1:3 or the substantially similar law of any other state or of the United States.
2. An individual who is ineligible to possess a firearm pursuant to §18.2-308.1:1 and who was discharged from the custody of the Commissioner pursuant to §19.2-182.7 less than five years before the date of his application for a concealed handgun permit.

3. An individual who was ineligible to possess a firearm pursuant to §18.2-308.1:2 and whose competency or capacity was restored pursuant to §37.2-1012 less than five years before the date of his application for a concealed handgun permit.

4. An individual who was ineligible to possess a firearm under §18.2-308.1:3 and who was released from commitment less than five years before the date of this application for a concealed handgun permit.

5. An individual who is subject to a restraining order, or to a protective order and prohibited by §18.2-308.1:4 from purchasing or transporting a firearm.

6. An individual who is prohibited by §18.2-308.2 from possessing or transporting a firearm, except that a permit may be obtained in accordance with subsection C of that section.

7. An individual who has been convicted of two or more misdemeanors within the five-year period immediately preceding the application, if one of the misdemeanors was a Class 1 misdemeanor, but the judge shall have the discretion to deny a permit for two or more misdemeanors that are not Class 1. Traffic infractions and misdemeanors set forth in Title 46.2 shall not be considered for purposes of this disqualification.

8. An individual who is addicted to, or is an unlawful user or distributor of, marijuana or any controlled substance.

9. An individual who has been convicted of a violation of §18.2-266 or a substantially similar local ordinance or of public drunkenness within the three-year period immediately preceding the application, or who is a habitual drunkard as determined pursuant to §4.1-333.

10. An alien other than an alien lawfully admitted for permanent residence in the United States.

11. An individual who has been discharged from the Armed Forces of the United States under dishonorable conditions.

12. An individual who is a fugitive from justice.

13. An individual who the court finds, by a preponderance of the evidence, based on specific acts by the applicant, is likely to use a weapon unlawfully or negligently to endanger others. The sheriff, chief of police, or attorney for the Commonwealth may submit to the court a sworn written statement indicating that, in the opinion of such sheriff, chief of police, or attorney for the Commonwealth, based upon a disqualifying conviction or upon the specific acts set forth in the statement, the applicant is likely to use a weapon unlawfully or negligently to endanger others. The statement of the sheriff, chief of police, or the attorney for the Commonwealth shall be based upon personal knowledge of such individual or of a deputy sheriff, police officer, or assistant attorney for the Commonwealth of the specific acts, or upon a written statement made under oath before a notary public of a competent person having personal knowledge of the specific acts.

14. An individual who has been convicted of any assault, assault and battery, sexual battery, discharging of a firearm in violation of §18.2-280 or 18.2-286.1 or brandishing of a firearm in violation of §18.2-282 within the three-year period immediately preceding the application.

15. An individual who has been convicted of stalking.

16. An individual whose previous convictions or adjudications of delinquency were based on an offense which would have been at the time of conviction a felony if committed by an adult under the laws of any state, the District of Columbia, the United States or its territories. For purposes of this disqualifier, only convictions occurring within 16 years following the later of the date of

(i) the conviction or adjudication or

(ii) release from any incarceration imposed upon such conviction or adjudication shall be deemed to be "previous convictions."

17. An individual who has a felony charge pending or a charge pending for an offense listed in subdivision 14 or 15.

18. An individual who has received mental health treatment or substance abuse treatment in a residential setting within five years prior to the date of his application for a concealed handgun permit.

19. An individual not otherwise ineligible pursuant to this section, who, within the three-year period immediately preceding the application for the permit, was found guilty of any criminal offense set forth in Article 1 (§18.2-247 et seq.) of Chapter 7 of this title or of a criminal offense of illegal possession or distribution of marijuana or any controlled substance, under the laws of any state, the District of Columbia, or the United States or its territories.

20. An individual, not otherwise ineligible pursuant to this section, with respect to whom, within the three-year period immediately preceding the application, upon a charge of any criminal offense set forth in Article 1 (§18.2-247 et seq.) of Chapter 7 of this title or upon a charge of illegal possession or distribution of marijuana or any controlled substance under the laws of any state, the District of Columbia, or the United States or its territories, the trial court found that the facts of the case were sufficient for a finding of guilt and disposed of the case pursuant to §18.2-251 or the substantially similar law of any other state, the District of Columbia, or the United States or its territories.

F. The making of a materially false statement in an application under this section shall constitute perjury, punishable as provided in §18.2-434.

G. The court shall require proof that the applicant has demonstrated competence with a handgun and the applicant may demonstrate such competence by one of the following, but no applicant shall be required to submit to any additional demonstration of competence, nor shall any proof of demonstrated competence expire:

1. Completing any hunter education or hunter safety course approved by the Department of Game and Inland Fisheries or a similar agency of another state;

2. Completing any National Rifle Association firearms safety or training course;

3. Completing any firearms safety or training course or class available to the general public offered by a law-enforcement agency, junior college, college, or private or public institution or organization or firearms training school utilizing instructors certified by the National Rifle Association or the Department of Criminal Justice Services;

4. Completing any law-enforcement firearms safety or training course or class offered for security guards, investigators, special deputies, or any division or subdivision of law enforcement or security enforcement;
5. Presenting evidence of equivalent experience with a firearm through participation in organized shooting competition or current military service or proof of an honorable discharge from any branch of the armed services;
6. Obtaining or previously having held a license to carry a firearm in the Commonwealth or a locality thereof, unless such license has been revoked for cause;
7. Completing any firearms training or safety course or class, <as of 7/1/09: including an electronic, video, or on-line course,> conducted by a state-certified or National Rifle Association-certified firearms instructor;
8. Completing any governmental police agency firearms training course and qualifying to carry a firearm in the course of normal police duties; or
9. Completing any other firearms training which the court deems adequate.
A photocopy of a certificate of completion of any of the courses or classes; an affidavit from the instructor, school, club, organization, or group that conducted or taught such course or class attesting to the completion of the course or class by the applicant; or a copy of any document which shows completion of the course or class or evidences participation in firearms competition shall constitute evidence of qualification under this subsection.
H. The permit to carry a concealed handgun shall specify only the following information: name, address, date of birth, gender, height, weight, color of hair, color of eyes, and signature of the permittee; the signature of the judge issuing the permit, or of the clerk of court who has been authorized to sign such permits by the issuing judge; and the date of issuance. The permit to carry a concealed handgun shall be no larger than two inches wide by three and one-fourth inches long and shall be of a uniform style prescribed by the Department of State Police. The person issued the permit shall have such permit on his person at all times during which he is carrying a concealed handgun and shall display the permit and a photo-identification issued by a government agency of the Commonwealth or by the United States Department of Defense or United States State Department (passport) upon demand by a law-enforcement officer.
H1. If a permit holder is a member of the Virginia National Guard, Armed Forces of the United States, or the Armed Forces reserves of the United States, and his five-year permit expires during an active-duty military deployment outside of the permittee's county or city of residence, such permit shall remain valid for 90 days after the end date of the deployment. In order to establish proof of continued validity of the permit, such a permittee shall carry with him and display, upon request of a law-enforcement officer, a copy of the permittee's deployment orders or other documentation from the permittee's commanding officer that order the permittee to travel outside of his county or city of residence and that indicate the start and end date of such deployment.
I. Persons who previously have held a concealed handgun permit shall be issued, upon application as provided in subsection D, a new five-year permit unless there is good cause shown for refusing to reissue a permit. If the new five-year permit is issued while an existing permit remains valid, the new five-year permit shall become effective upon the expiration date of the existing permit, provided that the application is received by the court at least 90 days but no more than 180 days prior to the expiration of the existing permit. If the circuit court denies the permit, the specific reasons for the denial shall be stated in the order of the court denying the permit. Upon denial of the application, the clerk shall provide the person with notice, in writing, of his right to an ore tenus hearing. Upon request of the applicant made within 21 days, the court shall place the matter on the docket for an ore tenus hearing. The applicant may be represented by counsel, but counsel shall not be appointed, and the rules of evidence shall apply. The final order of the court shall include the court's findings of fact and conclusions of law.
J. Any person convicted of an offense that would disqualify that person from obtaining a permit under subsection E or who violates subsection F shall forfeit his permit for a concealed handgun and surrender it to the court. Upon receipt by the Central Criminal Records Exchange of a record of the arrest, conviction or occurrence of any other event that would disqualify a person from obtaining a concealed handgun permit under subsection E, the Central Criminal Records Exchange shall notify the court having issued the permit of such disqualifying arrest, conviction or other event. Upon receipt of such notice of a conviction, the court shall revoke the permit of a person disqualified pursuant to this subsection, and shall promptly notify the State Police and the person whose permit was revoked of the revocation.
J1. Any person permitted to carry a concealed handgun, who is under the influence of alcohol or illegal drugs while carrying such handgun in a public place, shall be guilty of a Class 1 misdemeanor. Conviction of any of the following offenses shall be prima facie evidence, subject to rebuttal, that the person is "under the influence" for purposes of this section: manslaughter in violation of §18.2-36.1, maiming in violation of §18.2-51.4, driving while intoxicated in violation of §18.2-266, public intoxication in violation of §18.2-388, or driving while intoxicated in violation of §46.2-341.24. Upon such conviction that court shall revoke the person's permit for a concealed handgun and promptly notify the issuing circuit court. A person convicted of a violation of this subsection shall be ineligible to apply for a concealed handgun permit for a period of five years.
J2. An individual who has a felony charge pending or a charge pending for an offense listed in subdivision E 14 or E 15, holding a permit for a concealed handgun, may have the permit suspended by the court before which such charge is pending or by the court that issued the permit.
J3. No person shall carry a concealed handgun onto the premises of any restaurant or club as defined in §4.1-100 for which a license to sell and serve alcoholic beverages for on-premises consumption has been granted by the Virginia Alcoholic Beverage Control Board under Title 4.1 of the Code of Virginia; however, nothing herein shall prohibit any sworn law-enforcement officer <as of 7/1/09: or any retired law-enforcement officer who meets the definition of a "qualified retired law-enforcement officer" pursuant to 18 U.S.C. §926C and is carrying the identification required by such statute> from carrying a concealed handgun on the premises of such restaurant or

club or any owner or event sponsor or his employees from carrying a concealed handgun while on duty at such restaurant or club if such person has a concealed handgun permit.

J4. The court shall revoke the permit of any individual for whom it would be unlawful to purchase, possess or transport a firearm under §18.2-308.1:2 or 18.2-308.1:3, and shall promptly notify the State Police and the person whose permit was revoked of the revocation.

J5. The Department of State Police shall conduct a state and national criminal background check through the National Instant Criminal Background Check System (NICS) and the Virginia Criminal Information Network (VCIN) on all valid concealed handgun permits annually. Upon receipt of a record of the arrest, conviction or occurrence of any other event that would disqualify a person from obtaining a concealed handgun permit under subsections E, J1, J2 or J4, the Superintendent of the Department of State Police or his designee shall revoke the permit of a disqualified person. The Department of State Police shall notify the disqualified person in writing at his last known address of the revocation notice. The disqualified person shall forfeit and immediately surrender his permit for a concealed handgun to the Department of State Police. The Department of State Police shall notify the court having issued the permit of such disqualifying information. If the Department of State Police revokes the permit, the specific reasons for the revocation shall be stated in the revocation notice. The person shall have the right to appeal the decision of the Department of State Police with the issuing court as provided in subsection I. Any person who knowingly is in possession of a revoked concealed handgun permit while in possession of a concealed handgun is guilty of a Class 6 felony.

K. No fee shall be charged for the issuance of such permit to a person who has retired from service
(i) as a magistrate in the Commonwealth;
(ii) as a special agent with the Alcoholic Beverage Control Board or as a law-enforcement officer with the Department of State Police, the Department of Game and Inland Fisheries, or a sheriff or police department, bureau or force of any political subdivision of the Commonwealth, after completing 15 years of service or after reaching age 55;
(iii) as a law-enforcement officer with the United States Federal Bureau of Investigation, Bureau of Alcohol, Tobacco and Firearms, Secret Service Agency, Drug Enforcement Administration, United States Citizenship and Immigration Services, Customs Service, Department of State Diplomatic Security Service, U.S. Marshals Service or Naval Criminal Investigative Service, after completing 15 years of service or after reaching age 55;
(iv) as a law-enforcement officer with any police or sheriff's department within the United States, the District of Columbia or any of the territories of the United States, after completing 15 years of service; or
(v) as a law-enforcement officer with any combination of the agencies listed in clauses (ii) through (iv), after completing 15 years of service. The clerk shall charge a fee of $10 for the processing of an application or issuing of a permit, including his costs associated with the consultation with law-enforcement agencies. The local law-enforcement agency conducting the background investigation may charge a fee not to exceed $35 to cover the cost of conducting an investigation pursuant to this section. The $35 fee shall include any amount assessed by the Federal Bureau of Investigation for providing criminal history record information, and the local law-enforcement agency shall forward the amount assessed by the Federal Bureau of Investigation to the State Police with the fingerprints taken from the applicant. The State Police may charge a fee not to exceed $5 to cover their costs associated with processing the application. The total amount assessed for processing an application for a permit shall not exceed $50, with such fees to be paid in one sum to the person who accepts the application. Payment may be made by any method accepted by that court for payment of other fees or penalties. No payment shall be required until the application is accepted by the court as a complete application. The order issuing such permit, or the copy of the permit application certified by the clerk as a de facto permit pursuant to subsection D, shall be provided to the State Police and the law-enforcement agencies of the county or city. The State Police shall enter the permittee's name and description in the Virginia Criminal Information Network so that the permit's existence and current status will be made known to law-enforcement personnel accessing the Network for investigative purposes.

K1. The clerk of a circuit court that issued a valid concealed handgun permit shall, upon presentation of the valid permit and proof of a new address of residence by the permit holder, issue a replacement permit specifying the permit holder's new address. The clerk of court shall forward the permit holder's new address of residence to the State Police. The State Police may charge a fee not to exceed $5, and the clerk of court issuing the replacement permit may charge a fee not to exceed $5. The total amount assessed for processing a replacement permit pursuant to this subsection shall not exceed $10, with such fees to be paid in one sum to the person who accepts the information for the replacement permit.

L. Any person denied a permit to carry a concealed handgun under the provisions of this section may present a petition for review to the Court of Appeals. The petition for review shall be filed within 60 days of the expiration of the time for requesting an ore tenus hearing pursuant to subsection I, or if an ore tenus hearing is requested, within 60 days of the entry of the final order of the circuit court following the hearing. The petition shall be accompanied by a copy of the original papers filed in the circuit court, including a copy of the order of the circuit court denying the permit. Subject to the provisions of subsection B of §17.1-410, the decision of the Court of Appeals or judge shall be final. Notwithstanding any other provision of law, if the decision to deny the permit is reversed upon appeal, taxable costs incurred by the person shall be paid by the Commonwealth.

M. For purposes of this section:
"Handgun" means any pistol or revolver or other firearm, except a machine gun, originally designed, made and intended to fire a projectile by means of an explosion of a combustible material from one or more barrels when held in one hand.

"Lawfully admitted for permanent residence" means the status of having been lawfully accorded the privilege of residing permanently in the United States as an immigrant in accordance with the immigration laws, such status not having changed.

"Law-enforcement officer" means those individuals defined as a law-enforcement officer in §9.1-101, campus police officers appointed pursuant to Chapter 17 (§23-232 et seq.) of Title 23, law-enforcement agents of the Armed Forces of the United States, the Naval Criminal Investigative Service, and federal agents who are otherwise authorized to carry weapons by federal law. "Law-enforcement officer" shall also mean any sworn full-time law-enforcement officer employed by a law-enforcement agency of the United States or any state or political subdivision thereof, whose duties are substantially similar to those set forth in §9.1-101.

"Personal knowledge" means knowledge of a fact that a person has himself gained through his own senses, or knowledge that was gained by a law-enforcement officer or prosecutor through the performance of his official duties.

N. As used in this article:

"Ballistic knife" means any knife with a detachable blade that is propelled by a spring-operated mechanism.

"Spring stick" means a spring-loaded metal stick activated by pushing a button which rapidly and forcefully telescopes the weapon to several times its original length.

O. The granting of a concealed handgun permit shall not thereby authorize the possession of any handgun or other weapon on property or in places where such possession is otherwise prohibited by law or is prohibited by the owner of private property.

P. A valid concealed handgun or concealed weapon permit or license issued by another state shall authorize the holder of such permit or license who is at least 21 years of age to carry a concealed handgun in the Commonwealth, provided

(i) the issuing authority provides the means for instantaneous verification of the validity of all such permits or licenses issued within that state, accessible 24 hours a day, and

(ii) except for the age of the permit or license holder and the type of weapon authorized to be carried, the requirements and qualifications of that state's law are adequate to prevent possession of a permit or license by persons who would be denied a permit in the Commonwealth under this section. The Superintendent of State Police shall

(a) in consultation with the Office of the Attorney General determine whether states meet the requirements and qualifications of this section,

(b) maintain a registry of such states on the Virginia Criminal Information Network (VCIN), and

(c) make the registry available to law-enforcement officers for investigative purposes. The Superintendent of the State Police, in consultation with the Attorney General, may also enter into agreements for reciprocal recognition with any state qualifying for recognition under this subsection.

P1. Nonresidents of the Commonwealth 21 years of age or older may apply in writing to the Virginia Department of State Police for a five-year permit to carry a concealed handgun. Every applicant for a nonresident concealed handgun permit shall submit two photographs of a type and kind specified by the Department of State Police for inclusion on the permit and shall submit fingerprints on a card provided by the Department of State Police for the purpose of obtaining the applicant's state or national criminal history record. As a condition for issuance of a concealed handgun permit, the applicant shall submit to fingerprinting by his local or state law-enforcement agency and provide personal descriptive information to be forwarded with the fingerprints through the Central Criminal Records Exchange to the Federal Bureau of Investigation for the purpose of obtaining criminal history record information regarding the applicant and obtaining fingerprint identification information from federal records pursuant to criminal investigations by state and local law-enforcement agencies. The application shall be made under oath before a notary or other person qualified to take oaths on a form provided by the Department of State Police, requiring only that information necessary to determine eligibility for the permit. If the permittee is later found by the Department of State Police to be disqualified, the permit shall be revoked and the person shall return the permit after being so notified by the Department of State Police. The permit requirement and restriction provisions of subsections E and F shall apply, mutatis mutandis, to the provisions of this subsection.

The applicant shall demonstrate competence with a handgun by one of the following:

1. Completing a hunter education or hunter safety course approved by the Virginia Department of Game and Inland Fisheries or a similar agency of another state;

2. Completing any National Rifle Association firearms safety or training course;

3. Completing any firearms safety or training course or class available to the general public offered by a law-enforcement agency, junior college, college, or private or public institution or organization or firearms training school utilizing instructors certified by the National Rifle Association or the Department of Criminal Justice Services or a similar agency of another state;

4. Completing any law-enforcement firearms safety or training course or class offered for security guards, investigators, special deputies, or any division or subdivision of law enforcement or security enforcement;

5. Presenting evidence of equivalent experience with a firearm through participation in organized shooting competition approved by the Department of State Police or current military service or proof of an honorable discharge from any branch of the armed services;

6. Obtaining or previously having held a license to carry a firearm in the Commonwealth or a locality thereof, unless such license has been revoked for cause;

7. Completing any firearms training or safety course or class conducted by a state-certified or National Rifle Association-certified firearms instructor;

8. Completing any governmental police agency firearms training course and qualifying to carry a firearm in the course of normal police duties; or

9. Completing any other firearms training that the Virginia Department of State Police deems adequate.

A photocopy of a certificate of completion of any such course or class, an affidavit from the instructor, school, club, organization, or group that conducted or taught such course or class attesting to the completion of the course or class by the applicant, or a copy of any document which shows completion of the course or class or evidences participation in firearms competition shall satisfy the requirement for demonstration of competence with a handgun.

The Department of State Police may charge a fee not to exceed $100 to cover the cost of the background check and issuance of the permit. Any fees collected shall be deposited in a special account to be used to offset the costs of administering the nonresident concealed handgun permit program. The Department of State Police shall enter the permittee's name and description in the Virginia Criminal Information Network so that the permit's existence and current status are known to law-enforcement personnel accessing the Network for investigative purposes.

The permit to carry a concealed handgun shall contain only the following information: name, address, date of birth, gender, height, weight, color of hair, color of eyes, and photograph of the permittee; the signature of the Superintendent of the Virginia Department of State Police or his designee; the date of issuance; and the expiration date. The person to whom the permit is issued shall have such permit on his person at all times when he is carrying a concealed handgun in the Commonwealth and shall display the permit on demand by a law-enforcement officer.

The Superintendent of the State Police shall promulgate regulations, pursuant to the Administrative Process Act (§2.2-4000 et seq.), for the implementation of an application process for obtaining a nonresident concealed handgun permit.

Q. A valid concealed handgun permit issued by the State of Maryland shall be valid in the Commonwealth provided,

(i) the holder of the permit is licensed in the State of Maryland to perform duties substantially similar to those performed by Virginia branch pilots licensed pursuant to Chapter 9 (§54.1-900 et seq.) of Title 54.1 and is performing such duties while in the Commonwealth, and

(ii) the holder of the permit is 21 years of age or older.

R. For the purposes of participation in concealed handgun reciprocity agreements with other jurisdictions, the official government-issued law-enforcement identification card issued to an active-duty law-enforcement officer in the Commonwealth who is exempt from obtaining a concealed handgun permit under this section shall be deemed a concealed handgun permit.

S. For the purposes of understanding the law relating to the use of deadly and lethal force, the Department of State Police, in consultation with the Supreme Court on the development of the application for a concealed handgun permit under this section, shall include a reference to the Virginia Supreme Court website address or the Virginia Reports on the application.

2. That the provisions of this act creating subdivisions D1 and J5, amending subsection I, and amending subsection D, eliminating the five-year permit and subsection H referencing expiration of such a permit shall not become effective unless an appropriation of funds effectuating the purposes of these provisions is included in the general appropriations act for the period of July 1, 2006 through June 30, 2008, passed during the 2007 Session of the General Assembly, which become law; if such funds are appropriated, then such provisions of this act shall become effective on July 1, 2007.

§18.2-308.1. Possession of firearm, stun weapon, or other weapon on school property prohibited

A. If any person possesses any

(i) stun weapon as defined in this section;

(ii) knife, except a pocket knife having a folding metal blade of less than three inches; or

(iii) weapon, including a weapon of like kind, designated in subsection A of §18.2-308, other than a firearm; upon

(a) the property of any public, private or religious elementary, middle or high school, including buildings and grounds;

(b) that portion of any property open to the public and then exclusively used for school-sponsored functions or extracurricular activities while such functions or activities are taking place; or

(c) any school bus owned or operated by any such school, he shall be guilty of a Class 1 misdemeanor.

B. If any person possesses any firearm designed or intended to expel a projectile by action of an explosion of a combustible material while such person is upon

(i) any public, private or religious elementary, middle or high school, including buildings and grounds;

(ii) that portion of any property open to the public and then exclusively used for school-sponsored functions or extracurricular activities while such functions or activities are taking place; or

(iii) any school bus owned or operated by any such school, he shall be guilty of a Class 6 felony; however, if the person possesses any firearm within a public, private or religious elementary, middle or high school building and intends to use, or attempts to use, such firearm, or displays such weapon in a threatening manner, such person shall be sentenced to a mandatory minimum term of imprisonment of five years to be served consecutively with any other sentence.

The exemptions set out in §18.2-308 shall apply, mutatis mutandis, to the provisions of this section. The provisions of this section shall not apply to

(i) persons who possess such weapon or weapons as a part of the school's curriculum or activities;

(ii) a person possessing a knife customarily used for food preparation or service and using it for such purpose;

(iii) persons who possess such weapon or weapons as a part of any program sponsored or facilitated by either the school or any organization authorized by the school to conduct its programs either on or off the school premises;

(iv) any law-enforcement officer;

(v) any person who possesses a knife or blade which he uses customarily in his trade;

(vi) a person who possesses an unloaded firearm that is in a closed container, or a knife having a metal blade, in or upon a motor vehicle, or an unloaded shotgun or rifle in a firearms rack in or upon a motor vehicle; or

(vii) a person who has a valid concealed handgun permit and possesses a concealed handgun while in a motor vehicle in a parking lot, traffic circle, or other means of vehicular ingress or egress to the school. For the purposes of this paragraph, "weapon" includes a knife having a metal blade of three inches or longer "closed container" includes a locked vehicle trunk.

As used in this section:

"Stun weapon" means any device that emits a momentary or pulsed output, which is electrical, audible, optical or electromagnetic in nature and which is designed to temporarily incapacitate a person.

§18.2-308.1:1. Possession or transportation of firearms by persons acquitted by reason of insanity; penalty; permit

A. It shall be unlawful for any person acquitted by reason of insanity and committed to the custody of the Commissioner of Mental Health, Mental Retardation and Substance Abuse Services, pursuant to Chapter 11.1 (§19.2-182.2 et seq.) of Title 19.2, on a charge of treason, any felony or any offense punishable as a misdemeanor under Title 54.1 or a Class 1 or Class 2 misdemeanor under this title, except those misdemeanor violations of

(i) Article 2 (§18.2-266 et seq.) of Chapter 7 of this title <Boundaries, Jurisdiction and Emblems of the Commonwealth, now 7.1>,

(ii) Article 2 (§18.2-415 et seq.) of Chapter 9 of this title <Commissions, Boards and Institutions Generally>, or

(iii) §18.2-119, or

(iv) an ordinance of any county, city, or town similar to the offenses specified in (i), (ii), or (iii), to knowingly and intentionally purchase, possess, or transport any firearm. A violation of this section shall be punishable as a Class 1 misdemeanor.

B. Any person so acquitted may, upon discharge from the custody of the Commissioner, petition the general district court in which he resides for a permit to possess or carry a firearm. If the court determines that the circumstances regarding the disability referred to in subsection A and the person's criminal history, treatment record, and reputation are such that the person will not be likely to act in a manner dangerous to public safety and that the granting of the relief would not be contrary to the public interest, the court shall grant the petition. Any person denied relief by the general district court may petition the circuit court for a de novo review of the denial. Upon a grant of relief in any court, the court shall enter a written order granting the petition and issue a permit, in which event the provisions of subsection A do not apply. The clerk of court shall certify and forward forthwith to the Central Criminal Records Exchange, on a form provided by the Exchange, a copy of any such order.

§18.2-308.1:2. Purchase, possession or transportation of firearm by persons adjudicated legally incompetent or mentally incapacitated; penalty

It shall be unlawful for any person who has been adjudicated

i) legally incompetent pursuant to former §37.1-128.02 or former §37.1-134,

ii) mentally incapacitated pursuant to former §37.1-128.1 or former §37.1-132 or

iii) incapacitated pursuant to Article 1.1 (§37.1-134.6 et seq.) of Chapter 4 of Title 37.1 and whose competency or capacity has not been restored pursuant to former §37.1-134.1 or §37.1-134.16, to purchase, possess, or transport any firearm. A violation of this section shall be punishable as a Class 1 misdemeanor.

§18.2-308.1:3. Purchase, possession or transportation of firearm by persons involuntarily committed; penalty

A. It shall be unlawful for any person involuntarily admitted to a facility or ordered to mandatory outpatient treatment pursuant to §19.2-169.2, involuntarily admitted to a facility or ordered to mandatory outpatient treatment as the result of a commitment hearing pursuant to Article 5 (§37.2-814 et seq.) of Chapter 8 of Title 37.2, or who was the subject of a temporary detention order pursuant to §37.2-809 and subsequently agreed to voluntary admission pursuant to §37.2-805 to purchase, possess or transport a firearm. A violation of this subsection shall be punishable as a Class 1 misdemeanor.

B. Any person prohibited from purchasing, possessing or transporting firearms under this section may, at any time following his release from involuntary admission to a facility, his release from an order of mandatory outpatient treatment, or his release from voluntary admission pursuant to §37.2-805 following the issuance of a temporary detention order, petition the general district court in the city or county in which he resides to restore his right to purchase, possess or transport a firearm. If the court determines that the circumstances regarding the disabilities referred to in subsection A and the person's criminal history, treatment record, and reputation are such that the person will not likely to act in a manner dangerous to public safety and that granting the relief would not be contrary to the public interest, the court shall grant the petition. Any person denied relief by the general district court may petition the circuit court for a de novo review of the denial. Upon a grant of relief in any court, the court shall enter a written order granting the petition, in which event the provisions of subsection A shall no longer apply. The clerk of court shall certify and forward forthwith to the Central Criminal Records Exchange, on a form provided by the Exchange, a copy of any such order.

§18.2-308.1:4. Purchase or transportation of firearm by persons subject to protective orders; penalty

It shall be unlawful for any person who is subject to

i) a protective order entered pursuant to §§16.1-253, 16.1-253.1, 16.1-253.4, 16.1-279.1, 19.2-152.8, 19.2-152.9, or §19.2-152.10;

ii) an order issued pursuant to subsection B of §20-103;

iii) an order entered pursuant to subsection D of §18.2-60.3; or

iv) an order issued by a tribunal of another state, the United States or any of its territories, possessions or commonwealths, or the District of Columbia pursuant to a statute that is substantially similar to those cited in clauses (i), (ii), or (iii) to purchase or transport any firearm while the order is in effect. Any person with a concealed handgun permit shall be prohibited from carrying any concealed firearm, and shall surrender his permit to the court entering the order, for the duration of any protective order referred to herein. A violation of this section is a Class 1 misdemeanor.

§18.2-308.1:5. Purchase or transportation of firearm by persons convicted of certain drug offenses prohibited

Any person who, within a thirty-six consecutive month period, has been convicted of two misdemeanor offenses under §18.2-250 or §18.2-250.1 shall be ineligible to purchase or transport a handgun. However, upon expiration of a period of five years from the date of the second conviction and provided the person has not been convicted of any such offense within that period, the ineligibility shall be removed.

§18.2-308.2. Possession or transportation of firearms, stun weapons, explosives or concealed weapons by convicted felons; penalties; petition for permit; when issued

A. It shall be unlawful for

(i) any person who has been convicted of a felony;

(ii) any person adjudicated delinquent, as a juvenile 14 years of age or older at the time of the offense of murder in violation of §18.2-31 or 18.2-32, kidnapping in violation of §18.2-47, robbery by the threat or presentation of firearms in violation of §18.2-58, or rape in violation of §18.2-61; or

(iii) any person under the age of 29 who was adjudicated delinquent as a juvenile 14 years of age or older at the time of the offense of a delinquent act which would be a felony if committed by an adult, other than those felonies set forth in clause (ii), whether such conviction or adjudication occurred under the laws of the Commonwealth, or any other state, the District of Columbia, the United States or any territory thereof, to knowingly and intentionally possess or transport any firearm or stun weapon as defined by §18.2-308.1 or any explosive material, or to knowingly and intentionally carry about his person, hidden from common observation, any weapon described in subsection A of §18.2-308. However, such person may possess in his residence or the curtilage thereof a stun weapon as defined by §18.2-308.1. Any person who violates this section shall be guilty of a Class 6 felony. However, any person who violates this section by knowingly and intentionally possessing or transporting any firearm and who was previously convicted of a violent felony as defined in §17.1-805 shall be sentenced to a mandatory minimum term of imprisonment of five years. Any person who violates this section by knowingly and intentionally possessing or transporting any firearm and who was previously convicted of any other felony within the prior 10 years shall be sentenced to a mandatory minimum term of imprisonment of two years. The mandatory minimum terms of imprisonment prescribed for violations of this section shall be served consecutively with any other sentence.

B. The prohibitions of subsection A shall not apply to

(i) any person who possesses a firearm, explosive material or other weapon while carrying out his duties as a member of the Armed Forces of the United States or of the National Guard of Virginia or of any other state,

(ii) any law-enforcement officer in the performance of his duties, or

(iii) any person who has been pardoned or whose political disabilities have been removed pursuant to Article V, Section 12 of the Constitution of Virginia provided the Governor, in the document granting the pardon or removing the person's political disabilities, may expressly place conditions upon the reinstatement of the person's right to ship, transport, possess or receive firearms.

C. Any person prohibited from possessing, transporting or carrying a firearm or stun weapon under subsection A, may petition the circuit court of the jurisdiction in which he resides for a permit to possess or carry a firearm or stun weapon; however, no person who has been convicted of a felony shall be qualified to petition for such a permit unless his civil rights have been restored by the Governor or other appropriate authority. The court may, in its discretion and for good cause shown, grant such petition and issue a permit. The provisions of this section relating to firearms and stun weapons shall not apply to any person who has been granted a permit pursuant to this subsection.

C1. Any person who was prohibited from possessing, transporting or carrying explosive material under subsection A may possess, transport or carry such explosive material if his right to possess, transport or carry explosive material has been restored pursuant to federal law.

D. For the purpose of this section, "explosive material" means any chemical compound mixture, or device, the primary or common purpose of which is to function by explosion; the term includes, but is not limited to, dynamite and other high explosives, black powder, pellet powder, smokeless gun powder, detonators, blasting caps and detonating cord but shall not include fireworks or permissible fireworks as defined in §27-95.

§18.2-308.2:01. Possession or transportation of certain firearms by certain persons

A. It shall be unlawful for any person who is not a citizen of the United States or who is not a person lawfully admitted for permanent residence to knowingly and intentionally possess or transport any assault firearm or to knowingly and intentionally carry about his person, hidden from common observation, an assault firearm.

B. It shall be unlawful for any person who is not a citizen of the United States and who is not lawfully present in the United States to knowingly and intentionally possess or transport any firearm or to knowingly and intentionally carry about his person, hidden from common observation, any firearm. A violation of this section shall be punishable as a Class 6 felony.

C. For purposes of this section, "assault firearm" means any semi-automatic center-fire rifle or pistol that expels single or multiple projectiles by action of an explosion of a combustible material and is equipped at the time of the offense with a magazine which will hold more than 20 rounds of ammunition or designed by the manufacturer to accommodate a silencer or equipped with a folding stock.

§18.2-308.2:1. Prohibiting the selling, etc., of firearms to certain persons

Any person who sells, barters, gives or furnishes, or has in his possession or under his control with the intent of selling, bartering, giving or furnishing, any firearm to any person he knows is prohibited from possessing or transporting a firearm pursuant to §§18.2-308.1:1, 18.2-308.2, subsection B of §18.2-308.2:01, or §18.2-308.7 shall be guilty of a Class 6 felony. However, this prohibition shall not be applicable when the person convicted of the felony, adjudicated delinquent or acquitted by reason of insanity has

i) been issued a permit pursuant to subsection C of §18.2-308.2 or subsection B of §18.2-308.1:1,

ii) been pardoned or had his political disabilities removed in accordance with subsection B of §18.2-308.2 or

iii) obtained a permit to ship, transport, possess or receive firearms pursuant to the laws of the United States.

§18.2-308.2:2. Criminal history record information check required for the transfer of certain firearms

A. Any person purchasing from a dealer a firearm as herein defined shall consent in writing, on a form to be provided by the Department of State Police, to have the dealer obtain criminal history record information. Such form shall include only the written consent; the name, birth date, gender, race, citizenship, and social security number and/or any other identification number; the number of firearms by category intended to be sold, rented, traded, or transferred; and answers by the applicant to the following questions:

(i) has the applicant been convicted of a felony offense or found guilty or adjudicated delinquent as a juvenile 14 years of age or older at the time of the offense of a delinquent act that would be a felony if committed by an adult;

(ii) is the applicant subject to a court order restraining the applicant from harassing, stalking, or threatening the applicant's child or intimate partner, or a child of such partner, or is the applicant subject to a protective order; and

(iii) has the applicant ever been acquitted by reason of insanity and prohibited from purchasing, possessing or transporting a firearm pursuant to 18.2-308.1:1 or any substantially similar law of any other jurisdiction, been adjudicated legally incompetent, mentally incapacitated or adjudicated an incapacitated person and prohibited from purchasing a firearm pursuant to 18.2-308.1:2 or any substantially similar law of any other jurisdiction, or been involuntarily admitted to an inpatient facility or involuntarily ordered to outpatient mental health treatment and prohibited from purchasing a firearm pursuant to 18.2-308.1:3 or any substantially similar law of any other jurisdiction.

B. 1. No dealer shall sell, rent, trade or transfer from his inventory any such firearm to any other person who is a resident of Virginia until he has

(i) obtained written consent and the other information on the consent form specified in subsection A, and provided the Department of State Police with the name, birth date, gender, race, citizenship, and social security and/or any other identification number and the number of firearms by category intended to be sold, rented, traded or transferred and

(ii) requested criminal history record information by a telephone call to or other communication authorized by the State Police and is authorized by subdivision 2 of this subsection to complete the sale or other such transfer. To establish personal identification and residence in Virginia for purposes of this section, a dealer must require any prospective purchaser to present one photo-identification form issued by a governmental agency of the Commonwealth or by the United States Department of Defense, and other documentation of residence.

Except where the photo-identification was issued by the United States Department of Defense, the other documentation of residence shall show an address identical to that shown on the photo-identification form, such as evidence of currently paid personal property tax or real estate tax, or a current

(a) lease,

(b) utility or telephone bill,

(c) voter registration card,

(d) bank check,

(e) passport,

(f) automobile registration, or

(g) hunting or fishing license; other current identification allowed as evidence of residency by Part 178.124 of Title 27 of the Code of Federal Regulations and ATF Ruling 2001-5; or other documentation of residence determined to be acceptable by the Department of Criminal Justice Services, that corroborates that the prospective purchaser currently resides in Virginia. Where the photo-identification was issued by the Department of Defense, permanent orders assigning the purchaser to a duty post in Virginia shall be the only other required documentation of residence. For the purposes of this section and establishment of residency for firearm purchase, residency shall be deemed to be the permanent duty post of a member of the armed forces. When the photo-identification presented to a dealer by the prospective purchaser is a driver's license or other photo-identification issued by the Department of Motor Vehicles, and such identification form contains a date of issue, the dealer shall not, except for a renewed driver's license or other photo-identification issued by the Department of Motor Vehicles, sell or otherwise transfer a firearm to the prospective purchaser until 30 days after the date of issue of an original or duplicate driver's license unless the prospective purchaser also presents a copy of his Virginia Department of Motor Vehicles driver's record showing that the original date of issue of the driver's license was more than 30 days prior to the attempted purchase.

In addition, no dealer shall sell, rent, trade or transfer from his inventory any assault firearm to any person who is not a citizen of the United States or who is not a person lawfully admitted for permanent residence. To establish citizenship or lawful admission for a permanent residence for purposes of purchasing an assault firearm, a dealer shall require a prospective purchaser to present a certified birth certificate or a certificate of birth abroad issued by the United States State Department, a certificate of citizenship or a certificate of naturalization issued by the United States Citizenship and Immigration Services, an unexpired U.S. passport, a United States citizen identification card, a current voter registration card, a current selective service registration card, or an immigrant visa or other documentation of status as a person lawfully admitted for permanent residence issued by the United States Citizenship and Immigration Services.

Upon receipt of the request for a criminal history record information check, the State Police shall

(1) review its criminal history record information to determine if the buyer or transferee is prohibited from possessing or transporting a firearm by state or federal law,

(2) inform the dealer if its record indicates that the buyer or transferee is so prohibited, and

(3) provide the dealer with a unique reference number for that inquiry.

2. The State Police shall provide its response to the requesting dealer during the dealer's request, or by return call without delay. If the criminal history record information check indicates the prospective purchaser or transferee has a disqualifying criminal record or has been acquitted by reason of insanity and committed to the custody of the Commissioner of Mental Health, Mental Retardation and Substance Abuse Services, the State Police shall have until the end of the dealer's next business day to advise the dealer if its records indicate the buyer or transferee is prohibited from possessing or transporting a firearm by state or federal law. If not so advised by the end of the dealer's next business day, a dealer who has fulfilled the requirements of subdivision 1 of this subsection may immediately complete the sale or transfer and shall not be deemed in violation of this section with respect to such sale or transfer. In case of electronic failure or other circumstances beyond the control of the State Police, the dealer shall be advised immediately of the reason for such delay and be given an estimate of the length of such delay. After such notification, the State Police shall, as soon as possible but in no event later than the end of the dealer's next business day, inform the requesting dealer if its records indicate the buyer or transferee is prohibited from possessing or transporting a firearm by state or federal law. A dealer who fulfills the requirements of subdivision 1 of this subsection and is told by the State Police that a response will not be available by the end of the dealer's next business day may immediately complete the sale or transfer and shall not be deemed in violation of this section with respect to such sale or transfer.

3. Except as required by subsection D of §9.1-132, the State Police shall not maintain records longer than 30 days, except for multiple handgun transactions for which records shall be maintained for 12 months, from any dealer's request for a criminal history record information check pertaining to a buyer or transferee who is not found to be prohibited from possessing and transporting a firearm under state or federal law. However, the log on requests made may be maintained for a period of 12 months, and such log shall consist of the name of the purchaser, the dealer identification number, the unique approval number and the transaction date.

4. On the last day of the week following the sale or transfer of any firearm, the dealer shall mail or deliver the written consent form required by subsection A to the Department of State Police. The State Police shall immediately initiate a search of all available criminal history record information to determine if the purchaser is prohibited from possessing or transporting a firearm under state or federal law. If the search discloses information indicating that the buyer or transferee is so prohibited from possessing or transporting a firearm, the State Police shall inform the chief law-enforcement officer in the jurisdiction where the sale or transfer occurred and the dealer without delay.

5. Notwithstanding any other provisions of this section, rifles and shotguns may be purchased by persons who are citizens of the United States or persons lawfully admitted for permanent residence but residents of other states under the terms of subsections A and B upon furnishing the dealer with proof of citizenship or status as a person lawfully admitted for permanent residence and one photo-identification form issued by a governmental agency of the person's state of residence and one other form of identification determined to be acceptable by the Department of Criminal Justice Services.

6. For the purposes of this subsection, the phrase "dealer's next business day" shall not include December 25.

C. No dealer shall sell, rent, trade or transfer from his inventory any firearm, except when the transaction involves a rifle or a shotgun and can be accomplished pursuant to the provisions of subdivision B 5 to any person who is not a resident of Virginia unless he has first obtained from the Department of State Police a report indicating that a search of all available criminal history record information has not disclosed that the person is prohibited from possessing or transporting a firearm under state or federal law. The dealer shall obtain the required report by mailing or delivering the written consent form required under subsection A to the State Police within 24 hours of its execution. If the dealer has complied with the provisions of this subsection and has not received the required report from the State Police within 10 days from the date the written consent form was mailed to the Department of State Police, he shall not be deemed in violation of this section for thereafter completing the sale or transfer.

D. Nothing herein shall prevent a resident of the Commonwealth, at his option, from buying, renting or receiving a firearm from a dealer in Virginia by obtaining a criminal history record information check through the dealer as provided in subsection C.

E. If any buyer or transferee is denied the right to purchase a firearm under this section, he may exercise his right of access to and review and correction of criminal history record information under §9.1-132 or institute a civil action as provided in §9.1-135, provided any such action is initiated within 30 days of such denial.

F. Any dealer who willfully and intentionally requests, obtains, or seeks to obtain criminal history record information under false pretenses, or who willfully and intentionally disseminates or seeks to disseminate criminal history record information except as authorized in this section shall be guilty of a Class 2 misdemeanor.

G. For purposes of this section:

"Actual buyer" means a person who executes the consent form required in subsection B or C, or other such firearm transaction records as may be required by federal law.

"Antique firearm" means:

1. Any firearm (including any firearm with a matchlock, flintlock, percussion cap, or similar type of ignition system) manufactured in or before 1898;

2. Any replica of any firearm described in subdivision 1 of this definition if such replica

(i) is not designed or redesigned for using rimfire or conventional centerfire fixed ammunition or

(ii) uses rimfire or conventional centerfire fixed ammunition that is no longer manufactured in the United States and that is not readily available in the ordinary channels of commercial trade;

3. Any muzzle-loading rifle, muzzle-loading shotgun, or muzzle-loading pistol that is designed to use black powder, or a black powder substitute, and that cannot use fixed ammunition. For purposes of this subdivision, the term "antique firearm" shall not include any weapon that incorporates a firearm frame or receiver, any firearm that is converted into a muzzle-loading weapon, or any muzzle-loading weapon that can be readily converted to fire fixed ammunition by replacing the barrel, bolt, breech-block, or any combination thereof; or

4. Any curio or relic as defined in this subsection.

"Assault firearm" means any semi-automatic center-fire rifle or pistol which expels single or multiple projectiles by action of an explosion of a combustible material and is equipped at the time of the offense with a magazine which will hold more than 20 rounds of ammunition or designed by the manufacturer to accommodate a silencer or equipped with a folding stock.

"Curios or relics" means firearms that are of special interest to collectors by reason of some quality other than is associated with firearms intended for sporting use or as offensive or defensive weapons. To be recognized as curios or relics, firearms must fall within one of the following categories:

1. Firearms that were manufactured at least 50 years prior to the current date, which use rimfire or conventional centerfire fixed ammunition that is no longer manufactured in the United States and that is not readily available in the ordinary channels of commercial trade, but not including replicas thereof;

2. Firearms that are certified by the curator of a municipal, state, or federal museum that exhibits firearms to be curios or relics of museum interest; and

3. Any other firearms that derive a substantial part of their monetary value from the fact that they are novel, rare, bizarre, or because of their association with some historical figure, period, or event. Proof of qualification of a particular firearm under this category may be established by evidence of present value and evidence that like firearms are not available except as collectors' items, or that the value of like firearms available in ordinary commercial channels is substantially less.

"Dealer" means any person licensed as a dealer pursuant to 18 U.S.C. §921 et seq.

"Firearm" means any handgun, shotgun, or rifle that will or is designed to or may readily be converted to expel single or multiple projectiles by action of an explosion of a combustible material.

"Handgun" means any pistol or revolver or other firearm originally designed, made and intended to fire single or multiple projectiles by means of an explosion of a combustible material from one or more barrels when held in one hand.

"Lawfully admitted for permanent residence" means the status of having been lawfully accorded the privilege of residing permanently in the United States as an immigrant in accordance with the immigration laws, such status not having changed.

H. The Department of Criminal Justice Services shall promulgate regulations to ensure the identity, confidentiality and security of all records and data provided by the Department of State Police pursuant to this section.

I. The provisions of this section shall not apply to

(i) transactions between persons who are licensed as firearms importers or collectors, manufacturers or dealers pursuant to 18 U.S.C. §921 et seq.;

(ii) purchases by or sales to any law-enforcement officer or agent of the United States, the Commonwealth or any local government; or

(iii) antique firearms, curios or relics.

J. The provisions of this section shall not apply to restrict purchase, trade or transfer of firearms by a resident of Virginia when the resident of Virginia makes such purchase, trade or transfer in another state, in which case the laws and regulations of that state and the United States governing the purchase, trade or transfer of firearms shall apply. A National Instant Criminal Background Check System (NICS) check shall be performed prior to such purchase, trade or transfer of firearms.

J1. All licensed firearms dealers shall collect a fee of $2 for every transaction for which a criminal history record information check is required pursuant to this section, except that a fee of $5 shall be collected for every transaction involving an out-of-state resident. Such fee shall be transmitted to the Department of State Police by the last day of the month following the sale for deposit in a special fund for use by the State Police to offset the cost of conducting criminal history record information checks under the provisions of this section.

K. Any person willfully and intentionally making a materially false statement on the consent form required in subsection B or C or on such firearm transaction records as may be required by federal law, shall be guilty of a Class 5 felony.

L. Except as provided in §2.2-308.2:1, any dealer who willfully and intentionally sells, rents, trades or transfers a firearm in violation of this section shall be guilty of a Class 6 felony.

L1. Any person who attempts to solicit, persuade, encourage, or entice any dealer to transfer or otherwise convey a firearm other than to the actual buyer, as well as any other person who willfully and intentionally aids or abets such person, shall be guilty of a Class 6 felony. This subsection shall not apply to a federal law-enforcement officer or a law-enforcement officer as defined in §9.1-101, in the performance of his official duties, or other person under his direct supervision.

M. Any person who purchases a firearm with the intent to

(i) resell or otherwise provide such firearm to any person who he knows or has reason to believe is ineligible to purchase or otherwise receive from a dealer a firearm for whatever reason or

(ii) transport such firearm out of the Commonwealth to be resold or otherwise provided to another person who the transferor knows is ineligible to purchase or otherwise receive a firearm, shall be guilty of a Class 5 felony. However, if the violation of this subsection involves such a transfer of more than one firearm, the person shall be sentenced to a mandatory minimum term of imprisonment of five years.

N. Any person who is ineligible to purchase or otherwise receive or possess a firearm in the Commonwealth who solicits, employs or assists any person in violating subsection M shall be guilty of a Class 5 felony and shall be sentenced to a mandatory minimum term of imprisonment of five years.

O. All driver's licenses issued on or after July 1, 1994, shall carry a letter designation indicating whether the driver's license is an original, duplicate or renewed driver's license.

P. Except as provided in subdivisions 1, 2 and 3 of this subsection, it shall be unlawful for any person who is not a licensed firearms dealer to purchase more than one handgun within any 30-day period. A violation of this subsection shall be punishable as a Class 1 misdemeanor.

1. Purchases in excess of one handgun within a 30-day period may be made upon completion of an enhanced background check, as described herein, by special application to the Department of State Police listing the number and type of handguns to be purchased and transferred for lawful business or personal use, in a collector series, for collections, as a bulk purchase from estate sales and for similar purposes. Such applications shall be signed under oath by the applicant on forms provided by the Department of State Police, shall state the purpose for the purchase above the limit, and shall require satisfactory proof of residency and identity. Such application shall be in addition to the firearms sales report required by the Bureau of Alcohol, Tobacco and Firearms (ATF). The Superintendent of State Police shall promulgate regulations, pursuant to the Administrative Process Act (§2.2-4000 et seq.), for the implementation of an application process for purchases of handguns above the limit.

Upon being satisfied that these requirements have been met, the Department of State Police shall forthwith issue to the applicant a nontransferable certificate, which shall be valid for seven days from the date of issue. The certificate shall be surrendered to the dealer by the prospective purchaser prior to the consummation of such sale and shall be kept on file at the dealer's place of business for inspection as provided in §54.1-4201 for a period of not less than two years. Upon request of any local law-enforcement agency, and pursuant to its regulations, the Department of State Police may certify such local law-enforcement agency to serve as its agent to receive applications and, upon authorization by the Department of State Police, issue certificates forthwith pursuant to this subsection. Applications and certificates issued under this subsection shall be maintained as records as provided in subdivision B 3. The Department of State Police shall make available to local law-enforcement agencies all records concerning certificates issued pursuant to this subsection and all records provided for in subdivision B 3.

2. The provisions of this subsection shall not apply to:

a. A law-enforcement agency;

b. An agency duly authorized to perform law-enforcement duties;

c. State and local correctional facilities;

d. A private security company licensed to do business within the Commonwealth;

e. The purchase of antique firearms as herein defined;

f. A person whose handgun is stolen or irretrievably lost who deems it essential that such handgun be replaced immediately. Such person may purchase another handgun, even if the person has previously purchased a handgun within a 30-day period, provided

(i) the person provides the firearms dealer with a copy of the official police report or a summary thereof, on forms provided by the Department of State Police, from the law-enforcement agency that took the report of the lost or stolen handgun;

(ii) the official police report or summary thereof contains the name and address of the handgun owner, the description of the handgun, the location of the loss or theft, the date of the loss or theft, and the date the loss or theft was reported to the law-enforcement agency; and

(iii) the date of the loss or theft as reflected on the official police report or summary thereof occurred within 30 days of the person's attempt to replace the handgun. The firearms dealer shall attach a copy of the official police report or summary thereof to the original copy of the Virginia firearms transaction report completed for the transaction and retain it for the period prescribed by the Department of State Police;

g. A person who trades in a handgun at the same time he makes a handgun purchase and as a part of the same transaction, provided that no more than one transaction of this nature is completed per day;

h. A person who holds a valid Virginia permit to carry a concealed handgun;

i. A person who purchases a handgun in a private sale. For purposes of this subdivision, a private sale means purchase from a person who makes occasional sales, exchanges or purchases of firearms for the enhancement of a personal collection of curios or relics as herein defined, or who sells all or part of such collection of curios and relics; or

j. A law-enforcement officer. For purposes of this subdivision, a law-enforcement officer means any employee of a police department or sheriff's office that is part of or administered by the Commonwealth or any political subdivision thereof, and who is responsible for the prevention and detection of crime and the enforcement of the penal, traffic or highway laws of the Commonwealth.

3. For the purposes of this subsection, "purchase" shall not include the exchange or replacement of a handgun by a seller for a handgun purchased from such seller by the same person seeking the exchange or replacement within the 30-day period immediately preceding the date of exchange or replacement.

§18.2-308.2:3. Criminal background check required for employees of a gun dealer to transfer firearms; exemptions; penalties

A. No person, corporation or proprietorship licensed as a firearms dealer pursuant to 18 U.S.C. §921 et seq. shall employ any person to act as a seller, whether full-time or part-time, permanent, temporary, paid or unpaid, for the transfer of firearms under §18.2-308.2:2, if such employee would be prohibited from possessing a firearm under §§18.2-308.1:1, 18.2-308.1:2, 18.2-308.1:3, 18.2-308.2, or §18.2-308.2:01 or is an illegal alien, or is prohibited from purchasing or transporting a firearm pursuant to §18.2-308.1:4 or §18.2-308.1:5.

B. Prior to permitting an applicant to begin employment, the dealer shall obtain a written statement or affirmation from the applicant that he is not disqualified from possessing a firearm and shall submit the applicant's fingerprints and personal descriptive information to the Central Criminal Records Exchange to be forwarded to the Federal Bureau of Investigation (FBI) for the purpose of obtaining national criminal history record information regarding the applicant.

C. Prior to August 1, 2000, the dealer shall obtain written statements or affirmations from persons employed before July 1, 2000, to act as a seller under §18.2-308.2:2 that they are not disqualified from possessing a firearm. Within five working days of the employee's next birthday, after August 1, 2000, the dealer shall submit the employee's fingerprints and personal descriptive information to the Central Criminal Records Exchange to be forwarded to the Federal Bureau of Investigation (FBI) for the purpose of obtaining national criminal history record information regarding the request.

C1. In lieu of submitting fingerprints pursuant to this section, any dealer holding a valid federal firearms license (FFL) issued by the Bureau of Alcohol, Tobacco and Firearms (ATF) may submit a sworn and notarized affidavit to the Department of State Police on a form provided by the Department, stating that the dealer has been subjected to a record check prior to the issuance and that the FFL was issued by the ATF. The affidavit may also contain the names of any employees that have been subjected to a record check and approved by the ATF. This exemption shall apply regardless of whether the FFL was issued in the name of the dealer or in the name of the business. The affidavit shall contain the valid FFL number, state the name of each person requesting the exemption, together with each person's identifying information, including their social security number and the following statement: "I hereby swear, under the penalty of perjury, that as a condition of obtaining a federal firearms license, each person requesting an exemption in this affidavit has been subjected to a fingerprint identification check by the Bureau of Alcohol, Tobacco and Firearms and the Bureau of Alcohol, Tobacco and Firearms subsequently determined that each person satisfied the requirements of 18 U.S.C. §921 et seq. I understand that any person convicted of making a false statement in this affidavit is guilty of a Class 5 felony and that in addition to any other penalties imposed by law, a conviction under this section shall result in the forfeiture of my federal firearms license."

D. The Department of State Police, upon receipt of an individual's record or notification that no record exists, shall submit an eligibility report to the requesting dealer within 30 days of the applicant beginning his duties for new employees or within 30 days of the applicant's birthday for a person employed prior to July 1, 2000.

E. If any applicant is denied employment because of information appearing on the criminal history record and the applicant disputes the information upon which the denial was based, the Central Criminal Records Exchange shall, upon written request, furnish to the applicant the procedures for obtaining a copy of the criminal history record from the Federal Bureau of Investigation. The information provided to the dealer shall not be disseminated except as provided in this section.

F. The applicant shall bear the cost of obtaining the criminal history record unless the dealer, at his option, decides to pay such cost.

G. Upon receipt of the request for a criminal history record information check, the State Police shall establish a unique number for that firearm seller. Beginning September 1, 2001, the firearm seller's signature, firearm seller's number and the dealer's identification number shall be on all firearm transaction forms. The State Police shall void the firearm seller's number when a disqualifying record is discovered. The State Police may suspend a firearm seller's identification number upon the arrest of the firearm seller for a potentially disqualifying crime.

H. This section shall not restrict the transfer of a firearm at any place other than at a dealership or at any event required to be registered as a gun show.

I. Any person who willfully and intentionally requests, obtains, or seeks to obtain criminal history record information under false pretenses, or who willfully and intentionally disseminates or seeks to disseminate criminal history record information except as authorized by this section and §18.2-308.2:2, shall be guilty of a Class 2 misdemeanor.

J. Any person willfully and intentionally making a materially false statement on the personal descriptive information required in this section shall be guilty of a Class 5 felony. Any person who offers for transfer any firearm in violation of this section shall be guilty of a Class 1 misdemeanor. Any dealer who willfully and knowingly employs or permits a person to act as a firearm seller in violation of this section shall be guilty of a Class 1 misdemeanor.

K. There is no civil liability for any seller for the actions of any purchaser or subsequent transferee of a firearm lawfully transferred pursuant to this section.

L. The provisions of this section requiring a seller's background check shall not apply to a licensed dealer.

M. Any person who willfully and intentionally makes a false statement in the affidavit as set out in subdivision C 1 shall be guilty of a Class 5 felony.

N. For purposes of this section:

"Dealer" means any person, corporation or proprietorship licensed as a dealer pursuant to 18 U.S.C. §921 et seq.

"Firearm" means any handgun, shotgun, or rifle that will or is designed to or may readily be converted to expel single or multiple projectiles by action of an explosion of a combustible material.

"Place of business" means any place or premises where a dealer may lawfully transfer firearms.

"Seller" means for the purpose of any single sale of a firearm any person who is a dealer or an agent of a dealer, who may lawfully transfer firearms and who actually performs the criminal background check in accordance with the provisions of §18.2-308.2:2.

"Transfer" means any act performed with intent to sell, rent, barter, trade or otherwise transfer ownership or permanent possession of a firearm at the place of business of a dealer.

§18.2-308.3. Use or attempted use of restricted ammunition in commission or attempted commission of crimes prohibited; penalty

A. When used in this section:

"Restricted firearm ammunition" applies to bullets, projectiles or other types of ammunition that are:

(i) coated with or contain, in whole or in part, polytetrafluorethylene or a similar product,

(ii) commonly known as "KTW" bullets or "French Arcanes," or

(iii) any cartridges containing bullets coated with a plastic substance with other than lead or lead alloy cores, jacketed bullets with other than lead or lead alloy cores, or cartridges of which the bullet itself is wholly comprised of a metal or metal alloy other than lead. This definition shall not be construed to include shotgun shells or solid plastic bullets.

B. It shall be unlawful for any person to knowingly use or attempt to use restricted firearm ammunition while committing or attempting to commit a crime. Violation of this section shall constitute a separate and distinct felony and any person found guilty thereof shall be guilty of a Class 5 felony.

§18.2-308.4. Possession of firearms while in possession of certain controlled substances

A. It shall be unlawful for any person unlawfully in possession of a controlled substance classified in Schedule I or II of the Drug Control Act (§54.1-3400 et seq.) of Title 54.1 to simultaneously with knowledge and intent possess any firearm. A violation of this subsection is a Class 6 felony and constitutes a separate and distinct felony.

B. It shall be unlawful for any person unlawfully in possession of a controlled substance classified in Schedule I or II of the Drug Control Act (§54.1-3400 et seq.) to simultaneously with knowledge and intent possess any firearm on or about his person. A violation of this subsection is a Class 6 felony and constitutes a separate and distinct felony and any person convicted hereunder shall be sentenced to a mandatory minimum term of imprisonment of two years. Such punishment shall be separate and apart from, and shall be made to run consecutively with, any punishment received for the commission of the primary felony.

C. It shall be unlawful for any person to possess, use, or attempt to use any pistol, shotgun, rifle, or other firearm or display such weapon in a threatening manner while committing or attempting to commit the illegal manufacture, sale, distribution, or the possession with the intent to manufacture, sell, or distribute a controlled substance classified in Schedule I or Schedule II of the Drug Control Act (§54.1-3400 et seq.) of Title 54.1 or more than one pound of marijuana. A violation of this subsection is a Class 6 felony, and constitutes a separate and distinct felony and any person convicted hereunder shall be sentenced to a mandatory minimum term of imprisonment of five years. Such punishment shall be separate and apart from, and shall be made to run consecutively with, any punishment received for the commission of the primary felony.

§18.2-308.5. Manufacture, import, sale, transfer or possession of plastic firearm prohibited

It shall be unlawful for any person to manufacture, import, sell, transfer or possess any plastic firearm. As used in this section, "plastic firearm" means any firearm, including machine guns and sawed-off shotguns as defined in this chapter, containing less than 3.7 ounces of electromagnetically detectable metal in the barrel, slide, cylinder, frame or receiver of which, when subjected to inspection by X-ray machines commonly used at airports, does not generate an image that accurately depicts its shape. A violation of this section shall be punishable as a Class 5 felony.

222 The VIRGINIA Gun Owner's Guide

§18.2-308.6. Possession of unregistered firearm mufflers or silencers prohibited; penalty

It shall be unlawful for any person to possess any firearm muffler or firearm silencer which is not registered to him in the National Firearms Registration and Transfer Record. A violation of this section shall be punishable as a Class 6 felony.

§18.2-308.7. Possession or transportation of certain firearms by persons under the age of 18; penalty

It shall be unlawful for any person under 18 years of age to knowingly and intentionally possess or transport a handgun or assault firearm anywhere in the Commonwealth. For the purposes of this section, "handgun" means any pistol or revolver or other firearm originally designed, made and intended to fire single or multiple projectiles by means of an explosion of a combustible material from one or more barrels when held in one hand and "assault firearm" means any

(i) semi-automatic centerfire rifle or pistol which expels single or multiple projectiles by action of an explosion of a combustible material and is equipped at the time of the offense with a magazine which will hold more than 20 rounds of ammunition or designed by the manufacturer to accommodate a silencer or equipped with a folding stock or

(ii) shotgun with a magazine which will hold more than seven rounds of the longest ammunition for which it is chambered. A violation of this section shall be a Class 1 misdemeanor.

This section shall not apply to:

1. Any person
(i) while in his home or on his property;
(ii) while in the home or on the property of his parent, grandparent, or legal guardian; or
(iii) while on the property of another who has provided prior permission, and with the prior permission of his parent or legal guardian if the person has the landowner's written permission on his person while on such property;

2. Any person who, while accompanied by an adult, is at, or going to and from, a lawful shooting range or firearms educational class, provided that the weapons are unloaded while being transported;

3. Any person actually engaged in lawful hunting or going to and from a hunting area or preserve, provided that the weapons are unloaded while being transported; and

4. Any person while carrying out his duties in the Armed Forces of the United States or the National Guard of this Commonwealth or any other state.

§18.2-308.8. Importation, sale, possession or transfer of Striker 12's prohibited; penalty

It shall be unlawful for any person to import, sell, possess or transfer the following firearms: the Striker 12, commonly called a "streetsweeper," or any semi-automatic folding stock shotgun of like kind with a spring tension drum magazine capable of holding twelve shotgun shells. A violation of this section shall be punishable as a Class 6 felony.

§18.2-309. Furnishing certain weapons to minors; penalty

A. If any person sells, barters, gives or furnishes, or causes to be sold, bartered, given or furnished, to any minor a dirk, switchblade knife or bowie knife, having good cause to believe him to be a minor, such person shall be guilty of a Class 1 misdemeanor.

B. If any person sells, barters, gives or furnishes, or causes to be sold, bartered, given or furnished, to any minor a handgun, having good cause to believe him to be a minor, such person shall be guilty of a Class 6 felony. This subsection shall not apply to any transfer made between family members or for the purpose of engaging in a sporting event or activity.

§18.2-311. Prohibiting the selling or having in possession blackjacks, etc.

If any person sells or barters, or exhibits for sale or for barter, or gives or furnishes, or causes to be sold, bartered, given or furnished, or has in his possession, or under his control, with the intent of selling, bartering, giving or furnishing, any blackjack, brass or metal knuckles, any disc of whatever configuration having at least two points or pointed blades which is designed to be thrown or propelled and which may be known as a throwing star or oriental dart, switchblade knife, ballistic knife, or like weapons, such person shall be guilty of a Class 4 misdemeanor. The having in one's possession of any such weapon shall be prima facie evidence, except in the case of a conservator of the peace, of his intent to sell, barter, give or furnish the same.

§18.2-311.1. Removing, altering, etc., serial number or other identification on firearm

Any person, firm, association or corporation who or which intentionally removes, defaces, alters, changes, destroys or obliterates in any manner or way or who or which causes to be removed, defaced, altered, changed, destroyed or obliterated in any manner or way the name of the maker, model, manufacturer's or serial number, or any other mark or identification on any pistol, shotgun, rifle, machine gun or any other firearm shall be guilty of a Class 1 misdemeanor.

§18.2-311.2. Third conviction of firearm offenses; penalty
On a third or subsequent conviction of any offense contained in Article 4, 5, 6, or 7 of Chapter 7 (§18.2-247 et seq.) of Title 18.2, which would ordinarily be punished as a Class 1 misdemeanor, where it is alleged in the information or indictment on which the person is convicted, that
(i) such person has been twice previously convicted of a violation of any Class 1 misdemeanor or felony offense contained in either Article 4, 5, 6, or 7 of Chapter 7 of Title 18.2 or §18.2-53.1, or of a substantially similar offense under the law of any other jurisdiction of the United States, and
(ii) each such violation occurred on a different date, such person shall be guilty of a Class 6 felony.

§18.2-312. Illegal use of tear gas, phosgene and other gases
If any person maliciously release or cause or procure to be released in any private home, place of business or place of public gathering any tear gas, mustard gas, phosgene gas or other noxious or nauseating gases or mixtures of chemicals designed to, and capable of, producing vile or injurious or nauseating odors or gases, and bodily injury results to any person from such gas or odor, the offending person shall be guilty of a Class 3 felony.
If such act be done unlawfully, but not maliciously, the offending person shall be guilty of a Class 6 felony.
Nothing herein contained shall prevent the use of tear gas or other gases by police officers or other peace officers in the proper performance of their duties, or by any person or persons in the protection of person, life or property.

§18.2-405. What constitutes a riot; punishment
Any unlawful use, by three or more persons acting together, of force or violence which seriously jeopardizes the public safety, peace or order is riot.
If such person carried, at the time of such riot, any firearm or other deadly or dangerous weapon, he shall be guilty of a Class 5 felony.

§18.2-406. What constitutes an unlawful assembly; punishment
Whenever three or more persons assembled share the common intent to advance some lawful or unlawful purpose by the commission of an act or acts of unlawful force or violence likely to jeopardize seriously public safety, peace or order, and the assembly actually tends to inspire persons of ordinary courage with well-grounded fear of serious and immediate breaches of public safety, peace or order, then such assembly is an unlawful assembly. Every person who participates in any unlawful assembly shall be guilty of a Class 1 misdemeanor. If any such person carried, at the time of his participation in an unlawful assembly, any firearm or other deadly or dangerous weapon, he shall be guilty of a Class 5 felony.

§18.2-433.1. Definitions
As used in this article:
"Civil disorder" means any public disturbance within the United States or any territorial possessions thereof involving acts of violence by assemblages of three or more persons, which causes an immediate danger of or results in damage or injury to the property or person of any other individual.
"Explosive or incendiary device" means
(i) dynamite and all other forms of high explosives,
(ii) any explosive bomb, grenade, missile, or similar device, or
(iii) any incendiary bomb or grenade, fire bomb, or similar device, including any device which consists of or includes a breakable container including a flammable liquid or compound, and a wick composed of any material which, when ignited, is capable of igniting such flammable liquid or compound, and can be carried or thrown by one individual acting alone.
"Firearm" means any weapon that will or is designed to or may readily be converted to expel single or multiple projectiles by the action of an explosion of a combustible material; or the frame or receiver of any such weapon.
"Law-enforcement officer" means any officer as defined in §9.1-101 or any such officer or member of the armed forces of the United States, any state, any political subdivision of a state, or the District of Columbia, and such term shall specifically include, but shall not be limited to, members of the National Guard, as defined in §101 (9) of Title 10, United States Code, members of the organized militia of any state or territory of the United States, the Commonwealth of Puerto Rico, or the District of Columbia, not included within the definition of National Guard as defined by such §101 (9), and members of the Armed Forces of the United States.

§18.2-433.2. Paramilitary activity prohibited
A. person shall be guilty of unlawful paramilitary activity, punishable as a Class 5 felony if he:
1. Teaches or demonstrates to any other person the use, application, or making of any firearm, explosive or incendiary device, or technique capable of causing injury or death to persons, knowing or having reason to know or intending that such training will be employed for use in, or in furtherance of, a civil disorder; or
2. Assembles with one or more persons for the purpose of training with, practicing with, or being instructed in the use of any firearm, explosive or incendiary device, or technique capable of causing injury or death to persons, intending to employ such training for use in, or in furtherance of, a civil disorder.

§18.2-433.3. Exceptions
Nothing contained in this article shall be construed to apply to:
1. Any act of a law-enforcement officer performed in the otherwise lawful performance of the officer's official duties;

2. Any activity, undertaken without knowledge of or intent to cause or further a civil disorder, which is intended to teach or practice self-defense or self-defense techniques such as karate clubs or self-defense clinics, and similar lawful activity;

3. Any facility, program or lawful activity related to firearms instruction and training intended to teach the safe handling and use of firearms; or

4. Any other lawful sports or activities related to the individual recreational use or possession of firearms, including but not limited to hunting activities, target shooting, self-defense and firearms collection.

Notwithstanding any language contained herein, no activity of any individual, group, organization or other entity engaged in the lawful display or use of firearms or other weapons or facsimiles thereof shall be deemed to be in violation of this statute.

§18.2-434. What deemed perjury; punishment and penalty

If any person to whom an oath is lawfully administered on any occasion willfully swear falsely on such occasion touching any material matter or thing, or if a person falsely make oath that any other person is eighteen years of age in order to obtain a marriage license for such other person, he shall be guilty of perjury, punishable as a Class 5 felony. Upon the conviction of any person for perjury, such person thereby shall be adjudged forever incapable of holding any office of honor, profit or trust under the Constitution of Virginia, or of serving as a juror.

§18.2-474.1. Delivery of drugs, firearms, explosives, etc., to prisoners

Notwithstanding the provisions of §18.2-474, any person who shall willfully in any manner deliver, attempt to deliver, or conspire with another to deliver to any prisoner confined under authority of the Commonwealth of Virginia, or of any political subdivision thereof, any drug which is a controlled substance regulated by the Drug Control Act in Chapter 34 of Title 54.1 or marijuana, shall be guilty of a Class 5 felony. Any person who shall willfully in any manner so deliver or attempt to deliver or conspire to deliver to any such prisoner, firearms, ammunitions, or explosives of any nature shall be guilty of a Class 3 felony.

Nothing herein contained shall be construed to repeal or amend §18.2-473.

Title 19.2 Criminal Procedure

§19.2-53. What may be searched and seized

Search warrants may be issued for the search of or for specified places, things or persons, and seizure therefrom of the following things as specified in the warrant:

1. Weapons or other objects used in the commission of crime;

§19.2-59.1. Strip searches prohibited; exceptions; how strip searches conducted

A. No person in custodial arrest for a traffic infraction, Class 3 or Class 4 misdemeanor, or a violation of a city, county, or town ordinance, which is punishable by no more than thirty days in jail shall be strip searched unless there is reasonable cause to believe on the part of a law-enforcement officer authorizing the search that the individual is concealing a weapon. All strip searches conducted under this section shall be performed by persons of the same sex as the person arrested and on premises where the search cannot be observed by persons not physically conducting the search.

§19.2-120. Admission to bail

Prior to conducting any hearing on the issue of bail, release or detention, the judicial officer shall, to the extent feasible, obtain the person's criminal history.

B. The judicial officer shall presume, subject to rebuttal, that no condition or combination of conditions will reasonably assure the appearance of the person or the safety of the public if the person is currently charged with:

4. A violation of §§18.2-308.1, 18.2-308.2, or §18.2-308.4 and which relates to a firearm and provides for a minimum, mandatory sentence;

§19.2-123. Release of accused on unsecured bond or promise to appear; conditions of release

A. Any person arrested for a felony who has previously been convicted of a felony, or who is presently on bond for an unrelated arrest in any jurisdiction, or who is on probation or parole, may be released only upon a secure bond. This provision may be waived with the approval of the judicial officer and with the concurrence of the attorney for the Commonwealth or the attorney for the county, city or town. Subject to the foregoing, when a person is arrested for either a felony or a misdemeanor, any judicial officer may impose any one or any combination of the following conditions of release:

3a. Require that the person do any or all of the following:

(v) refrain from possessing a firearm, destructive device, or other dangerous weapon;

§19.2-386.11. Judgment of condemnation; destruction

A. If the forfeiture is established, the judgment shall be that the property be condemned as forfeited to the Commonwealth subject to any remission granted under subsection A of §19.2-386.10 and further that the same be sold, unless

(i) a sale thereof has been already made under §19.2-386.7,

(ii) the court determines that the property forfeited is of such minimal value that the sale would not be in the best interest of the Commonwealth or

(iii) the court finds that the property may be subject to return to a participating agency. If the court finds that the property may be subject to return to an agency participating in the seizure in accordance with subsection C of §19.2-386.14, the order shall provide for storage of the property until the determination to return it is made or, if return is not made, for sale of the property as provided in this section and §19.2-386.12. If sale has been made, the judgment shall be against the proceeds of sale, subject to the rights of any lien holder whose interest is not forfeited. If the property condemned has been delivered to the claimant under §19.2-386.6, further judgment shall be against the obligors in the bond for the penalty thereof, to be discharged by the payment of the appraised value of the property, upon which judgment, process of execution shall be awarded and the clerk shall endorse thereon, "No security is to be taken."

C. Contraband, the sale or possession of which is unlawful, weapons and property not sold because of the minimal value thereof, may be ordered destroyed by the court.

§19.2-386.27. Forfeiture of firearms carried in violation of §18.2-308

Any weapon used in the commission of a violation of §18.2-308 shall be forfeited to the Commonwealth and may be seized by an officer as forfeited, and such as may be needed for police officers, conservators of the peace, and the Department of Forensic Science shall be devoted to that purpose, subject to any registration requirements of federal law, and the remainder shall be disposed of as provided in §19.2-386.29.

§19.2-386.28. Forfeiture of weapons that are concealed, possessed, transported or carried in violation of law

Any firearm, stun weapon as defined by §18.2-308.1, or any weapon concealed, possessed, transported or carried in violation of §§18.2-283.1, 18.2-287.4, 18.2-308.1:2, 18.2-308.1:3, 18.2-308.1:4, 18.2-308.2, 18.2-308.2:01, 18.2-308.2:1, 18.2-308.4, 18.2-308.5, 18.2-308.7, or §18.2-308.8 shall be forfeited to the Commonwealth and disposed of as provided in §19.2-386.29.

§19.2-386.29. Forfeiture of certain weapons used in commission of criminal offense

All pistols, shotguns, rifles, dirks, bowie knives, switchblade knives, ballistic knives, razors, slingshots, brass or metal knucks, blackjacks, stun weapons, and other weapons used by any person in the commission of a criminal offense, shall, upon conviction of such person, be forfeited to the Commonwealth by order of the court trying the case. The court shall dispose of such weapons as it deems proper by entry of an order of record. Such disposition may include the destruction of the weapons or, subject to any registration requirements of federal law, sale of the firearms to a licensed dealer in such firearms in accordance with the provisions of Chapter 22 (§19.2-369 et seq.) of this title regarding sale of property forfeited to the Commonwealth.

The proceeds of any sale of such weapon shall be paid in accordance with the provisions of Article VIII, Section 8 of the Constitution of Virginia. In addition, the court may authorize the seizing law-enforcement agency to use the weapon for a period of time as specified in the order. When the seizing agency ceases to so use the weapon, it shall be disposed of as otherwise provided in this section.

However, upon petition to the court and notice to the attorney for the Commonwealth, the court, upon good cause shown, shall return any such weapon to its lawful owner after conclusion of all relevant proceedings if such owner

i) did not know and had no reason to know of the conduct giving rise to the forfeiture and

ii) is not otherwise prohibited by law from possessing the weapon. The owner shall acknowledge in a sworn affidavit to be filed with the record in the case or cases that he has retaken possession of the weapon involved.

§19.2-389.1. Dissemination of juvenile record information

Record information maintained in the Central Criminal Records Exchange pursuant to the provisions of §16.1-299 shall be disseminated only

(i) to make the determination as provided in §18.2-308.2 and §18.2-308.2:2 of eligibility to possess or purchase a firearm;

Title 22.1 Education

§22.1-3.2. Notice of student's school status required as condition of admission

Prior to admission to any public school of the Commonwealth, a school board shall require the parent, guardian, or other person having control or charge of a child of school age to provide, upon registration, a sworn statement or affirmation indicating whether the student has been expelled from school attendance at a private school or in a public school division of the Commonwealth or in another state for an offense in violation of school board policies relating to weapons, alcohol or drugs, or for the willful infliction of injury to another person. Any person making a materially false statement or affirmation shall be guilty upon conviction of a Class 3 misdemeanor. The registration document shall be maintained as a part of the student's scholastic record.

§22.1-277.07. Expulsion of students under certain circumstances; exceptions

A. In compliance with the federal Improving America's Schools Act of 1994 (Part F-Gun-Free Schools Act of 1994), a school board shall expel from school attendance for a period of not less than one year any student whom such school board has determined, in accordance with the procedures set forth in this article, to have brought a firearm onto school property or to a school-sponsored activity as prohibited by §18.2-308.1, or to have brought a firearm or destructive device as defined in subsection E, a firearm muffler or firearm silencer, or a pneumatic gun as defined in subsection E of §15.2-915.4 onto school property or to a school-sponsored activity. A school administrator, pursuant to school board policy, or a school board may, however, determine, based on the facts of a particular situation, that special circumstances exist and no disciplinary action or another disciplinary action or another term of expulsion is appropriate. A school board may promulgate guidelines for determining what constitutes special circumstances. In addition, a school board may, by regulation, authorize the division superintendent or his designee to conduct a preliminary review of such cases to determine whether a disciplinary action other than expulsion is appropriate. Such regulations shall ensure that, if a determination is made that another disciplinary action is appropriate, any such subsequent disciplinary action is to be taken in accordance with the procedures set forth in this article.

B. The Board of Education is designated as the state education agency to carry out the provisions of the federal Improving America's Schools Act of 1994, and shall administer the funds to be appropriated to the Commonwealth under this act.

C. Each school board shall revise its standards of student conduct no later than three months after the date on which this act becomes effective. Local school boards requesting moneys apportioned to the Commonwealth through the federal Improving America's Schools Act of 1994 shall submit to the Department of Education an application requesting such assistance. Applications for assistance shall include:

1. Documentation that the local school board has adopted and implemented student conduct policies in compliance with this section; and

2. A description of the circumstances pertaining to expulsions imposed under this section, including

(i) the schools from which students were expelled under this section,

(ii) the number of students expelled from each such school in the school division during the school year, and

(iii) the types of firearms involved in the expulsions.

D. No school operating a Junior Reserve Officers Training Corps (JROTC) program shall prohibit the JROTC program from conducting marksmanship training when such training is a normal element of such programs. Such programs may include training in the use of pneumatic guns. The administration of a school operating a JROTC program shall cooperate with the JROTC staff in implementing such marksmanship training.

E. As used in this section:

"Destructive device" means

(i) any explosive, incendiary, or poison gas, bomb, grenade, rocket having a propellant charge of more than four ounces, missile having an explosive or incendiary charge of more than one-quarter ounce, mine, or other similar device;

(ii) any weapon, except a shotgun or a shotgun shell generally recognized as particularly suitable for sporting purposes, by whatever name known that will, or may be readily converted to, expel a projectile by the action of an explosive or other propellant, and that has any barrel with a bore of more than one-half inch in diameter that is homemade or was not made by a duly licensed weapon manufacturer, any fully automatic firearm, any sawed-off shotgun or sawed-off rifle as defined in §18.2-299 or any firearm prohibited from civilian ownership by federal law; and

(iii) any combination of parts either designed or intended for use in converting any device into any destructive device described in this subsection and from which a destructive device may be readily assembled. "Destructive device" shall not include any device that is not designed or redesigned for use as a weapon, or any device originally designed for use as a weapon and that is redesigned for use as a signaling, pyrotechnic, line-throwing, safety, or other similar device, nor shall it include any antique firearm as defined in subsection G of §18.2-308.2:2.

"Firearm" means any weapon prohibited on school property or at a school-sponsored activity pursuant to §18.2-308.1, or any weapon, including a starter gun, that will, or is designed or may readily be converted to, expel single or multiple projectiles by the action of an explosion of a combustible material or the frame or receiver of any such weapon. "Firearm" shall not include any pneumatic gun, as defined in subsection E of §15.2-915.4.

"One year" means 365 calendar days as required in federal regulations.

"School property" means any real property owned or leased by the school board or any vehicle owned or leased by the school board or operated by or on behalf of the school board.

F. The exemptions set out in §18.2-308 regarding concealed weapons shall apply, mutatis mutandis, to the provisions of this section. The provisions of this section shall not apply to persons who possess such firearm or firearms or pneumatic guns as a part of the curriculum or other programs sponsored by the schools in the school division or any organization permitted by the school to use its premises or to any law-enforcement officer while engaged in his duties as such.

G. This section shall not be construed to diminish the authority of the Board of Education or the Governor concerning decisions on whether, or the extent to which, Virginia shall participate in the federal Improving America's Schools Act of 1994, or to diminish the Governor's authority to coordinate and provide policy direction on official communications between the Commonwealth and the United States government.

§22.1-277.07:1. Policies prohibiting possession of firearms

Notwithstanding any other provision of law to the contrary, each school division may develop and implement procedures addressing disciplinary actions against students, and may establish disciplinary policies prohibiting the possession of firearms on school property, school buses, and at school-sponsored activities.

§22.1-277.2:1. Disciplinary authority of school boards under certain circumstances; alternative education program.

A. A school board may, in accordance with the procedures set forth in this article, require any student who has been
(i) charged with an offense relating to the Commonwealth's laws, or with a violation of school board policies, on weapons, alcohol or drugs, or intentional injury to another person;
(ii) found guilty or not innocent of an offense relating to the Commonwealth's laws on weapons, alcohol, or drugs, or of a crime that resulted in or could have resulted in injury to others, or of an offense that is required to be disclosed to the superintendent of the school division pursuant to subsection G of §16.1-260;
(iii) found to have committed a serious offense or repeated offenses in violation of school board policies;
(iv) suspended pursuant to §22.1-277.05; or
(v) expelled pursuant to §§22.1-277.06, 22.1-277.07, or §22.1-277.08, or subsection B of §22.1-277, to attend an alternative education program. A school board may require such student to attend such programs regardless of where the crime occurred. School boards may require any student who has been found, in accordance with the procedures set forth in this article, to have been in possession of, or under the influence of, drugs or alcohol on a school bus, on school property, or at a school-sponsored activity in violation of school board policies, to undergo evaluation for drug or alcohol abuse, or both, and, if recommended by the evaluator and with the consent of the student's parent, to participate in a treatment program.
As used in this section, the term "charged" means that a petition or warrant has been filed or is pending against a pupil.

B. A school board may adopt regulations authorizing the division superintendent or his designee to require students to attend an alternative education program consistent with the provisions of subsection A after
(i) written notice to the student and his parent that the student will be required to attend an alternative education program and
(ii) notice of the opportunity for the student or his parent to participate in a hearing to be conducted by the division superintendent or his designee regarding such placement. The decision of the superintendent or his designee regarding such alternative education placement shall be final unless altered by the school board, upon timely written petition, as established in regulation, by the student or his parent, for a review of the record by the school board.

§22.1-278. Guidelines for school board policies; school board regulations governing student conduct; Board standards for compliance with federal law requiring expulsion under certain circumstances by school board

B. The Board of Education shall establish standards to ensure compliance with the federal Improving America's Schools Act of 1994 (Part F--"Gun-Free Schools Act of 1994"), in accordance with Sec. 22.1-277.01, to be effective on July 1, 1995.
This subsection shall not be construed to diminish the authority of the Board of Education or the Governor concerning decisions on whether, or the extent to which, Virginia shall participate in the federal Improving America's Schools Act of 1994, or to diminish the Governor's authority to coordinate and provide policy direction on official communications between the Commonwealth and the United States government.

§22.1-278.1. School safety audits and school crisis and emergency management plans required

A. For the purposes of this section, unless the context requires otherwise:
"School crisis and emergency management plan" means the essential procedures, operations, and assignments required to prevent, manage, and respond to a critical event or emergency, including natural disasters involving fire, flood, tornadoes, or other severe weather; loss or disruption of power, water, communications or shelter; bus or other accidents; medical emergencies; student or staff member deaths; explosions; bomb threats; gun, knife or other weapons threats; spills or exposures to hazardous substances; the presence of unauthorized persons or trespassers; the loss, disappearance or kidnapping of a student; hostage situations; violence on school property or at school activities; and other incidents posing a serious threat of harm to students, personnel, or facilities.

D. Each school board shall ensure that every school that it supervises shall develop a written school crisis and emergency management plan, consistent with the definition provided in this section. The Department of Education and the Virginia Center for School Safety shall provide technical assistance to the school divisions of the Commonwealth in the development of the school crisis and emergency management plans.
Upon consultation with local school boards, division superintendents, the Virginia Center for School Safety, and the Coordinator of Emergency Management, the Board of Education shall develop, and may revise as it deems necessary, a model school crisis and emergency management plan for the purpose of assisting the public schools in Virginia in developing viable, effective crisis and emergency management plans.

§22.1-279.3:1. Reports of certain acts to school authorities

A. Reports shall be made to the division superintendent and to the principal or his designee on all incidents involving
(i) the assault or assault and battery, without bodily injury, of any person on a school bus, on school property, or at a school-sponsored activity;
(ii) the assault and battery that results in bodily injury, sexual assault, death, shooting, stabbing, cutting, or wounding of any person, or stalking of any person as described in§18.2-60.3, on a school bus, on school property, or at a school-sponsored activity;

(iii) any conduct involving alcohol, marijuana, a controlled substance, imitation controlled substance, or an anabolic steroid on a school bus, on school property, or at a school-sponsored activity, including the theft or attempted theft of student prescription medications;

(iv) any threats against school personnel while on a school bus, on school property or at a school-sponsored activity;

(v) the illegal carrying of a firearm, as defined in §22.1-277.07, onto school property;

(vi) any illegal conduct involving firebombs, explosive materials or devices, or hoax explosive devices, as defined in §18.2-85, or explosive or incendiary devices, as defined in §18.2-433.1, or chemical bombs, as described in §18.2-87.1, on a school bus, on school property, or at a school-sponsored activity;

(vii) any threats or false threats to bomb, as described in §18.2-83, made against school personnel or involving school property or school buses; or

(viii) the arrest of any student for an incident occurring on a school bus, on school property, or at a school-sponsored activity, including the charge therefor.

B. Notwithstanding the provisions of Article 12 (§16.1-299 et seq.) of Chapter 11 of Title 16.1, local law-enforcement authorities shall report, and the principal or his designee and the division superintendent shall receive such reports, on offenses, wherever committed, by students enrolled at the school if the offense would be a felony if committed by an adult or would be a violation of the Drug Control Act (§54.1-3400 et seq.) and occurred on a school bus, on school property, or at a school-sponsored activity, or would be an adult misdemeanor involving any incidents described in clauses (i) through (viii) of subsection A.

C. The principal or his designee shall submit a report of all incidents required to be reported pursuant to this section to the superintendent of the school division. The division superintendent shall annually report all such incidents to the Department of Education for the purpose of recording the frequency of such incidents on forms that shall be provided by the Department and shall make such information available to the public.

In submitting reports of such incidents, principals and division superintendents shall accurately indicate any offenses, arrests, or charges as recorded by law-enforcement authorities and required to be reported by such authorities pursuant to subsection B.

A division superintendent who knowingly fails to comply or secure compliance with the reporting requirements of this subsection shall be subject to the sanctions authorized in §22.1-65. A principal who knowingly fails to comply or secure compliance with the reporting requirements of this section shall be subject to sanctions prescribed by the local school board, which may include, but need not be limited to, demotion or dismissal.

The principal or his designee shall also notify the parent of any student involved in an incident required pursuant to this section to be reported, regardless of whether disciplinary action is taken against such student or the nature of the disciplinary action. Such notice shall relate to only the relevant student's involvement and shall not include information concerning other students.

Whenever any student commits any reportable incident as set forth in this section, such student shall be required to participate in such prevention and intervention activities as deemed appropriate by the superintendent or his designee. Prevention and intervention activities shall be identified in the local school division's drug and violence prevention plans developed pursuant to the federal Improving America's Schools Act of 1994 (Title IV - Safe and Drug-Free Schools and Communities Act).

D. Except as may otherwise be required by federal law, regulation, or jurisprudence, the principal shall immediately report to the local law-enforcement agency any act enumerated in clauses (ii) through (vii) of subsection A that may constitute a criminal offense and may report to the local law-enforcement agency any incident described in clause (i) of subsection A.

Further, except as may be prohibited by federal law, regulation, or jurisprudence, the principal shall also immediately report any act enumerated in clauses (ii) through (v) of subsection A that may constitute a criminal offense to the parents of any minor student who is the specific object of such act. Further, the principal shall report that the incident has been reported to local law enforcement as required by law and that the parents may contact local law enforcement for further information, if they so desire.

E. A statement providing a procedure and the purpose for the requirements of this section shall be included in school board policies required by §22.1-253.13:7.

The Board of Education shall promulgate regulations to implement this section, including, but not limited to, establishing reporting dates and report formats.

F. For the purposes of this section, "parent" or "parents" means any parent, guardian or other person having control or charge of a child.

G. This section shall not be construed to diminish the authority of the Board of Education or to diminish the Governor's authority to coordinate and provide policy direction on official communications between the Commonwealth and the United States government.

§22.1-280.1. Reports of certain acts to school authorities

A. Reports shall be made to the principal or his designee on all incidents involving

(i) the assault, assault and battery, sexual assault, death, shooting, stabbing, cutting, or wounding of any person on a school bus, on school property, or at a school-sponsored activity;

(iv) the illegal carrying of a firearm onto school property;

(v) any illegal conduct involving firebombs, explosive materials or devices, or hoax explosive devices, as defined in §18.2-85, or explosive or incendiary devices, as defined in §18.2-433.1, or chemical bombs, as described in §18.2-87.1, on a school bus, on school property, or at a school-sponsored activity; or

(vi) any threats or false threats to bomb, as described in §18.2-83, made against school personnel or involving school property or school buses.

B. Notwithstanding the provisions of Article 12 (§16.1-299 et seq.) of Chapter 11 of Title 16.1, local law-enforcement authorities may report, and the principal or his designee may receive such reports, on offenses, wherever committed, by students enrolled at the school if the offense would be a felony if committed by an adult or would be a violation of the Drug Control Act (§54.1-3400 et seq.) and occurred on a school bus, on school property, or at a school-sponsored activity, or would be an adult misdemeanor involving any incidents described in clauses (i) through (iv) of subsection A.

C. The principal or his designee shall submit a report of all incidents required or authorized to be reported pursuant to this section to the superintendent of the school division. The division superintendent shall annually report all such incidents to the Department of Education for the purpose of recording the frequency of such incidents on forms which shall be provided by the Department and shall make such information available to the public. A division superintendent who knowingly fails to comply or secure compliance with the reporting requirements of this subsection shall be subject to the sanctions authorized in §22.1-65. A principal who knowingly fails to comply or secure compliance with the reporting requirements of this section shall be subject to sanctions prescribed by the local school board, which may include but need not be limited to demotion or dismissal.

The principal or his designee shall also notify the parent of any student involved in an incident required by subsection A or authorized by subsection B to be reported, regardless of whether disciplinary action is taken against such student or the nature of the disciplinary action. Such notice shall relate to only the relevant student's involvement and shall not include information concerning other students.

Whenever any student commits any reportable incident as set forth in this section, such student shall be required to participate in such prevention and intervention activities as deemed appropriate by the superintendent or his designee. Prevention and intervention activities shall be identified in the local school division's drug and violence prevention plans developed pursuant to the federal Improving America's Schools Act of 1994 (Title IV - Safe and Drug-Free Schools and Communities Act).

D. The principal shall immediately report to the local law-enforcement agency any act enumerated in subsection A which may constitute a criminal offense.

F. A statement providing a procedure and the purpose for the requirements of this section shall be included in the policy manual of all school divisions.

The Board of Education shall promulgate regulations to implement this section, including, but not limited to, establishing reporting dates and report formats.

Title 29.1 Game, Inland Fisheries and Boating

§29.1-100. Definitions

As used in and for the purposes of this title only, or in any of the regulations of the Board, unless the context clearly requires a different meaning:

"Firearm" means any weapon that will or is designed to or may readily be converted to expel single or multiple projectiles by the action of an explosion of a combustible material.

"Muzzleloading pistol" means a firearm originally designed, made or intended to fire a projectile (bullet) from one or more barrels when held in one hand and that is loaded from the muzzle or forward end of the cylinder.

"Muzzleloading rifle" means a firearm firing a single projectile that is loaded along with the propellant from the muzzle of the gun.

"Muzzleloading shotgun" means a firearm with a smooth bore firing multiple projectiles that are loaded along with the propellant from the muzzle of the gun.

"Pistol" means a weapon originally designed, made, and intended to fire a projectile (bullet) from one or more barrels when held in one hand, and having one or more chambers as an integral part of or permanently aligned with the bore and a short stock at an angle to and extending below the line of the bore that is designed to be gripped by one hand.

"Revolver" means a projectile weapon of the pistol type, having a breechloading chambered cylinder arranged so that the cocking of the hammer or movement of the trigger rotates it and brings the next cartridge in line with the barrel for firing.

"Rifle" means a weapon designed or redesigned, made or remade, and intended to be fired from the shoulder, and designed or redesigned and made or remade to use the energy of the explosive in a fixed metallic cartridge to fire only a single projectile through a rifled bore for each single pull of the trigger.

"Shotgun" means a weapon designed or redesigned, made or remade, and intended to be fired from the shoulder, and designed or redesigned and made or remade to use the energy of the explosive in a fixed shotgun shell to fire through a smooth bore or rifled shotgun barrel either a number of ball shot or a single projectile for each single pull of the trigger.

§29.1-101. Game Protection Fund

The amount received by the State Treasurer from the collection of admittance, parking, or other use fees, sale of hunting, trapping and fishing licenses, revenue generated from the sales and use tax pursuant to subsection E of §58.1-638, and such other items as may accrue to the Board shall be set aside and shall constitute the Game Protection Fund. The income and principal of this Fund, including any unexpended balance, shall be a separate fund in the state treasury and shall only be used for the payment of the salaries, allowances, wages, and expenses incident to carrying out the provisions of the hunting, trapping and inland fish laws and for no other purpose, except as provided in §§29.1-101.01, 29.1-701, 58.1-345 and 58.1-1410.

§29.1-208. Searches and seizures

All conservation police officers are vested with the authority to search any person arrested as provided in §29.1-205 together with any box, can, package, barrel or other container, hunting bag, coat, suit, trunk, grip, satchel or fish basket carried by, in the possession of, or belonging to such person. Conservation police officers shall also have the authority, immediately subsequent to such arrest, to enter and search any refrigerator, building, vehicle, or other place in which the officer making the search has reasonable ground to believe that the person arrested has concealed or placed any wild bird, wild animal or fish, which will furnish evidence of a violation of the hunting, trapping and inland fish laws. Such a search may be made without a warrant, except that a dwelling may not be searched without a warrant. Should any container as described in this section reveal any wild bird, wild animal or fish, or any part thereof, which has been illegally taken, possessed, sold, purchased or transported, the conservation police officer shall seize and hold as evidence the container, together with such wild bird, wild animal or fish, and any unlawful gun, net, or other device of any kind for taking wild birds, wild animals or fish which he may find.

§29.1-300.1. Certification of competence in hunter education

A. Except as provided in subsection B of this section and §29.1-300.4, no hunting license shall be issued to
(i) a person who has never obtained a license to hunt in any state or country, or
(ii) a person who is under the age of sixteen, unless such a person presents to the Board of Game and Inland Fisheries or one of its authorized license vendors, a certificate of completion in hunter education issued or authorized by the Board under the hunter education program, or proof that he holds the equivalent certificate obtained from an authorized agency or association of another state or country.
B. Although a resident under the age of twelve is not required to obtain a license to hunt, any person under the age of twelve, or an individual on his behalf, may purchase a Virginia hunting license or a junior lifetime hunting license pursuant to §29.1-302.1, without completing a hunter education program as required in subsection A of this section, provided that no person under the age of twelve shall hunt unless accompanied and directly supervised by an adult who has, on his person, a valid Virginia hunting license. The junior lifetime hunting license issued to an individual under the age of twelve shall become invalid on the individual's twelfth birthday and remain invalid until certification of competence in hunter education is shown as provided in this section. A lifetime license, indicating the completion of hunter education or an equivalent certificate, shall be reissued at no cost when such proof is provided.
The adult shall be responsible for such supervision. For the purposes of this section, "adult" means the parent or legal guardian of the person under age twelve, or such person over the age of eighteen designated by the parent or legal guardian.
"Accompanied and directly supervised" means that the adult is within sight of the person under the age of twelve.
C. This section shall not apply to persons while on horseback hunting foxes with hounds but without firearms.

§29.1-300.4. Apprentice hunting license; deferral of hunter education.

A. There is hereby established an apprentice hunting license. The license shall be a one-time nonrenewable license that shall be valid for two years from the date of purchase and shall entitle the licensee to a one-time deferral of completion of hunter education required under §29.1-300.1. The apprentice hunting licensee shall not hunt unless accompanied and directly supervised by an adult over the age of 18 who has, on his person, a valid Virginia hunting license. For the purposes of this section, "accompanied and directly supervised" occurs when a person over 18 maintains a close visual and verbal contact with, provides adequate direction to, and can immediately assume control of the firearm from the apprentice hunter. The cost of the license shall be $10 for a resident and $20 for a nonresident.

§29.1-301. Exemptions from license requirements

A. No license shall be required of landowners, their spouses, their children and grandchildren and the spouses of such children and grandchildren, or the landowner's parents, resident or nonresident, to hunt, trap and fish within the boundaries of their own lands and inland waters or while within such boundaries or upon any private permanent extension therefrom, to fish in any abutting public waters.
B. No license shall be required of any stockholder owning 50 percent or more of the stock of any domestic corporation owning land in this Commonwealth, his or her spouse and children and minor grandchildren, resident or nonresident, to hunt, trap and fish within the boundaries of lands and inland waters owned by the domestic corporation.
C. No license shall be required of bona fide tenants, renters or lessees to hunt, trap or fish within the boundaries of the lands or waters on which they reside or while within such boundaries or upon any private permanent extension therefrom, to fish in any abutting public waters if such individuals have the written consent of the landlord upon their person. A guest of the owner of a private fish pond shall not be required to have a fishing license to fish in such pond.
D. No license shall be required of resident persons under 16 years old to fish.
D1. No license shall be required of resident persons under 12 years old to hunt, provided such person is accompanied and directly supervised by an adult who has, on his person, a valid Virginia hunting license as described in subsection B of §29.1-300.1.

E. No license shall be required of a resident person 65 years of age or over to hunt or trap on private property in the county or city in which he resides. An annual license at a fee of $1 shall be required of a resident person 65 years of age or older to fish in any inland waters of the Commonwealth, which shall be in addition to a license to fish for trout as specified in subsection B of §29.1-310 or a special lifetime trout fishing license as specified in §29.1-302.4. A resident 65 years of age or older may, upon proof of age satisfactory to the Department and the payment of a $1 fee, apply for and receive from any authorized agent of the Department a nontransferable annual license permitting such person to hunt or an annual license permitting such person to trap in all cities and counties of the Commonwealth. Any lifetime license issued pursuant to this article prior to July 1, 1988, shall remain valid for the lifetime of the person to whom it was issued. Any license issued pursuant to this section includes any damage stamp required pursuant to Article 3 (§29.1-352 et seq.) of this chapter.

F. No license to fish, except for trout as provided in §29.1-302.4 or subsection B of §29.1-310, shall be required of nonresident persons under 12 years of age when accompanied by a person possessing a valid license to fish in Virginia.

G. No license shall be required to trap rabbits with box traps.

H. No license shall be required of resident persons under 16 years of age to trap when accompanied by any person 18 years of age or older who possesses a valid state license to trap in this Commonwealth.

I. No license to hunt, trap or fish shall be required of any Indian who habitually resides on an Indian reservation or of a member of the Virginia recognized tribes who resides in the Commonwealth; however, such Indian must have on his person an identification card or paper signed by the chief of his tribe, a valid tribal identification card, written confirmation through a central tribal registry, or certification from a tribal office. Such card, paper, confirmation, or certification shall set forth that the person named is an actual resident upon such reservation or member of the recognized tribes in the Commonwealth, and such card, paper, confirmation or certification shall create a presumption of residence, which may be rebutted by proof of actual residence elsewhere.

J. No license to fish shall be required of legally blind persons.

K. No fishing license shall be required in any inland waters of the Commonwealth, except those stocked with trout by the Department or other public body, on free fishing days. The Board shall designate no more than three free fishing days in any calendar year.

L. No license to fish, except for trout as provided in §29.1-302.4 or subsection B of §29.1-310, in Laurel Lake and Beaver Pond at Breaks Interstate Park shall be required of a resident of the State of Kentucky who (i) possesses a valid license to fish in Kentucky or (ii) is exempt under Kentucky law from the requirement of possessing a valid fishing license.

M. No license to hunt or fish shall be required of any person who is not hunting or fishing but is aiding a disabled person to hunt or fish when such disabled person possesses a valid Virginia hunting or fishing license under §29.1-302, 29.1-302.1 or 29.1-302.2

§29.1-307. Special muzzleloading license

There shall be a license for hunting with a muzzleloader during the special muzzleloading seasons, which shall be in addition to the license required to hunt small game. The fee for the special license shall be $12 for a resident and $25 for a nonresident. The special muzzleloader license may be obtained from the clerk or agent whose duty it is to sell licenses in any county or city.

§29.1-519. Guns, pistols, revolvers, etc., which may be used; penalty

A. All wild birds and wild animals may be hunted with the following weapons unless shooting is expressly prohibited:

1. A shotgun or muzzleloading shotgun not larger than ten gauge;
2. An automatic-loading or hand-operated repeating shotgun capable of holding not more than three shells the magazine of which has been cut off or plugged with a one-piece filler incapable of removal through the loading end, so as to reduce the capacity of the gun to not more than three shells at one time in the magazine and chamber combined, unless otherwise allowed by Board regulations;
3. A rifle, a muzzleloading rifle, or an air rifle;
4. A bow and arrow; or
5. A crossbow, which is a type of bow and arrow, used by disabled individuals. Such individuals who meet criteria established by the Department and attested to by a licensed physician on a standardized form provided by the Department, which shall be in the individual's possession while hunting, shall be allowed to participate in hunting seasons under the same rules, regulations, laws, and conditions that apply to hunters using standard archery equipment.

B. A pistol, muzzle-loading pistol or revolver may be used to hunt nuisance species of birds and animals.

C. In the counties west of the Blue Ridge Mountains, and counties east of the Blue Ridge where rifles of a caliber larger than .22 caliber may be used for hunting wild birds and animals, game birds and animals may be hunted with pistols or revolvers firing cartridges rated in manufacturers' tables at 350 foot pounds of energy or greater and under the same restrictions and conditions as apply to rifles, provided that no cartridge shall be used with a bullet of less than .23 caliber. In no event shall pistols or revolvers firing cartridges rated in manufacturers' tables at 350 foot pounds of energy or greater be used if rifles of a caliber larger than .22 caliber are not authorized for hunting purposes.

D. The use of muzzle-loading pistols and .22 caliber rimfire handguns is permitted for hunting small game where .22 caliber rifles are permitted.

E. The hunting of wild birds and wild animals with fully automatic firearms, defined as a machine gun in §18.2-288, is prohibited.

F. The hunting of wild birds or wild animals with
(i) weapons other than those authorized by this section or
(ii) weapons that have been prohibited by this section shall be punishable as a Class 3 misdemeanor.

§29.1-521. Unlawful to hunt, trap, possess, sell or transport wild birds and wild animals except as permitted; penalty

A. The following shall be unlawful:
1. To hunt or kill any wild bird or wild animal, including any nuisance species, with a gun, firearm or other weapon on Sunday, which is hereby declared a rest day for all species of wild bird and wild animal life, except raccoons, which may be hunted until 2:00 a.m. on Sunday mornings. However, a person lawfully carrying a gun, firearm or other weapon on Sunday in an area that could be used for hunting shall not be presumed to be hunting on Sunday, absent evidence to the contrary.
3. To hunt or attempt to kill or trap any species of wild bird or wild animal after having obtained the daily bag or season limit during such day or season. However, any properly licensed person, or a person exempt from having to obtain a license, who has obtained such daily bag or season limit while hunting may assist others who are hunting game by calling game, retrieving game, handling dogs, or conducting drives if the weapon in his possession is an unloaded firearm, a bow without a nocked arrow or an unloaded crossbow. Any properly licensed person, or person exempt from having to obtain a license, who has obtained such season limit prior to commencement of the hunt may assist others who are hunting game by calling game, retrieving game, handling dogs, or conducting drives, provided he does not have a firearm, bow or crossbow in his possession.
5. To kill or capture any wild bird or wild animal adjacent to any area while a field or forest fire is in progress.
6. To shoot or attempt to take any wild bird or wild animal from an automobile or other vehicle, except as provided in §29.1-521.3.
C. A violation of subdivisions 1 through 10 of subsection A of this section shall be punishable as a Class 3 misdemeanor.

§29.1-521.1. Willfully impeding hunting or trapping; penalty

A. It shall be unlawful to willfully and intentionally impede the lawful hunting or trapping of wild birds or wild animals.
B. Any person convicted of a violation of this section shall be guilty of a Class 3 misdemeanor.

§29.1-521.2. Violation of §18.2-286 while hunting; forfeiture of certain weapons; revocation of license

A. Any firearm, crossbow or bow and arrow used by any person to hunt any game bird or game animal in a manner which violates §18.2-286 may, upon conviction of such person violating §18.2-286, be forfeited to the Commonwealth by order of the court trying the case. The forfeiture shall be enforced as provided in Chapter 22 (§19.2-369 et seq.) of Title 19.2. The officer or other person seizing the property shall immediately give notice to the attorney for the Commonwealth.
B. The court may revoke the current hunting license, if any, of a person hunting any game bird or game animal in a manner that constitutes a violation of §18.2-286. The court may prohibit the issuance of any hunting license to that person for a period of up to five years. If found hunting during this prohibited period, the person shall be guilty of a Class 2 misdemeanor. Notification of such revocation or prohibition shall be forwarded to the Department pursuant to subsection C of §29.1-56.1.

§29.1-521.3. Shooting wild birds and wild animals from stationary vehicles by disabled persons

Any person, upon application to a conservation police officer and the presentation of a medical doctor's written statement based on a physical examination that such person is permanently unable to walk due to impaired mobility, may, in the discretion of the conservation police officer, be issued a permit to shoot wild birds and wild animals from a stationary automobile or other vehicle during established open hunting seasons and in accordance with other laws and regulations. Permits issued pursuant to this section shall
(i) be issued on a form provided by the Department,
(ii) not authorize shooting from a stationary vehicle less than 50 feet from nor in or across any public road or highway subject to the provisions of §29.1-526,
(iii) be issued for the lifetime of the permittee and be issued only to those persons who are properly licensed to hunt, and
(iv) be nontransferable. Any permit found in the possession of any person not entitled to such permit shall be subject to confiscation by a conservation police officer.

§29.1-523. Killing deer by use of certain lights; acts raising presumption of attempt to kill

Any person who kills or attempts to kill any deer between a half hour after sunset and a half hour before sunrise by use of a light attached to any vehicle or a spotlight or flashlight shall be guilty of a Class 2 misdemeanor. The flashing of a light attached to any vehicle or a spotlight or flashlight from any vehicle between a half hour after sunset and half hour before sunrise by any person or persons, then in possession of a firearm, crossbow, or bow and arrow or speargun, without good cause, shall raise a presumption of an attempt to kill deer in violation of this section. Every person in or on any such vehicle shall be deemed a principal in the second degree and subject to the same punishment as a principal in the first degree. Every person who, in any manner, aids, abets or acts in concert with any person or persons violating this section shall be deemed a principal in the second degree and subject to the same punishment as a principal in the first degree.

In addition to the penalty prescribed herein, the court shall revoke the current hunting license, if any, of the person convicted of violating this section and prohibit the issuance of any hunting license to that person for the next license year. If found hunting during this prohibited period, the person shall be guilty of a Class 2 misdemeanor. Notification of such revocation or prohibition shall be forwarded to the Department pursuant to subsections C and D of §18.2-56.1.

This section shall not apply to persons duly authorized to kill deer according to the provisions of §29.1-529.

§29.1-524. Forfeiture of vehicles and weapons used for killing or attempt to kill

Every vehicle, firearm, crossbow, bow and arrow, or speargun used with the knowledge or consent of the owner or lienholder thereof, in killing or attempting to kill deer between a half hour after sunset and a half hour before sunrise in violation of §29.1-523, and every vehicle used in the transportation of the carcass, or any part thereof, of a deer so killed shall be forfeited to the Commonwealth. Upon being condemned as forfeited in proceedings under Chapter 22 (§19.2-369 et seq.) of Title 19.2, the proceeds of sale shall be disposed of according to law.

§29.1-525. Employment of lights under certain circumstances upon places used by deer

A. Any person in any vehicle and then in possession of any firearm, crossbow, bow and arrow or speargun who employs a light attached to the vehicle or a spotlight or flashlight to cast a light beyond the water or surface of the roadway upon any place used by deer shall be guilty of a Class 2 misdemeanor. Every person in or on any such vehicle shall be deemed prima facie a principal in the second degree and subject to the same punishment as a principal in the first degree. This subsection shall not apply to a landowner in possession of a weapon when he is on his own land and is making a bona fide effort to protect his property from damage by deer and not for the purpose of killing deer unless the landowner is in possession of a permit to do so pursuant to the provisions of §29.1-529.

B. Any person in any motor vehicle who deliberately employs a light attached to such vehicle or a spotlight or flashlight to cast a light beyond the surface of the roadway upon any place used by deer, except upon his own land or upon land on which he has an easement or permission for such purpose, shall be guilty of a Class 4 misdemeanor. Every person in or on any such vehicle shall be deemed prima facie a principal in the second degree and subject to the same punishment as a principal in the first degree.

C. In addition to the penalties prescribed in subsection A of this section, the court shall revoke the current hunting license, if any, of the person convicted of a violation of subsection A of this section and prohibit the issuance of any hunting license to that person for the next license year. In addition to the penalties prescribed in subsection B of this section, the court may revoke the current hunting license, if any, of the person convicted of a violation of subsection B of this section and prohibit the issuance of any hunting license to that person for the next license year. If a person convicted of a violation of subsection A or subsection B of this section is found hunting during the prohibited period, the person shall be guilty of a Class 2 misdemeanor. Notification of such revocation or prohibition shall be forwarded to the Department pursuant to subsections C and D of §18.2-56.1.

§29.1-526. Counties and cities may prohibit hunting or trapping near primary and secondary highways

The governing body of any county or city may prohibit by ordinance the hunting, with a firearm, of any game bird or game animal while the hunting is on or within 100 yards of any primary or secondary highway in such county or city and may provide that any violation of the ordinance shall be a Class 3 misdemeanor. In addition, the governing body of any county or city may prohibit by ordinance the trapping of any game animal or furbearer within fifty feet of the shoulder of any primary or secondary highway in the county or city and may provide that any violation of the ordinance shall be a Class 3 misdemeanor. No such ordinance shall prohibit such trapping where the written permission of the landowner is obtained. It shall be the duty of the governing body enacting an ordinance under the provisions of this section to notify the Director by registered mail no later than May 1 of the year in which the ordinance is to take effect. If the governing body fails to make such notice, the ordinance shall be unenforceable.

For the purpose of this section, the terms "hunt" and "trap" shall not include the necessary crossing of highways for the bona fide purpose of going into or leaving a lawful hunting or trapping area.

§29.1-527. Counties, cities or towns may prohibit hunting near public schools and county, city, town or regional parks

The governing body of any county, city or town may prohibit by ordinance, shooting or hunting with a firearm, or prohibit hunters from traversing an area while in possession of a loaded firearm, within 100 yards of any property line of a public school or a county, city, town or regional park. The governing body may, in such ordinance, provide that any violation thereof shall be a Class 4 misdemeanor. Nothing in this section shall give any county, city or town the authority to enforce such an ordinance on lands within a national or state park or forest, or wildlife management area.

§29.1-528. Counties or cities may prohibit hunting with certain firearms

A. The Board shall promulgate regulations establishing model ordinances for hunting with firearms that may be adopted by counties or cities. Such model ordinances developed by the Board shall address such items as, but are not limited to, firearm caliber, type of firearm (e.g., rifle, shotgun, muzzleloader), and type of ammunition. The governing body of any county or city may, by ordinance, prohibit hunting in such county or city with a shotgun loaded with slugs, or with a rifle of a caliber larger than .22 rimfire. However, such ordinance may permit the hunting of groundhogs with a rifle of a caliber larger than .22 rimfire between March 1 and August 31. Such ordinance may also permit the use of muzzle-loading rifles during the prescribed open seasons for the hunting of game species. Any such ordinance may also specify permissible type of ammunition to be used for such hunting.

B. No such ordinance shall be enforceable unless the governing body notifies the Director by registered mail prior to May 1 of the year in which the ordinance is to take effect.

C. In adopting an ordinance pursuant to the provisions of this section the governing body of any county or city may provide that any person who violates the provisions of the ordinance shall be guilty of a Class 3 misdemeanor.

§29.1-529. Killing of deer or bear damaging fruit trees, crops, livestock, or personal property or creating a hazard to aircraft or motor vehicles

B. Subject to the provisions of subsection A, the Director or his designee may issue a written authorization to kill deer causing damage to residential plants, whether ornamental, noncommercial agricultural, or other types of residential plants. The Director may charge a fee not to exceed actual costs. The holder of this written authorization shall be subject to local ordinances, including those regulating the discharge of firearms.

F. The Director or his designee may revoke or refuse to reissue any authorization granted under this section when it has been shown by a preponderance of the evidence that an abuse of the authorization has occurred. Such evidence may include a complaint filed by any person with the Department alleging that an abuse of the written authorization has occurred. Any person aggrieved by the issuance, denial or revocation of a written authorization can appeal the decision to the Department of Game and Inland Fisheries. Any person convicted of violating any provision of the hunting and trapping laws and regulations shall be entitled to receive written authorization to kill deer or bear. However, such person shall not

(i) be designated as a shooter nor

(ii) carry out the authorized activity for a person who has received such written authorization for a period of at least two years and up to five years following his most recent conviction for violating any provision of the hunting and trapping laws and regulations. In determining the appropriate length of this restriction, the Director shall take into account the nature and severity of the most recent violation and of any past violations of the hunting and trapping laws and regulations by the applicant. No person shall be designated as a shooter under this section during a period when such person's hunting license or privileges to hunt have been suspended or revoked.

§29.1-530. Open and closed season for trapping, bag limits, etc.

B. In addition, the following general rules shall be applicable to any person trapping in the Commonwealth:

3. Licensed trappers may shoot wild animals caught in traps during the open hunting season if the trapper has a license to hunt.

§29.1-530.1. Blaze orange clothing required at certain times

During any firearms deer season, except during the special season for hunting deer with a muzzle-loading rifle only, in counties and cities designated by the Board, every hunter, or any person accompanying a hunter, shall wear a blaze orange hat, except that the bill or brim of the hat may be a color or design other than solid blaze orange, or blaze orange upper body clothing that is visible from 360 degrees or display at least 100 square inches of solid blaze orange material at shoulder level within body reach visible from 360 degrees.

Any person violating the provisions of this section shall, upon conviction, pay a fine of $25.

Violations of this section shall not be admissible in any civil action for personal injury or death as evidence of negligence, contributory negligence or assumption of the risk.

This section shall not apply when

(i) hunting waterfowl from stationary or floating blinds,

(ii) hunting waterfowl over decoys,

(iii) hunting waterfowl in wetlands as defined in §28.2-1300,

(iv) hunting waterfowl from a boat or other floating conveyance,

(v) participating in hunting dog field trials permitted by the Board of Game and Inland Fisheries,

(vi) on horseback while hunting foxes with hounds but without firearms, or

(vii) hunting with a bow and arrow in areas where the discharge of firearms is prohibited by state law or local ordinance.

§29.1-544. Dressing, packing and selling bobwhite quail

A. It shall be lawful for the licensee of a shooting preserve or his designated agents to dress, pack and sell bobwhite quail raised by him for use as food, under rules or regulations to be prescribed by the Board.

§29.1-549. Hunting deer from watercraft; confiscation of watercraft and weapons used

A. Any person who kills or attempts to kill any deer while the person is in a boat or other type watercraft shall be guilty of a Class 4 misdemeanor.

B. Every boat or other watercraft and their motors, and any firearm, crossbow, bow and arrow, or speargun used with the knowledge or consent of the owner or lienholder thereof, in killing or attempting to kill deer in violation of this section, shall be forfeited to the Commonwealth, and upon being condemned as forfeited in proceedings under Chapter 22 (§19.2-369 et seq.) of Title 19.2 the proceeds of sale shall be disposed of according to law.

§29.1-556. Unlawful devices to be destroyed

Any firearm, trap, net, or other device of any kind or nature for taking wild birds, wild animals, or fish, except as specifically permitted by law, shall be considered unlawful. Any person who violates the provisions of this section shall be guilty of a Class 3 misdemeanor, and the device shall be forfeited to the Commonwealth. Nets, traps or other such devices, excluding firearms, shall be destroyed by the conservation police officer if the owner or user of the device cannot be located within thirty days. Unlawful fixed devices may be destroyed by the conservation police officer at the place where the devices are found.

Title 37.2 Mental Health, Mental Retardation, and Substance Abuse Services

§37.2-134.18. Clerk to index findings of incapacity or restoration; notice to Commissioner, commissioner of accounts, Secretary of Board of Elections and CCRE

B. The clerk shall certify and forward forthwith to the Central Criminal Records Exchange, on a form provided by the Exchange, a copy of any order adjudicating a person incapacitated under this article and any order of restoration of capacity under §37.1-134.16. The copy of the form and the order shall be kept confidential in a separate file and used only to determine a person's eligibility to possess, purchase or transfer a firearm.

§37.2-814. Commitment hearing for involuntary admission; written explanation; right to counsel; rights of petitioner.

B. At the commencement of the commitment hearing, the district court judge or special justice shall inform the person whose involuntary admission is being sought of his right to apply for voluntary admission for inpatient treatment as provided for in §37.2-805 and shall afford the person an opportunity for voluntary admission. The district court judge or special justice shall advise the person whose involuntary admission is being sought that if the person chooses to be voluntarily admitted pursuant to §37.2-805, such person will be prohibited from possessing or purchasing a firearm pursuant to §18.2-308.1:3. The judge or special justice shall ascertain if the person is then willing and capable of seeking voluntary admission for inpatient treatment. If the judge or special justice finds that the person is capable and willingly accepts voluntary admission for inpatient treatment, the judge or special justice shall require him to accept voluntary admission for a minimum period of treatment not to exceed 72 hours. After such minimum period of treatment, the person shall give the facility 48 hours' notice prior to leaving the facility. During this notice period, the person shall not be discharged except as provided in §37.2-837, 37.2-838, or 37.2-840. The person shall be subject to the transportation provisions as provided in §37.2-829 and the requirement for preadmission screening by a community services board as provided in §37.2-805.

§37.2-819. Order of involuntary admission or involuntary outpatient treatment forwarded to CCRE; certain voluntary admissions forwarded to CCRE; firearm background check.

B. The clerk of court shall also, prior to the close of that business day, forward upon receipt to the Central Criminal Records Exchange, on a form provided by the Exchange, certification of any person who has been the subject of a temporary detention order pursuant to §37.2-809, and who, after being advised by the judge or special justice that he will be prohibited from possessing a firearm pursuant to §18.2-308.1:3, subsequently agreed to voluntary admission pursuant to §37.2-805.

C. The copy of the forms and orders sent to the Central Criminal Records Exchange pursuant to subsection A, and the forms and certifications sent to the Central Criminal Records Exchange regarding voluntary admission pursuant to subsection B, shall be kept confidential in a separate file and used only to determine a person's eligibility to possess, purchase, or transfer a firearm. No medical records shall be forwarded to the Central Criminal Records Exchange with any form, order, or certification required by subsection A or B. The Department of State Police shall forward only a person's eligibility to possess, purchase, or transfer a firearm to the National Instant Criminal Background Check System.

Title 44 Military and Emergency Laws

§44-54.12. Arms, equipment and facilities

The Virginia State Defense Force, to the extent authorized by the Governor and funded by the General Assembly, shall be equipped as needed for training and for state active duty. The Adjutant General, by regulation or otherwise, may authorize the use of privately owned real and personal property if deemed in the best interest of the Commonwealth.

To the extent permitted by federal law and contracts with the federal government or localities and to the extent that space is available, the Adjutant General in his discretion may authorize the use of armories and other facilities of the National Guard, other state facilities under his control, and all or portions of privately owned facilities under contract for the storage and maintenance of arms, equipment and supplies of the Virginia State Defense Force and for the assembly, drill, training and instruction of its members.

Members of the Virginia State Defense Force shall not be armed with firearms during the performance of training duty or state active duty, except under circumstances and in instances authorized by the Governor.

§44-146.15. Construction of chapter
Nothing in this chapter is to be construed to:
(3) Empower the Governor, any political subdivision, or any other governmental authority to in any way limit the rights of the people to keep and bear arms as guaranteed by Article I, Section 13 of the Constitution of Virginia or the Second Amendment of the Constitution of the United States, including the lawful possession, sale, or transfer of firearms except to the extent necessary to ensure public safety in any place or facility designated or used by the Governor, any political subdivision of the Commonwealth or any other governmental entity as an emergency shelter or for the purpose of sheltering persons;

Title 46.2 Motor Vehicles

§46.2-345. Issuance of special identification cards; fee; confidentiality; penalties
A. On the application of any person who is a resident of the Commonwealth or the parent or legal guardian of any such person who is under the age of 15, the Department shall issue a special identification card to the person provided:
I. Any person who uses a false or fictitious name or gives a false or fictitious address in any application for an identification card or knowingly makes a false statement or conceals a material fact or otherwise commits a fraud in any such application shall be guilty of a Class 2 misdemeanor. However, where the name or address is given, or false statement is made, or fact is concealed, or fraud committed, with the intent to purchase a firearm or where the identification card is obtained for the purpose of committing any offense punishable as a felony, a violation of this section shall constitute a Class 4 felony.

§46.2-348. Fraud or false statements in applications for license; penalties
Any person who uses a false or fictitious name or gives a false or fictitious address in any application for a driver's license, or any renewal or duplicate thereof, or knowingly makes a false statement or conceals a material fact or otherwise commits a fraud in his application shall be guilty of a Class 2 misdemeanor. However, where the license is used, or the fact concealed, or fraud is done, with the intent to purchase a firearm, a violation of this section shall be punishable as a Class 4 felony.

§46.2-749.6. Special license plates for supporters of the National Rifle Association
On receipt of an application therefor, the Commissioner shall issue special license plates to supporters of the National Rifle Association.

Title 52 Police (State)

§52-4.4. Duties relating to criminal history record information checks required by licensed firearms dealers
The Superintendent of the Department of State Police shall establish a toll-free telephone number which shall be operational seven days a week between the hours of 8:00 a.m. and 10:00 p.m., except December 25, for purposes of responding to inquiries from licensed firearms dealers, as such term is defined in 18 U.S.C. §921 et seq., pursuant to the provisions of §18.2-308.2:2. The Department shall hire and train such personnel as are necessary to administer the provisions of this section.

§52-8.4:1. Regulations for firearms shows
The Superintendent of State Police shall provide a form for use by promoters of firearms shows for the purpose of notifying the State Police and the chief of police, or the sheriff in localities without police departments, of their intent to conduct a firearms show pursuant to §54.1-4201.1.

§52-11.4. Disposal of unclaimed property in the possession of State Police; exemption from the Uniform Disposition of Unclaimed Property Act
The Department of State Police may provide for
(i) the public sale in accordance with the provisions of this section or
(ii) the retention for use by the State Police or other law-enforcement agency of any unclaimed personal property that has been in the possession of the State Police and unclaimed for a period of more than 60 days. For the purposes of this section, "unclaimed personal property" means any personal property, other than firearms or other weapons, belonging to another that has been acquired by a law-enforcement officer pursuant to his duties, that is not needed in any criminal prosecution, that has not been claimed by its rightful owner and that the State Treasurer has indicated will be declined if remitted under the Uniform Disposition of Unclaimed Property Act (§55-210.1 et seq.).
Prior to the sale or retention for use by the State Police of any unclaimed personal property, the Superintendent or his designee shall make reasonable attempts to
(i) notify by mail the rightful owner of the property,
(ii) obtain from the attorney for the Commonwealth of the jurisdiction in which the unclaimed item came into the possession of the State Police in writing a statement advising that the item is not needed in any criminal prosecution,

(iii) cause to be published on the website maintained by the State Police for a period of 60 days notice that there will be a public display and sale of unclaimed personal property, including property selected for retention by the State Police, which shall be described generally in the notice, together with the date, time and place of the sale and shall be made available for public viewing at the sale, and

(iv) cause to be published in a newspaper of general circulation in the locality where the sale is to be held once a week for two successive weeks prior to the sale, a notice that includes the date, time, place of the sale, general description of items to be sold and the State Police website address. The Superintendent or his designee shall pay from the proceeds of sale the costs of advertisement, removal, storage, investigation as to ownership and liens, and notice of sale. The balance of the funds shall be held by the Superintendent or his designee for the owner and paid to the owner upon satisfactory proof of ownership. Any unclaimed item retained for use by the State Police shall become the property of the Commonwealth and any property provided to other law-enforcement agencies shall become the property of the locality served by the agency and shall be retained only if, in the opinion of the Superintendent or chief law-enforcement officer, there is a legitimate use for the property by the agency and that retention of the item is a more economical alternative than purchase of a similar or equivalent item.

If no claim has been made by the owner for the property or proceeds of such sale within 60 days of the sale, the remaining funds shall be deposited in the Literary Fund of the Commonwealth and the retained property may be placed into use by the State Police or other law-enforcement agency. Any such owner shall be entitled to apply to the Commonwealth within one year from the date of the sale and, if timely application is made therefor and satisfactory proof of ownership of the funds or property is made, the Commonwealth shall pay the remaining proceeds of the sale or return the property to the owner without interest or other charges or compensation. No claim shall be made nor any suit, action or proceeding be instituted for the recovery of such funds or property after one year from the date of the sale.

§52-11.5. Disposal of unclaimed firearms or other weapons in possession of the State Police

Subject to the provisions of §19.2-386.29, the State Police may destroy unclaimed firearms and other weapons that have been in the possession of the Department for a period of more than 60 days and that have been determined by the Superintendent or his designee to be unsuitable to be placed in service with the Department. For the purposes of this section, "unclaimed firearms and other weapons" means any firearm or other weapon belonging to another that has been acquired by a law-enforcement officer pursuant to his duties, that is not needed in any criminal prosecution, that has not been claimed by its rightful owner and that the State Treasurer has indicated will be declined if remitted under the Uniform Disposition of Unclaimed Property Act (§55-210.1 et seq.).

At the discretion of the Superintendent or his designee, unclaimed firearms or other weapons may be destroyed by any means that render the firearms or other weapons permanently inoperable. Prior to the destruction of such firearms or other weapons, the Superintendent or his designee shall comply with the notice provisions contained in §52-11.4.

§52-25.1. Reporting of confiscated firearms

The Superintendent shall establish and maintain within the Department of State Police a Criminal Firearms Clearinghouse as a central repository of information regarding all firearms seized, forfeited, found or otherwise coming into the possession of any state or local law-enforcement agency of the Commonwealth which are believed to have been used in the commission of a crime. The Superintendent shall adopt and promulgate regulations prescribing the form for reporting this information and the time and manner of submission of the form.

In addition to any other information which the Superintendent may require, the form shall require

(i) the serial number or other identifying information on the firearm, if available,

(ii) a brief description of the circumstances under which the firearm came into the possession of the law-enforcement agency, including the crime which was or may have been committed with the firearm,

(iii) the name of or other identifying information on the person from whom the firearm was taken,

(iv) the original place of sale and, if known, the chain of possession of the firearm, and

(v) the disposition of the firearm.

Title 53.1 Prisons and Other Methods of Correction

§53.1-109.01. Authority for regional jail officers to carry weapons

It shall be lawful for any regional jail officer who has been designated by the superintendent, and who has completed the basic course in firearms for jailers and custodial officers pursuant to subdivision 7 of §9-170, to carry and use sufficient weapons to prevent escapes, suppress rebellion, and defend or protect himself or others in the course of his assigned duties.

§53.1-151. Eligibility for parole

A. Except as herein otherwise provided, every person convicted of a felony and sentenced and committed by a court under the laws of this Commonwealth to the Department of Corrections, whether or not such person is physically received at a Department of Corrections facility, or as provided for in §19.2-308.1:

4. B. 1. Any person convicted of three separate felony offenses of

(i) murder,

(ii) rape or

(iii) robbery by the presenting of firearms or other deadly weapon, or any combination of the offenses specified in subdivisions (i), (ii) or (iii) when such offenses were not part of a common act, transaction or scheme shall not be eligible for parole.

§53.1-203. Felonies by prisoners; penalties
It shall be unlawful for a prisoner in a state, local or community correctional facility or in the custody of an employee thereof to:

7. Introduce into a correctional facility or have in his possession firearms or ammunition for firearms;

§53.1-233. Death chamber; who to execute death sentence
The Director is hereby authorized and directed to provide and maintain a permanent death chamber and necessary appurtenant facilities within the confines of a state correctional facility. The death chamber shall have all the necessary appliances for the proper execution of prisoners by electrocution or by continuous intravenous injection of a substance or combination of substances sufficient to cause death. Any such substance shall be applied until the prisoner is pronounced dead by a physician licensed in the Commonwealth. All prisoners upon whom the death penalty has been imposed shall be executed in the death chamber. Each execution shall be conducted by the Director or one or more assistants designated by him.

§53.1-234. Transfer of prisoner; how death sentence executed; who to be present
The clerk of the circuit court in which is pronounced the sentence of death against any person shall, after such judgment becomes final in the circuit court, deliver a certified copy thereof to the Director. Such person so sentenced to death shall be confined prior to the execution of the sentencing a state correctional facility designated by the Director. Prior to the time fixed in the judgment of the court for the execution of the sentence, the Director shall cause the condemned prisoner to be conveyed to the state correctional facility housing the death chamber.

The Director, or the assistants appointed by him, shall at the time named in the sentence, unless a suspension of execution is ordered, cause the prisoner under sentence of death to be electrocuted or injected with a lethal substance, until he is dead. The method of execution shall be chosen by the prisoner. In the event the prisoner refuses to make a choice at least fifteen days prior to the scheduled execution, the method of execution shall be by lethal injection.

Execution by lethal injection shall be permitted in accordance with procedures developed by the Department. At the execution there shall be present the Director or an assistant, a physician employed by the Department or his assistant, such other employees of the Department as may be required by the Director and, in addition thereto, at least six citizens who shall not be employees of the Department. In addition, the counsel for the prisoner and a clergyman may be present.

Title 54.1 Professions and Occupations

§54.1-2967. Physicians and others rendering medical aid to report certain wounds
Any physician or other person who renders any medical aid or treatment to any person for any wound which such physician or other person knows or has reason to believe is a wound inflicted by a weapon specified in §18.2-308 and which wound such physician or other person believes or has reason to believe was not self-inflicted shall as soon as practicable report such fact, including the wounded person's name and address, if known, to the sheriff or chief of police of the county or city in which treatment is rendered. If such medical aid or treatment is rendered in a hospital or similar institution, such physician or other person rendering such medical aid or treatment shall immediately notify the person in charge of such hospital or similar institution, who shall make such report forthwith.

Any physician or other person failing to comply with this section shall be guilty of a Class 3 misdemeanor. Any person participating in the making of a report pursuant to this section or participating in a judicial proceeding resulting therefrom shall be immune from any civil liability in connection therewith, unless it is proved that such person acted in bad faith or with malicious intent.

§54.1-4200. Definitions
For the purpose of this chapter, unless the context requires a different meaning:
"Dealer in firearms" means
(i) any person, firm, partnership, or corporation engaged in the business of selling, trading or transferring firearms at wholesale or retail;
(ii) any person, firm, partnership, or corporation engaged in the business of making or fitting special barrels, stocks, or trigger mechanisms to firearms; or
(iii) any person, firm, partnership, or corporation that is a pawnbroker.
"Engaged in business" means as applied to a dealer in firearms a person, firm, partnership, or corporation that devotes time, attention, and labor to dealing in firearms as a regular course of trade or business with the principal objective of livelihood and profit through repetitive purchase or resale of firearms, but such term shall not involve a person who makes occasional sales, exchanges, or purchases of firearms for the enhancement of a personal collection or for a hobby, or who sells all or part of his personal collection of firearms.

"Firearms show" means any gathering or exhibition, open to the public, not occurring on the permanent premises of a dealer in firearms, conducted principally for the purposes of exchanging, selling or trading firearms as defined in Sec. 18.2-308.2:2.

§54.1-4201. Inspection of records

A. Every dealer in firearms shall keep at his place of business, for not less than a period of two years, the original consent form required to be completed by §18.2-308.2:2 for each firearm sale.

B. Every dealer in firearms shall admit to his place of business during regular business hours the chief law-enforcement officer, or his designee, of the jurisdiction in which the dealer is located, or any law-enforcement official of the Commonwealth, and shall permit such law-enforcement officer, in the course of a bona fide criminal investigation, to examine and copy those federal and state records related to the acquisition or disposition of a particular firearm required by this section. This section shall not be construed to authorize the seizure of any records.

§54.1-4201.1. Notification by sponsor of firearms show to State Police and local law-enforcement authorities required; records; penalty

A. No promoter of a firearms show shall hold such show without giving notice at least 30 days prior to the show to the State Police and the sheriff or chief of police of the locality in which the firearms show will be held. The notice shall be given on a form provided by the State Police. A separate notice shall be required for each firearms show.
"Promoter" means every person, firm, corporation, club, association, or organization holding a firearms show in the Commonwealth.
The promoter shall maintain for the duration of the show a list of all vendors or exhibitors in the show for immediate inspection by any law-enforcement authorities, and within five days after the conclusion of the show, by mail, by hand, by email, or by fax, transmit a copy of the complete vendor or exhibitor list to the law-enforcement authorities to which the 30-day prior notice was required. The vendor or exhibitor list shall contain the full name and residence address and the business name and address, if any, of the vendors or exhibitors.

B. A willful violation of this section shall be a Class 3 misdemeanor.

C. The provisions of this section shall not apply to firearms shows held in any town with a population of not less than 1,995 and not more than 2,010, according to the 1990 United States census.

§54.1-4202. Penalties for violation of the provisions of this chapter

Any person convicted of a first offense for willfully violating the provisions of this chapter shall be guilty of a Class 2 misdemeanor. Any person convicted of a second or subsequent offense under the provisions of this chapter shall be guilty of a Class 1 misdemeanor.

Title 55 Property and Conveyances

§55-248.9. Prohibited provisions in rental agreements

A. A rental agreement shall not contain provisions that the tenant:

6. Agrees as a condition of tenancy in public housing to a prohibition or restriction of any lawful possession of a firearm within individual dwelling units unless required by federal law or regulation.

B. A provision prohibited by subsection A included in a rental agreement is unenforceable. If a landlord brings an action to enforce any of the prohibited provisions, the tenant may recover actual damages sustained by him and reasonable attorney's fees.

Title 58.1 Taxation

§58.1-638. Disposition of state sales and use tax revenue; localities' share; Game Protection Fund

E. Beginning July 1, 2000, of the remaining sales and use tax revenue, the revenue generated by a two percent sales and use tax, up to an annual amount of $13 million, collected from the sales of hunting equipment, auxiliary hunting equipment, fishing equipment, auxiliary fishing equipment, wildlife-watching equipment, and auxiliary wildlife-watching equipment in Virginia, as estimated by the most recent U.S. Department of the Interior, Fish and Wildlife Service and U.S. Department of Commerce, Bureau of the Census National Survey of Fishing, Hunting, and Wildlife-Associated Recreation, shall be paid into the Game Protection Fund established under §29.1-101 and shall be used, in part, to defray the cost of law enforcement.

§58.1-3504. Classification of certain household goods and personal effects for taxation; governing body may exempt

A. Notwithstanding any provision of §58.1-3503, household goods and personal effects are hereby defined as separate items of taxation and classified as follows:

2. Household and kitchen furniture, including gold and silver plates, plated ware, watches and clocks, sewing machines, refrigerators, automatic refrigerating machinery of any type, vacuum cleaners and all other household machinery, books, firearms and weapons of all kinds.

Title 59.1 Trade and Commerce

§59.1-148.3. Purchase of handguns of certain officers

A. The Department of State Police, the Department of Game and Inland Fisheries, the Department of Alcoholic Beverage Control, the State Lottery Department, the Marine Resources Commission, the Capitol Police, the Department of Conservation and Recreation, the Department of Forestry, any sheriff, any regional jail board or authority and any local police department may allow any full-time sworn law-enforcement officer, deputy, or regional jail officer, a local fire department may allow any full-time sworn fire marshal, the Department of Motor Vehicles may allow any law-enforcement officer, and any institution of higher learning named in §23-14 may allow any campus police officer appointed pursuant to Chapter 17 (§23-232 et seq.) of Title 23, retiring on or after July 1, 1991, who retires after at least 20 years of service or as a result of a service-incurred disability to purchase the service handgun issued to him by the agency or institution at a price of $1. This privilege shall also extend to any former Superintendent of the Department of State Police who leaves service after a minimum of five years. Other weapons issued by the Department of State Police for personal duty use of an officer, may, with approval of the Superintendent be sold to the officer subject to the qualifications of this section at a fair market price determined as in subsection B, so long as the weapon is a type and configuration that can be purchased at a regular hardware or sporting goods store by a private citizen without restrictions other than the instant background check.

B. The agencies listed above may allow any full-time sworn law-enforcement officer who retires with 10 or more years of service, but less than 20, to purchase the service handgun issued to him by the agency at a price equivalent to the weapon's fair market value on the date of the officer's retirement. Any full-time sworn law-enforcement officer employed by any of the agencies listed above who is retired for disability as a result of a nonservice-incurred disability may purchase the service handgun issued to him by the agency at a price equivalent to the weapon's fair market value on the date of the officer's retirement. Determinations of fair market value may be made by reference to a recognized pricing guide.

C. The agencies listed above may allow the immediate survivor of any full-time sworn law-enforcement officer (i) who is killed in the line of duty or (ii) who dies in service and has at least 20 years of service to purchase the service handgun issued to the officer by the agency at a price of $1.

D. The governing board of any institution of higher learning named in §23-14 may allow any campus police officer appointed pursuant to Chapter 17 (§23-232 et seq.) of Title 23 who retires on or after July 1, 1991, to purchase the service handgun issued to him at a price equivalent to the weapon's fair market value on the date of the officer's retirement. Determinations of fair market value may be made by reference to a recognized pricing guide.

E. The Department of State Police may allow any full-time sworn state police law-enforcement officer who retires as a result of a service-incurred disability and who was on disability leave at the time the Department issued 10-mm semiautomatic handguns to its officers to purchase one of the 10-mm semiautomatic handguns used by the Department of State Police at a price of $1.

F. The Department of State Police may allow any officer who at the time of his retirement was a full-time sworn law-enforcement officer and who retires after 20 years of state service, even if a portion of his service was with another state agency, to purchase the service handgun issued to him by the Department at a price of $1.

G. The sheriff of Hanover County may allow any auxiliary or volunteer deputy sheriff with a minimum of 15 years of service, upon leaving office, to purchase for $1 the service handgun issued to him.

H. Any sheriff or local police department, in accordance with written authorization or approval from the local governing body, may allow any auxiliary law-enforcement officer with more than 20 years of service to purchase the service handgun issued to him by the agency at a price that is equivalent to or less than the weapon's fair market value on the date of purchase by the officer.

I. The agencies listed in subsection A may allow any full-time sworn law-enforcement officer currently employed by the agency to purchase his service handgun, with the approval of the chief law-enforcement officer of the agency, at a fair market price. This subsection shall only apply when the agency has purchased new service handguns for its officers, and the handgun subject to the sale is no longer used by the agency or officer in the course of duty.

§59.1-148.4. Sale of firearms by law-enforcement agencies prohibited; exception

A law-enforcement agency of this Commonwealth shall not sell or trade any firearm owned and used or otherwise lawfully in its possession except
(i) to another law-enforcement agency of the Commonwealth,
(ii) to a licensed firearms dealer,
(iii) to the persons as provided in §59.1-148.3 or
(iv) as authorized by a court in accordance with §19.2-386.29.

§59.1-443.2. Restricted use of social security numbers

A. Except as otherwise specifically provided by law, a person shall not:
1. Intentionally communicate another individual's social security number to the general public;
2. Print an individual's social security number on any card required for the individual to access or receive products or services provided by the person;
3. Require an individual to use his social security number to access an Internet website, unless a password, unique personal identification number or other authentication device is also required to access the site; or

4. Send or cause to be sent or delivered any letter, envelope, or package that displays a social security number on the face of the mailing envelope or package, or from which a social security number is visible, whether on the outside or inside of the mailing envelope or package.

B. This section does not prohibit the collection, use, or release of a social security number as permitted by the laws of the Commonwealth or the United States, or the use of a social security number for internal verification or administrative purposes unless such use is prohibited by a state or federal statute, rule, or regulation.

C. In the case of any

(i) health care provider as defined in §8.01-581.1,

(ii) manager of a pharmacy benefit plan,

(iii) insurer as defined in §38.2-100,

(iv) corporation providing a health services plan,

(v) health maintenance organization providing a health care plan for health care services, or

(vi) contractor of any such person, the prohibition contained in subdivision 2 of subsection A shall become effective on January 1, 2006.

D. This section shall not apply to public bodies as defined in §2.2-3701.

E. No person shall embed an encrypted or unencrypted social security number in or on a card or document, including, but not limited to, using a bar code, chip, magnetic strip, or other technology, in place of removing the social security number as required by this section.

About Steve Maniscalco

Steve Maniscalco served in the U.S. Navy from 1980 to 1986, achieving the rank of Petty Officer First Class. As a Submarine Sonar Technician he traveled extensively throughout the Atlantic, Arctic and Mediterranean Oceans and the Caribbean Islands. Steve observed that, remarkably, it all looks like the inside of a nuclear submarine.

Since 1986, Steve has worked for the U.S. government as a technical writer and an electronic technician. The majority of his government service was in the Norfolk, Va., area as a sailor and then as a civilian employee.

Steve moved to Phoenix, Ariz., in 1994, and made the switch from submarines to F-16 jet aircraft, writing technical manuals for aircraft trainers at Luke Air Force base. He is an active competitive shooter, having participated in literally hundreds of matches.

In 1995, Steve approached Bloomfield Press, proposing to co-author a book about Virginia gun laws. Steve brings to *The Virginia Gun Owner's Guide* his ambition as a writer, his passion for competitive shooting and an abiding interest in constitutional issues.

Mr. Maniscalco quit his secure government position to devote himself as a full-time dad to his new son, Steven Blaise, a full-time husband to his wife, Leslie and a full-time writer to just about anyone who will pay him fairly for quality work. You are holding a sample of his abilities in your hands. To see his work as a web-page designer visit www.gunlaws.com.

About Alan Korwin

Alan Korwin, author of three books and co-author of eight others, is a full-time freelance writer, consultant and businessman with a twenty-five-year track record. He is a founder and two-term past president of the Arizona Book Publishing Association, which has presented him with its Visionary Leadership award, named in his honor, the Korwin Award. He has received national awards for his publicity work as a member of the Society for Technical Communication, and is a past board member of the Arizona chapter of the Society of Professional Journalists.

Mr. Korwin wrote the business plan that raised $5 million in venture capital and launched the in-flight catalog *SkyMall;* he did the publicity for Pulitzer Prize cartoonist Steve Benson's fourth book; working with American Express, he wrote the strategic plan that defined their worldwide telecommunications strategy for the 1990s; and he had a hand in developing ASPED, Arizona's economic strategic plan. Korwin's writing appears nationally regularly.

Korwin turned his first book, *The Arizona Gun Owner's Guide,* into a self-published best-seller, now in its 23rd edition. With his wife Cheryl he operates Bloomfield Press, which has grown into the largest publisher and distributor of gun-law books in the country. It is built around eight books he has completed on the subject, including the unabridged federal guide, *Gun Laws of America*, an expanding line of related items, and countless radio and TV appearances. His 12th book, on the rapidly growing limits to free speech, is underway.

Alan Korwin is originally from New York City, where his clients included IBM, AT&T, NYNEX and others, many with real names. He is a pretty good guitarist and singer, with a penchant for parody (his current band is The Cartridge Family). In 1986, finally married, he moved to the Valley of the Sun.
It was a joyful and successful move.

In The Gravest Extreme
Massad Ayoob, 132 pgs. #ITGE $12.95. Widely recognized as the definitive work on the use of deadly force. This former law enforcement officer describes what you actually face in a lethal confrontation, a criminal's mind-set, gun-fight tactics, judicial system's view on self-defense cases, more. Dispels the myths, truly excellent—a must for any armed household & especially CCW permit holders. Ayoob has written for most major gun magazines for decades.

The Truth About Self-Protection
Massad Ayoob, 418 pgs. #TASP $7.99. Get the facts on every aspect of personal safety, from evasive driving to planting cactus by your windows. Lifesaving techniques will help keep you, your family and your possessions safe, prepare you for defense if it becomes absolutely necessary, and guide you in buying lethal and less-than-lethal goods, from locks to firearms. Crime-avoidance techniques.

Gun-Proof Your Children
Masaad Ayoob, 52 pgs. #GPYC $4.95. One of the world's leading experts on lethal-force issues, this father of two shares his thoughts and very practical ideas on gun safety for kids in a classic short booklet. Also includes a primer on handguns for the novice. Here is a parent's guide that does not advocate avoidance, and instead proposes that knowledge should trump ignorance, and that education is the best choice.

You and The Police
Boston T. Party, 128 pgs. #YATP $16.00. If you're like most people, you don't have a clue what to do if you're stopped by the police. This book tells you how to handle a stop with dignity, and reviews the rights you do and do not have. What should you say or do if a peace officer wants to search your car, or if you're arrested? Can you talk your way out of a ticket? What are the limits on warrantless searches, and how can you respond to intimidation?

The Concealed Handgun Manual
Chris Bird, 416 pgs. #CHM $22.95. The standard for people who carry for self defense. Detailed accounts of S/D incidents, latest on laws and licenses, packed with nitty gritty on picking and packing a gun, advanced shooting technique, street-wise tactics, how to see trouble coming and avoid it. What to expect after you have shot someone.

Principles of Personal Defense
Col. Jeff Cooper, 44 pgs. #POPD $14.00. Hard-boiled wisdom from "The Father of the Modern Techniques of Shooting." His seven principles are stark and brutal (Alertness, Decisiveness, Aggressiveness, Speed, Coolness, Ruthlessness and Surprise). Too much for the squeamish. An instant, violent counterattack is a total surprise to most criminals. "The perfect fight is one that is over before the loser really understands what is going on."

Stressfire—
Gunfighting Tactics for Police
Massad Ayoob, 150 pgs. #SF $11.95. Heavy-duty reading for advanced students and those who want the deepest understanding of lethal confrontations and how to survive a deadly encounter. Ayoob pours on the experience and techniques that make him a sought-after world-class expert, in a real page-turner. Not for the faint of heart, it will make you think. You may be able to shoot straight, but can you "clear" a house?

No Second Place Winner
Jordan, 114 pgs. #NSPW $14.95. Unique discussion of armed response by a man who made it his trade. Jordan worked the U.S. Border Patrol of the old days and lived to tell about it. He became one of the deadliest shots of modern times. In an easy going style he describes with chilling clarity what it takes to win gun fights. "Be first or be dead… there are no second place winners." Filled with draw-and-shoot techniques, wonderful B&W stop-action

DVDs
"Providing a brave new world of education, from basic to very advanced."

Handgun Basics For Self Defense And Target Shooting

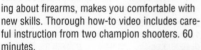

#D-HBF $34.95 list, our price only $29.95. Perfect for the newcomer, learn about handling and shooting revolvers and semi-auto pistols. Easy-to-follow info on how the guns work, safety, loading and unloading, at-home self defense, and a review of the most popular models and ammo for basic home use. 90 minutes.

A Woman's Guide To Firearms

#D-AWG $24.95 list, our price only $21.95. Host Gerald McRaney (TV's "Major Dad") leads you through a step-by-step program designed with women in mind. Helps reduce fear some women feel when learning about firearms, makes you comfortable with new skills. Thorough how-to video includes careful instruction from two champion shooters. 60 minutes.

Basic Self-Defense Handgun Use & Safety

#D-BSD $34.95 list, our price only $29.95. Experts Bill Wilson, Ken Hackathorn and Lenny Magill take you through the shooting basics of grip, stance, sight alignment, trigger pull; Weaver and Isosceles stances and interesting variations too. Preparation for real life situations, info on self defense, dry fire practice you can do at home. 60 minutes.

Advanced Self-Defense Shooting Tactics & Techniques

#D-ASD $34.95 list, our price only $29.95. Designed for more experienced shooters, learn to shoot on the move, what to expect at 3, 7 and 10 yards and beyond. Practice techniques help you learn quickly. Then learn to shoot while moving away from an adversary, a crucial survival skill for gunfights. 60 minutes.

Concealed Carry Techniques And Secrets Of The Pros

#D-CCT $24.95 list, our price only $21.95. How to select, wear and draw from more than 40 different concealment methods. Think you know how to carry? Wait till you see some of the options you've never thought about, which may be right for you. Includes an incredible display of draw and shoot from concealed carry, a mind-opening experience. 110 minutes.

Practical Concealed Carry Self-Defense Shooting Drills

#D-PCC $39.95 list, our price only $34.95. Practice makes perfect and that's what this video is all about. Gain proficiency in both marksmanship and ability to draw quickly, present arms and pull the trigger. Ken Hackathorn and Bill Wilson demonstrate carry and draw techniques you can model. Focuses on six main methods of carry, live and dry fire drills you can use, pocket holsters, pocket carry and fanny packs. 90 minutes.

Advanced Concealed Carry, Faster, More Accurately

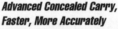

#D-ACC $34.95 list, our price only $29.95. The followup to *Practical Concealed Carry*. Deep concealment techniques and real gunfight survival tools, shooting on the move, the five-step draw method, and popular methods of carry and concealment with modern handguns. 110 minutes.

Move! Shoot! Live!

#D-MSL $34.95 list, our price only $29.95. Based on studies of actual gunfights, learn where, how and why people get shot or not, in actual lethal confrontations. Movement is a key, so your first goal is to move out of the line of fire, then keep moving while you return fire. This video takes self-defense up a notch. Plus actual gunfight footage with analysis. 80 minutes.

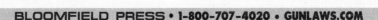

Published by

BLOOMFIELD PRESS

THE TEXAS GUN OWNERS Guide
Who can bear arms?
Where are guns forbidden?
When can you shoot?
by Alan Korwin
and Georgene Lockwood

THE VIRGINIA GUN OWNERS Guide
Who can bear arms?
Where are guns forbidden?
When can you shoot?
by Alan Korwin
and Steve Maniscalco

THE CALIFORNIA GUN OWNERS Guide
by Georgene Lockwood
and Alan Korwin

THE FLORIDA GUN OWNERS Guide

THE ARIZONA GUN OWNERS Guide
Who can bear arms?
Where are guns forbidden?
When can you shoot?

THE Heller CASE GUN RIGHTS AFFIRMED!
A DEFINING MOMENT IN HISTORY
Supreme Court Embraces the Second Amendment
Alan Korwin   David B. Kopel
ALL 96 SUPREME COURT GUN CASES EXPLAINED

SUPREME COURT GUN CASES
Two Centuries of Gun Rights Re...
EVERY WORD OF EVERY KEY...
David B. Kopel
Stephen P. Halbrook, Ph.D.
plus the nearly forgotten self-defense...

GUN LAWS of AMERICA
Every Federal Gun La... on the books.
WITH PLAIN ENGLISH SUMM...
By Alan Korwin
with Attorney Michael P. An...

THE LIBERTY POLL
by Attorney Michael P. Anthony, Author Alan Korwin and Syndicated Columnist Vin Suprynowicz

"Hello, politician—What's the purpose of government? It's time to start asking tough questions the "news" media avoids, to really learn what sort of leaders we elect. Although reporters can seem like they play hardball with candidates, they almost never do.

• If you're elected to the office you seek: a) what laws will you repeal; b) what taxes will you reduce or eliminate; c) what agencies will you shrink or close?

• Can you name any areas where government might serve the public interest, but where it has no authority to act? If not, is it still accurate to say we have a "government of limited powers"? Does this matter?

• Can you name any current areas of government operations that are outside the authority delegated to government?

• Regarding jury trials, should judges be required to inform jurors they have the power, in the sanctity of the jury room, to decide whether a law in question is just, or constitutional? Should schools teach this?

• Regarding law enforcement, are you in favor of police using deadly force when absolutely necessary to protect innocent lives from criminal attack? Do you believe that people, even people with no training of any kind, have less right to defend themselves than authorities do?

• When did you last read the state and federal Constitutions?

THE ONLY QUESTION ABOUT GUN REGISTRATION by Alan Korwin

Only one thing is overlooked in the common sense proposals to register guns. How exactly would writing down my name, or your name, help arrest criminals or make you safer? The unfortunate answer is that, no matter how good it feels when the words first pass your ears, registering honest gun owners doesn't stop criminals, and in fact focuses in the opposite direction. Gun registration schemes lack a crime-prevention component.

• Registering 90 million Americans is extremely expensive. A database that big needs 24,000 changes daily, just to keep up with people who move every ten years. Floor after floor of cubicle after cubicle—it's a federal jobs program all by itself. How many criminals will register? That's right, none, and planners know that. In fact, crooks can't register—the ban on self incrimination makes it illegal to force them. All that money and time, invested on tracking the innocent.

• Americans who fail to register would become felons without harming anyone.

• Registration, if enacted, will create an underground market for guns bigger than the drug trade. The last thing you want to encourage is import programs and price supports that drug dealers enjoy, for gun runners.

• You don't really think authorities would use registration lists to confiscate guns from people, do you? Despite examples of exactly that in New York and California, and global history for the past century, this couldn't really happen, do you think?

WHY DON'T POLICE ARREST ALL THE BRADY CRIMINALS THEY FIND? by Alan Korwin

It's well known by now, that of all the people stopped by the Brady law's FBI background check, very few are arrested—even though it's a five-year felony for them to try to buy a gun. If the goal is to stop crime, why aren't these people arrested? Here's why:

• Because the Brady law is neither designed nor intended to increase the annual number of federal prosecutions. (from BATF, FBI, White House)

• Because the last thing you want is for police to be constantly showing up at gunstores and making arrests of felons who want guns.... it's too potentially dangerous for the customers. (Arizona Police Lieut.)

• Because there isn't enough time for all the arraignments, dockets would gridlock, detention cells would burst, prisons would overflow, and nobody in the system wants to even attempt it.

• Because unless we have more crime and violence we won't be able to justify taking everybody's gun away.

• Because the real purpose of the Brady law is to build a federal gun-registration infrastructure, and it has been wildly successful.

POLITICALLY CORRECTED GLOSSARY

We've all talked about losing the war of words in the struggle for our liberties.

Well here comes the cavalry—

Certain words hurt you when you talk about your rights and liberties.

People who would deny your rights have done a good job of manipulating the language so far. Without even realizing it, you're probably using terms that actually help people who want to disarm you.

To preserve, protect and defend your rights in the critical debate of where power should reside in America, you need effective word choices. Try out some of the ideas in this chart the next time you deal with this subject.

This is just a small part of my full Politically Corrected Glossary. Get the rest in ready-to-print form (a PDF file) on our website. Feel free to share this with your friends, journalists, anti-gun bigots, and anyone else who needs a refreshing perspective on the liberties your personal firearms represent.

THEY WIN IF YOU SAY:	YOU WIN IF YOU SAY:
pro gun	pro rights
gun control	crime control
reasonable gun-control laws	illegal infringement laws
anti-gun movement	anti-self-defense movement
semiautomatic handgun	sidearm
concealed carry	discreet carry or right to carry
assault weapon or lethal weapon	household firearms
Saturday night specials	racist gun laws
junk guns	the affordability issue
high-capacity magazines	normal-capacity magazines
Second Amendment	Bill of Rights
the powerful gun lobby	civil rights organizations
common-sense legislation	dangerous utopian ideas
anti gun	anti-gun bigotry
anti gun	anti-gun prejudice
anti gun	anti rights

WHEN THEY SAY:	YOU SAY:
Guns kill	Guns save lives
Guns cause crime	Guns stop crime
Guns are bad	Guns are why America is still free
Assault weapons are bad	Assault is a type of behavior
Guns are too dangerous to own	You should take a safety class
People shouldn't have guns	Maybe you shouldn't have one
People don't need guns	Only good people need guns
Gun owners should be registered	Bad guys first
They should take away all the guns	Bad guys first. Who is "they"?
The purpose of a gun is to kill	The purpose of a gun is to protect
We need more gun laws	Criminal activity is already banned
Do you really have a gun?	Of course, don't you?

The Massad Ayoob Video Series—

Most people will never in their lives see real-life footage of tactical instruction like this. Ayoob, world-renowned, has produced recorded recordings that truly stand out.

Judicious Use Of Deadly Force

#D-JUO $34.95 list, our price only $29.95. In this video, police captain Massad Ayoob, generally recognized as the leading authority on use of deadly weapons by civilians in self defense, goes beyond his book, "In the Gravest Extreme" to deal from the ground up in the core principles of law, ethics, and tactics of using lethal force. Ideal for the instructor or attorney, and vital for citizens who keep or carry a loaded gun. 130 minutes.

LFI Handgun Safety

#D-LFIH $34.95 list, our price only $29.95. Seen by every Lethal Force Institute student before training begins. Ayoob pulls no punches showing how old-fashioned "Manuals of Arms" set the stage for accidents, and demonstrating the safest, most modern techniques of loading, unloading, drawing, and handling revolvers and semiautomatics. This is the video LFI grads bring back to their gun clubs on special

Cute Lawyer Tricks

#D-CLT $34.95 list, our price only $29.95. Ayoob reveals the slick side of "the suits" and how to prevail in court. Prepares police and civilians for the antics lawyers play to discredit you, your testimony and evidence. How they sway judges and juries, and how to fight back and win. Available again at last. 30 minutes.

Shoot to Live! Gunfight Survival

#STL $34.95 list, our price only $29.95. An in-depth interview with Ayoob about how to survive an on-the-street gunfight. Hard-hitting, practical, witty information about where to shoot an offender for maximum stopping power. .45 vs. 9mm vs .22 calibers, training vs. real life, what happens when you get shot and lots more. 80 minutes.

ON A LIGHTER NOTE and A UNIQUE EXPERIENCE

The Good Citizen's Handbook

J. M. Trontz, 140 pgs. #GCH $12.95. Lessons from civics, scouting, even government guides from decades ago. Real wisdom from before America's values were debased. With old drawings of wholesome life-styles from 1920s to 1950s, here is what made America great—the dignity, courtesy, values we stood for. Re-awakens long forgotten goals and ideals—penmanship matters, a good little boy doesn't talk back, Jr. Rifleman's Code of Conduct (Rule #9): "I will seek the advice of better marksmen than myself."

The Worst-Case Scenario Survival Handbook

Piven & Borgenicht, 176 pgs. #WCS $14.95. Survival experts provide illustrated, step-by-step instructions on what you need to do in dire straights: How to take a punch; How to deliver a baby in a taxi; How to jump from a moving car; How to stop a car with no brakes; How to escape killer bees; How to treat a bullet or knife wound; How to use a defibrillator; How to do a tracheotomy; How to land the plane and more!

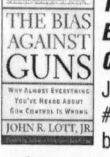
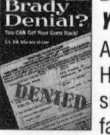